Whole Grains FOR A NEW GENERATION

P9-COP-830

Whole Grains

FOR A NEW GENERATION

Light Dishes, Hearty Meals, Sweet Treats,
and Sundry Snacks for the Everyday Cook

By Liana Krissoff
Photographs by Rinne Allen

STEWART, TABORI & CHANG | NEW YORK

Published in 2012 by Stewart, Tabori & Chang
An imprint of ABRAMS

Copyright © 2012 Liana Krissoff
Photographs copyright © 2012 Rinne Allen

All rights reserved. No portion of this book may be reproduced, stored in a retrieval system, or transmitted in any form or by any means, mechanical, electronic, photocopying, recording, or otherwise, without written permission from the publisher.

Library of Congress Cataloging-in-Publication Data

Krissoff, Liana.
Whole grains for a new generation : light dishes, hearty meals, sweet treats, and sundry snacks for the everyday cook / by Liana Krissoff.
p. cm.
Includes bibliographical references and index.
ISBN 978-1-61769-001-3
1. Cooking (Cereals) 2. Grain. I. Title.
TX808.K75 2012
641.6'31—dc23
                    2011053260

Editor: Elinor Hutton
Designer: Matthew Egan
Production Manager: Tina Cameron

The text of this book was typeset using Omnes.

Printed and bound in China

10 9 8 7 6 5 4 3 2 1

Stewart, Tabori & Chang books are available at special discounts when purchased in quantity for premiums and promotions as well as fundraising or educational use. Special editions can also be created to specification. For details, contact specialsales@abramsbooks.com or the address below.

115 West 18th Street
New York, NY 10011
www.abramsbooks.com

For Thalia

Contents

Introduction

M ention whole grains, and many people, even if they've been hearing more and more in recent years about the wonderful variety of grains available today and their many health benefits, still immediately envision earnest piles of brown rice and steamed broccoli served up by do-gooder parents or radical roommates. Dusty bulk bins in medicinal, humorless health food stores on the largely unpopulated side of town. Wan slabs of tofu leaning against some sad, plain spelt berries. In other words, food that's a duty to eat, not a pleasure. I want to be one of the many new voices helping to change that perception.

I'm certainly not the kind of person who eats food just because it's good for me or because I need to eat to survive. There's far too much fun to be had cooking and eating to let that everyday opportunity for subtle happiness slip by. Mealtime in my family has always been something to look forward to, to plan for, to enjoy. My parents didn't often cook fancy meals for us kids, and we rarely went to restaurants, but they were (and still are) open to trying different foods and unusual ingredients, confident that they could learn how to cook anything on the planet, and so they did. Much of it was decidedly not health food. Sure, my mom had a carob period (short-lived, thank goodness—we all knew that wasn't chocolate), and experimented with other "healthful" foods that didn't gain traction with my dad and my brother and me. But for the most part, she cooked just plain delicious food for us, whether the dish grew out of an interest in Georgia's lost Cherokee culture (well, that oven-dried corn wasn't delicious so much as *memorable*), a monthlong trek through Thailand with a notebook and a curious intellect (hence the coconut-milk pancakes and other street-food delights we devoured on her return), or challenges issued by culinary entities from Julia Child to *Sunset* magazine (French bread and the best sopaipillas ever, respectively).

She also cooked whole grains and served them well. I may be one of the few children of the '80s who has fond memories of wheat berries: steaming bowls of the little grains, plump and chewy, sprinkled ever so judiciously with white sugar and swimming in cold milk, spooned up on winter mornings before the school bus came in the dark. Cracked wheat porridge with a touch of cinnamon—nothing elaborate—warming me and my brother after an afternoon ice skating on the snow-covered lake. Tiny whole wheat buns halved to sandwich shredded venison shoulder and red pepper relish in my lunch bag. So I suppose when I started to learn to cook

more whole grains a couple years ago, I came to the project with an ingrained appreciation of how tasty they could be, but I understand if others need more convincing before they pull the trigger on that first bag of quinoa, or millet, or farro.

With a few exceptions, the food in this book is far from austere. Spices are used with abandon, as are fresh chiles and herbs, creamy Greek yogurt and homemade crème fraîche (so easy to make it's ridiculous), bursting ripe vegetables and sweet-tart fruits, succulent meats and oily fish, and all-important salt. This is food made by someone who drinks wine and coffee just about every day, and who butters her bread. It's both homey everyday food you and your family will love and fun but super-easy dinner-party food. It's Indian, Mexican, Thai, and all-American Southern—my cooking is inspired by all that's flavorful, and I hope it serves as inspiration to you in turn.

Now let's get the fascinating grain anatomy and taxonomy and whatnot out of the way so we can dive into the recipes as quickly as possible.

WHAT'S A GRAIN, ANYWAY, AND WHAT MAKES ONE WHOLE?

A grain is, quite simply, the whole seed of a plant. True grains are those that come from plants in the grass family, Poaceae. They're also known as cereals: Wheat, corn, rice, oats, rye, barley, millet, sorghum, teff, triticale, and wild rice are all cereal crops, true grains. Seeds that do not come from a grass but that have culinary uses and nutritional profiles that are similar to those of true grains are called pseudograins, and they usually come from broadleaf plant varieties; these include buckwheat, quinoa, and amaranth.

Each grain or pseudograin, each seed, consists of three main parts, all of which are found inside an inedible layer called the hull. You may remember cross-section diagrams of grains from such classes as middle-school science. In all the illustrations, at the bottom of the seed near the stem and looking, very appropriately, like an egg yolk, is the germ: the tiny part of the interior of the grain that when fertilized will sprout (hence the term *germinate*) and grow into a new plant. The endosperm, which makes up the bulk of the interior and is the source of energy for the germ, surrounds it. The bran is the outer protective layer. Each part of the grain has different nutritional characteristics and content:

- GERM vitamins B and E, essential amino acids, oils
- ENDOSPERM mostly starch (carbohydrate)
- BRAN fiber, B vitamins

When a grain is processed, first the hull or outer husk is removed. At this point it's a fully edible whole grain. If processing continues and the germ and the bran are removed, the grain is no longer whole—only the starchy, carbohydrate-rich endosperm is left, and that's what we're eating when we eat refined grains. There are some good reasons for doing this: Refined grains, like white flour, degerminated cornmeal, and white rice, keep longer in storage than whole grains because they lack the oils that can turn rancid on the shelf over time. Refined grains also tend to taste lighter and more delicate than those made with whole grains. And, at least in the case of white rice and fine degerminated cornmeal, refined grains cook more quickly than whole grains.

FITTING WHOLE GRAINS INTO YOUR EVERYDAY MEALS

You can see that for most people and most modern diets, the most useful parts of the grain would be the germ and bran. They're incredibly nutritious, and yet most of the grains produced for consumption today are ultra-processed to remove them. While it's my feeling that there are many applications for which only white flour or white rice will do—a perfect pizza crust, a holey loaf of ciabatta, a fine white layer cake, a traditional risotto—I think that for most of us those foods should, ideally, be considered special treats, and if it's possible to replace refined grains with whole grains without any reduction in deliciousness we should do so. Luckily, whole grains offer a variety of fun, crazy textures to play with and a ton of flavor in each bite, so there's certainly no need to worry about giving up an ounce of cooking or eating pleasure. In fact, I find that whole grains are so much more satisfying than refined grains that when they're part of my meal I'm less likely to overeat.

The dishes in this book cover a lot of ground—there are whole grains for every meal, after all. But I don't want to suggest that eating whole grains (or any grains) three times a day is a viable diet for me or for anyone. Whole grains, as tasty and as good for you as they are, shouldn't replace nutrient-dense fresh vegetables, and on their own they won't provide as much protein as most people need. Basically, when I crave grains, whether it's a hunk of bread or a bowl of cereal or a pie or something to go with kung pao chicken, I try to make the grains whole. When I buy cornmeal, I make sure it says it's made from whole corn or hominy. When I buy dried pasta, unless it's a special occasion, I pick one made with at least some whole wheat. If I happen to be desperate for a store-bought cold cereal (I was addicted to mixed Nutty Nuggets and Toasted Oats for a while), I know that one of the many varieties of unsweetened puffed whole grains is a good option. That said, it's my hope that this book will help you go far beyond simple substitutions like this to discover new ways of cooking and enjoying the enormous variety of interesting and unusual grains that are readily available today.

You'll probably notice that most of the dishes—the salads, the sides, and the main courses especially—are loaded with fresh produce. Good meats and fish are used moderately and, I think, wisely here and in the foods my family and I cook. When they appear in these recipes, meats and fish take center stage: I believe that when you indulge in something

special like a rosy rare grilled flank steak, you should truly enjoy and appreciate it, and it shouldn't be hidden, the meat used only as a "flavoring" for grains and vegetables. When you have meat or fish, it deserves to be the focus of the meal!

Though many traditional food cultures relied on whole grains for the bulk of their nutritional intake, I think an approach in which whole grains are balanced with other healthful ingredients is more appropriate in a modern diet. So you'll find a posole rojo that's reasonably authentic in its flavor profile—brick-red guajillo chiles, garlic, and onion forming the base—but one in which sharp-tasting, tender mustard greens are wilted into the hot stew right alongside the pork and whole hominy. You'll find as much zucchini as couscous in the stuffing for whole rainbow trout. In a quinoa dish, the roasted butternut squash, shallots, and sausage dominate. The salads are similarly balanced. You're getting your grains here, but also your dark leafy greens, nonstarchy vegetables, lesser cuts of meat, small sustainable fish and shellfish, your good cheeses, cream, and yogurt—lots of yogurt. Usually, just a cup's worth of grain can cook up into three or four servings, often more.

PROTEIN BENEFITS OF WHOLE GRAINS

Every person's protein requirement is different, and some people feel better when they have more or less than the feds recommend. If you eat meat and fish and you live in the developed world, you probably don't need to think about your protein intake at all. If you prefer to limit meat and fish in your diet, instead relying mostly on other sources for your protein, these Centers for Disease Control numbers (based on findings and conclusions published in 2005 by the Institute of Medicine of the National Academies) may be helpful as a baseline recommended daily allowance:

INDIVIDUALS	AGE	GRAMS
Children	1 to 8	13 to 19
Children	9 to 13	34
Girls	14 to 18	46
Boys	14 to 18	52
Women	19 and older	46
Men	19 and older	56

Vegetarians and vegans may be especially interested in whole grains, not just because they're tasty and fun to cook, but also because they can provide a surprising amount of protein, especially when compared to refined grains. Quinoa is the grain highest in protein by weight when cooked (at 4 to 5 percent), and it's a complete protein, meaning it contains all nine essential amino acids—the ones the human body can't produce on its own and requires to survive. It's one of very few nonmeat or nondairy sources of complete protein. Amaranth and buckwheat, barley, millet, teff, and wild rice crowd close behind at 3 to 4 percent. And it would be a mistake to discount the mighty oat: one ½-cup (80 g) serving of raw rolled oats—plus 2 tablespoons sliced almonds to improve the protein (think muesli)—is actually considerably higher in protein than one 1-cup (180 g) serving of cooked quinoa. Compare these with a serving of tofu or a large egg (other complete proteins):

- ½ CUP (80 g) RAW ROLLED OATS (10 g protein) PLUS 2 TABLE-SPOONS SLICED ALMONDS (2.5 g protein): 12.5 g protein
- 1 CUP (180 g) COOKED QUINOA: 8 g protein
- ¼ BLOCK EXTRA-FIRM TOFU: 8 g protein
- 1 LARGE EGG: 6 g protein

(And just for the heck of it: A can of tuna has about 14 g protein, and a nice, big, juicy sirloin steak clocks in at around 30 g protein—complete, of course.)

[THE TAKEAWAY? As far as grain-based protein is concerned, quinoa is great, and oats (especially with nuts or another source of nongrain protein, such as milk) are awesome.]

BUYING AND STORING WHOLE GRAINS

I buy most of my grains from bulk sources: the bins at the local specialty food store, a small bakery-café in the next town over that also sells whole grains and flours at reasonable prices, and the big world market called Your Dekalb Farmers Market, which has just about every grain-related product I could want in convenient quantities. (See sources on page 262 for mail-order options.) I also pick up unusual rices when I become intrigued by them in Asian and Indian grocery stores. In other words, I buy whole grains just about everywhere but the supermarket, where they're usually overpriced and often stale due to lack of turnover.

However, if avoiding gluten is a goal—if you're very sensitive to it or have celiac disease or are cooking for someone who can't eat any gluten—you should steer clear of the bulk bins, where the scoop used for wheat flour by the person before you may be the one that's now in the buckwheat groats bin, contaminating its contents. Fine particles from one bin easily make their way to another through the air. If gluten is a concern, you should buy your grains already packaged, and the labels should specify that the contents are indeed gluten free to avoid any chance of contamination. Online retailers may be another option, especially if you buy enough to make the shipping costs worthwhile; see page 262 for a list of a few reputable sources.

Whole grains, even though they contain oils that can turn rancid over time, don't necessarily have to be stored in the refrigerator or freezer. I store mine in airtight containers (usually in large glass canning jars) in a dark cupboard as far from the heat of the oven as possible. It's very rare that under these conditions a batch of flour or whole grains will become unusable.

One common annoyance in stored grains, however, is the group of resourceful little pests called pantry moths. If you bring grains home in bags from the bulk bin, even if they're well sealed, it's a good idea to transfer the grains to glass containers as soon as possible. The easiest way to prevent moths from taking over is to freeze the grains for a few days before transferring them to the cupboard, which will neutralize any of the (minuscule, unnoticeable, harmless) eggs that might already be in them. You can also scatter a few dried bay leaves in the cupboard among the containers; the essential oils help repel pests.

[KEY WORDS: airtight, dark, and cool.]

MAKING WHOLE GRAINS EASY

When I decided to write this book, I flung myself into what turned out to be weeks of experimenting with basic grain-cooking techniques. In the past, I'd always simply put some grains in a pot with some water and simmered them until they were tender. Surely it must be more complicated than that, I thought. So I set about measuring, toasting, frying, salting, soaking, steaming, rinsing, adding grains to boiling water, adding boiling water to grains, and every combination thereof. I discovered that, in large part, cooking grains involves, well, putting some grains in a pot with some water and simmering them until they're tender. Yes, some of them benefit from a brief pretoasting (millet, farro, cracked wheat); one grain does need to be presoaked for even cooking (Chinese black rice); some are best added to already boiling water (cornmeal, polenta, grits); some ideally should be parboiled and then steamed the rest of the way (brown basmati and long-grain brown rices); and some of the firmer whole grains (wheat berries and the like) should not be salted too early in the cooking process or cooked in acidic liquids, similar to cooking dried beans. But overall, you can rest assured that this is pretty much all you need to know about cooking whole grains (though there are another couple hundred pages in this book you might wish to peruse anyway). In short, don't sweat the details. Grains are forgiving, and so are your family and friends.

MAKING LAST-MINUTE WHOLE GRAINS

It's true that many whole grains take longer to cook than their refined counterparts, but if you prepare a few meals' worth at one time, it's a simple matter to pull them out when you need them for a quick last-minute meal—indeed, dumping out a bag of precooked whole grains is faster and easier than cooking the refined version fresh for each meal. Many of the recipes in this book, even those in which the grain appears in a brothy soup or stew, call for cooked grains, not because I'm a lazy recipe writer but because most grains should be cooked at least most of the way in plain unsalted water with no added acid and because it's so easy to cook them in advance.

The larger, firmer whole grains—farro; wheat, rye, and spelt berries; wild rice; hulled barley; whole hominy; oat and buckwheat groats and kasha—can be cooked in large batches (double or triple the amounts listed in the Grain Cooking Cheat Sheet on page 259), then divided among quart-size freezer bags and stacked flat in the freezer for long-term storage. They can be thawed in just a minute or so.

The smaller, more delicate grains—such as quinoa and millet, bulgur, whole wheat couscous, cracked wheat, and freekeh—can be cooked ahead, frozen, and thawed to add to soups and stews or to use in baked goods, but for salads or other dishes where the integrity of the individual grains is more important, I'd only go as far as cooking ahead and refrigerating for a few days. These quick-cooking grains are best cooked in smaller quantities (like those listed on the cheat sheet on page 259) so they stay fluffy and don't get mushy or overcooked in the pot.

TO SOAK OR NOT?

If you're the kind of person who plans ahead, you might wish to presoak the firmer, longer-cooking grains—wheat berries, farro, spelt berries, rye berries, oat groats—so they'll cook more quickly the day you serve them. Soak in cool water at room temperature for about 8 hours or overnight, drain, then proceed as usual, checking frequently to see if the grains are cooked through: Soaked grains will cook in two-thirds to half the time. You can also soak oats overnight in the amount of water called for in the recipes that follow; in the morning it's basically just a matter of sticking the pot on the stove and heating them up.

Some folks have found that the whole grains that are high in the antinutrient phytic acid (such as wheat, rye, and oats) may be easier to digest and their nutrients may be more readily absorbed if they've been soaked in water with a culture of some sort added (a spoonful of yogurt, for example) for a certain period. If you do have trouble digesting whole grains, please look into the Weston A. Price Foundation's recommendations for pretreating grains, as it's very possible you'll be able to add these valuable whole grains (and the flours made from them) to your diet if you follow its suggestions.

Brown and red rices can be parboiled in batches as large as you wish and then refrigerated or frozen, to be pulled out and finished just before serving (see page 29). In fact, I think their texture benefits from this simple two-stage cooking process.

Porridge-cooked grains—oatmeal, amaranth, teff, and cornmeal—don't freeze very well (or, rather, they don't thaw quickly enough for me to make it worth it). Refrigerated leftovers reheat easily, though, in a heavy covered pan with a little extra water.

TO REHEAT REFRIGERATED OR FROZEN GRAINS
Put the refrigerated or frozen grains in a deep sieve or steamer basket, set the sieve or basket over or in a saucepan with an inch of boiling water in the bottom, put the pan lid on the sieve as tight as it'll go (just inside the rim of the pan, if possible), and steam until hot. Or put the grains and a little water in a saucepan, cover, and place over medium-high heat; cook, gently stirring occasionally, until hot. Drain if necessary. Or use a microwave oven (I don't have one, but I know they work): Put the grains in a microwave-safe bowl with a splash of water, cover loosely with a lid or vented plastic wrap or waxed paper, and heat on full power until heated through or thawed, stopping every 30 to 60 seconds to uncover and check them, stirring if necessary so they heat evenly and don't overcook.

TO THAW FROZEN GRAINS WITHOUT HEATING
Dump the frozen grains into a sieve or colander and run it under cold water for a minute, gently breaking up the grains with your fingers or a spatula. Drain well, then reheat as above or use cold. Or, if you have more time, submerge the bag or container of grains in a bowl of cold water set in the sink under a barely running faucet (this could take 30 minutes or so for a couple cups of grain), or put it in the refrigerator overnight.

SUBSTITUTING GRAINS

Do it. By all means, do it. With some simple adjustments in cooking time and maybe liquid quantity (check the Grain-Cooking Cheat Sheet on page 259), you can substitute just about any grain in any recipe for any other similarly sized and textured grain, especially if they're cooked separately and then combined with the other ingredients in a dish. For example, a quinoa salad can be made with any similar (delicate or small) grain—and vice versa; a wheat berry dish can be made with any larger, firmer grain.

PORRIDGE-Y GRAINS:
- Amaranth
- Barley grits (broken-up hulled barley)
- Cornmeal, grits, or polenta
- Oatmeal
- Short-grain or sweet brown rice, stirred while cooking
- Teff

DELICATE, SMALL GRAINS:
- Bulgur
- Cracked wheat
- Freekeh
- Millet
- Quinoa
- Whole wheat couscous

FIRMER, LARGER GRAINS:
- Buckwheat groats
- Farro
- Hulled or hull-less barley
- Kamut berries
- Kasha
- Long-grain or basmati brown rice
- Oat groats
- Rye berries
- Spelt berries
- Triticale berries
- Wheat berries
- Whole hominy
- Wild rice

USEFUL COOKWARE FOR THE WHOLE GRAIN KITCHEN

Most of the recipes in this book don't require any special equipment or tools, but the following basic vessels and utensils will be useful. With a few exceptions (a good nonstick surface for the occasional injera, a cast-iron skillet for cornbread), I prefer heavy tri-ply stainless-steel saucepans, pots, and sauté pans. They heat evenly, the surface results in beautiful browning and nice crusts, and they're super easy to clean and maintain.

HEAVY 2-QUART (2-L) SAUCEPAN WITH A TIGHT-FITTING LID:

You can cook the larger, firmer whole grains, wheat berries and the like, in any kind of vessel that you can boil water in. Quinoa, millet, and rice are best cooked in a heavy saucepan with a tight-fitting lid, preferably in smaller batches and smaller pans. To cook 1 to 1½ cups (170 to 300 g) of any of these, a 1½- to 2-quart (2-L) saucepan is ideal—these grains like being a bit snug in the pot, I think. For larger batches, a 3-quart (2.8-L) saucepan is useful, though you could also use a . . .

HEAVY 6-QUART (5.7-L) DUTCH OVEN:
I cook soups and stews, boil pasta, braise meats, and make paella-type dishes in my trusty tri-ply stainless-steel Dutch oven. I like the ease factor of stainless, but those fancy enameled cast-iron Dutch ovens are nice too.

HEAVY SAUTÉ PANS WITH LIDS:
There are three I use most often: a small 8-inch (20-cm) for toasting spices and nuts, frying eggs, and reheating single servings of leftovers; a larger 12-inch (30.5-cm) for most pasta sauces, pan-searing fish or chicken, risottos, and so on; and a deeper, steep-sided large sauté pan for big batches of one-pot dishes or stovetop braises.

WELL-SEASONED 12-INCH (30.5-CM) CAST-IRON SKILLET AND FLAT GRIDDLE:

For cornbread, pancakes, and the occasional tomato-based braise so we all get our iron.

NONSTICK GRIDDLE OR SAUTÉ PAN:
For injera. Sometimes I use a large griddle for pancakes.

SIEVE AND STEAMER BASKET:
Find a deep fine-mesh sieve or two for draining and reheating grains. If you cook rice often, and want to use the two-stage method I describe on page 29, a collapsible metal steamer basket will make it easy.

HEATPROOF SILICONE SPATULAS, A WOODEN SPURTLE, AND A RUBBER SPATULA:

For stirring, natch. (See page 26 for more on the spurtle.)

SPICE MILL, MINI FOOD PROCESSOR, AND BLENDER:

For grinding spices fresh, making oat or quinoa flour, pureeing hummus and other condiments and sauces. I don't have or need a full-size food processor, and you won't need any top-of-the-line high-powered processing or blending equipment for these recipes.

WHOLE GRAIN COOKING FOR VEGETARIANS, VEGANS, GLUTEN FREES, AND THE EMPHATICALLY NOT

I'm not vegetarian, vegan, or gluten free. I eat everything (except fava beans), and so do the people I regularly cook for (well, my husband, Derek, won't eat lettuce, and our daughter, Thalia, won't eat onions or fermented long beans at the moment). But there are enough people in my life who prefer not to eat meat, or dairy, or gluten-containing grains that I wanted these recipes to be useful to them or at least easily adaptable to their needs. Each recipe that conforms to these dietary restrictions indicates that next to the yield for quick reference.

If you're very sensitive to gluten or have celiac disease, be sure to read labels of any grains or prepared ingredients to be sure they are explicitly gluten free, and buy your grains in sealed packages from trusted sources rather than from bulk bins. Take special care when using oats: Oats themselves are gluten free, but they're often grown or processed near enough to gluten-containing grains that they may contain trace amounts. Oats that are truly gluten free will be labeled as such.

You might notice that there are very few dishes in this book that use high-demand premium cuts of meat or larger, rarer fish species. Because they offer more flavor and because it's a more responsible way to eat meat and fish, I prefer to use, for example, chicken thighs or whole chicken over bland boneless, skinless breasts; beef chuck roast and pork shoulder over steaks and loin chops; small fish and shellfish over tuna steaks; wild-caught salmon over farmed. I love a good New York strip steak or a perfectly pan-seared piece of halibut as much as anyone, but one of my goals here is to provide examples of how to use lesser cuts and smaller fish to make satisfying, delicious everyday meals.

The Grains

In this book, I focus on whole grains that are readily available in good supermarkets or whole foods stores. Some are more unusual than others, and I hope that even if you're familiar with every grain stocking the bins at your local health food store, you'll find something curious and intriguing in these pages. Even as I write this, new grains—or, rather, newly rediscovered ancient grains—are coming into markets all over the world, but since they're not yet easy to obtain, I think it would be a frustrating tease to include recipes using them here. For example, fonio, a tiny grain from West Africa, may well become as common as quinoa, but it's still so rare that I haven't even found a good online source for it. (Perhaps, if it's tasty, fonio will appear in my next book. For now, it's omitted.) Likewise, there are a multitude of whole grain flours on the market these days, and given the health benefits of moving away from refined flours, it's well worth exploring each and every one of them. In the recipes in this book, however, I've limited myself to those I'm currently most familiar with, that I enjoy using, and that are readily available offline.

Following are brief descriptions of each of the grains featured in the recipes—where they come from, what they look and taste like, how to cook with them. Gluten-free grains are noted so they will be easy for the gluten-concerned to reference. Against the advice of my editor, I've also listed the botanical names of the grains—not to be pedantic but because I myself found knowing those names, and thus where each grain fit into the order of the universe of plants, to be extremely helpful in understanding what exactly a grain is and how the different grains are related to other plants. After the introduction to each grain, I describe how to cook it in the most basic way. You'll notice that the starting quantities and yields vary a bit from grain to grain; this is because I imagine you'll want to cook some grains in smaller quantities (like a single serving of rolled oats for breakfast) than others (like wheat berries intended for the freezer and later use). Porridgey, soft-cooked grains can be cooked in any quantity but aren't great options for freezing; fluffy, pilaf-style grains are best cooked in small quantities (1 or 2 cups / 225 or 455 g) so they don't become mushy, but can be frozen and thawed with reasonable success; large, firm grains can be cooked in industrial-size quantities and frozen and thawed easily.

AMARANTH

Amaranthus, fam. Amaranthaceae
gluten free

Amaranth

Native to the Americas, the pseudograin amaranth was first domesticated five to seven thousand years ago, probably in central Mexico, and to the Aztecs and Incas, it was as important a crop as maize and legumes. It's believed that the blood-red seed heads of amaranth played an important role in Mexican religious rituals, and when the Spanish arrived in the 1500s, they so strongly discouraged the production of amaranth ("discouraged" is putting it mildly; they burned acres of amaranth to the ground) that the grain eventually fell into obscurity until it was rediscovered by U.S. growers and health-food types in the 1970s. It's not hard to understand why amaranth was so important to pre-Columbian peoples as well as to those bell-bottomed vegetarians: Amaranth is a well-balanced complete protein that's high in lysine (an amino acid uncommon in grains); is relatively drought-, pest-, and disease-resistant; and can be cultivated under a variety of conditions.

Assuming you're not going to mix it with blood to make figurines to offer to

your pagan gods, what can you do with this wondrous pseudograin, and what does it taste like? To be honest, amaranth is a relative newcomer to my own kitchen, and at first it was a somewhat challenging one. The individual seeds are very tiny and pale brown, and when cooked in water, porridge style, they stick together in a mass of little spheres that are tender but so minuscule it's hard to know if you've even crushed them between your teeth or not. They don't, no matter what I've tried, cook into a fluffy pilaf—it's just not what they do, and there's no use trying to make them into something like a pilaf. Their texture is actually very similar to that of beluga caviar, and in fact at one point in my experiments, I dusted a bowlful of well-salted soft-cooked amaranth with powdered toasted nori seaweed, closed my eyes, and almost tasted that delightful roe. I suspect there aren't many vegans who miss caviar so much that they'd go to the trouble of trying to produce a substitute, but if you're out there, I have these words for you: Start chilling the vodka.

I'm no supertaster, but I've read a lot of descriptions of the flavor of amaranth that don't seem very accurate. To me, soft-cooked amaranth tastes—and smells—grassy and herbal. It doesn't taste or smell like any other grain, but rather more like a fresh green vegetable, and once I came to understand that, I learned to appreciate it on its own terms. Sure, it can be served as a sort of "polenta," but instead of (or in addition to) stirring in grated Parmesan, I'd suggest pairing it with an ingredient that highlights the green flavor, like barely wilted spinach. I also find amaranth to work exceptionally well in brothy soups, filling them out and providing a welcome hearty

texture without weighing them down the way that a nuttier or "grainier" grain could. The tomatillo and amaranth soup with chicken on page 121 would be a good jumping-off point for other similar dishes with tangy, vegetal elements—tomato, citrus, unripe plums, green mango.

The other way to get your amaranth fix is to pop it: Tossed into a very hot dry pan, the little seeds immediately puff and turn bright white like popcorn and take on an entirely different flavor that I can only describe as toasty, browned, warm. Keep a jar of popped amaranth in the cupboard and sprinkle the puffs on salads or breakfast cereal, yogurt, or ice cream. Or pop a whole lot of amaranth to make the Mexican sweets called alegrías (page 230), or—and this is probably my favorite use of amaranth yet—fold popped amaranth into melted dark chocolate to make crisp, delicate, toasty-tasting chocolates (page 229).

TO SOFT-COOK AMARANTH

Grain	1 cup (200 g)	2 cups (330 g)
Water	3 cups (720 ml)	6 cups (1.4 L)
Salt	Pinch	¼ teaspoon
Pan size	2-quart (2-L)	3-quart (2.8-L)
Yield	2 cups (330 g)	4 cups (660 g)

In a heavy saucepan over medium-high heat, toast the amaranth, stirring frequently, until a shade darker and just beginning to crackle. Stir in the water and salt and bring to a boil, stirring, then lower the heat and simmer briskly, stirring occasionally, until the grains are tender and translucent and the mixture is thick, about 20 minutes. (The mixture won't start to thicken until the last few minutes.) If not using right away, transfer to an airtight container and refrigerate. Amaranth doesn't freeze especially well. To reheat, see page 15.

TO POP AMARANTH

Use a large, heavy, stainless-steel sauté pan or wide saucepan that has a lid (preferably a glass lid so you can see what's going on inside). Heat the pan over high heat, on a burner that fully covers the bottom of the pan, for several minutes—it needs to be blisteringly hot. Toss a few drops of water into the pan; if they don't evaporate right away but rather dance crazily around the pan for several seconds first, the pan is the right temperature. Add 1 to 2 tablespoons amaranth to the pan, quickly put the lid on, and shake the pan back and forth over the heat. The amaranth should start to pop within a couple seconds. Lift the lid if necessary after about 5 seconds and check to see if the grains have puffed up into little white balls. If they have, and you see many more white puffs than brown grains, remove from the heat and immediately pour them out onto a plate to cool. Return the pan to the heat, make sure it's good and hot, and repeat with more amaranth.

Some batches, it must be said, will burn before the grains pop. If they don't start popping almost as soon as they hit the hot pan, dump them out onto a plate (before they burn) and try popping that batch again after the grains have cooled. On a good day, ¼ cup (56 g) raw amaranth yields over 1 cup (60 g) popped amaranth. Store popped amaranth in an airtight container at room temperature for up to 1 month.

BARLEY
Hordeum vulgare, fam. Poaceae
contains gluten

Purple barley / Hulled barley

Cheap and versatile, barley is truly an ancient grain. First cultivated at least ten thousand years ago in Africa and southeast Asia and used as currency by the Sumerians, it can be grown just about anywhere, in extremely hot and extremely cold climates. Today in the United States, more than half of the barley grown is used for animal feed, and almost half is used to make barley malt syrup and sweeteners (sprouted barley is high in maltose) and beer; a paltry 2 percent is used as a grain for human consumption. Most of that is either ground for flour or "pearled," meaning that not just the hull but also most of the bran is removed to make it slightly quicker cooking. Pearl barley, as it's called, is fine and delicious, but it's not really a whole grain. In these recipes, I use what's usually labeled "hulled" barley: The grains have been stripped of their hulls but most of the bran remains. Not all of the bran is left on the grain because the abrasion necessary to remove the barley's especially stubborn hull results in some loss of bran as well. There are new varieties

of "hull-less" barley, which, as the name implies, do not need to be hulled and so retain all of the bran, but they're not nearly as widely available as the hulled barley. Barley is also commonly sold as flakes, which are simply rolled-flat barley grains, and barley grits, which are toasted and ground grains; however, these two processed forms of the grain can be made with either hulled or pearl barley, and it's often difficult to tell which has been used, so I stick with the hulled or hull-less variety.

Cooked whole barley is absorbent and has a mild and pleasant flavor that adapts very well to whatever other ingredients you cook with it, and it works in salads as well as it does in liquidy soups like mushroom-barley soup. It releases its starch into the cooking liquid reluctantly, but is still a good option for a risotto-like dish that's much more healthful than the white rice version.

Barley's main claim to fame in the age of vitamin-fortified flours and rice is its fiber content. Just a cup (160 g) of cooked barley provides over 13 g of dietary fiber, which is about half of the RDA, and barley's insoluble fiber, as it ferments in the colon, produces a certain acid that may help lower blood cholesterol. It's also a lower-glycemic food, meaning that for most people, it does not result in a blood-sugar spike.

TO COOK HULLED OR HULL-LESS BARLEY

Grain	1 cup (200 g)	3 cups (600 g)
Water	3 cups (720 ml)	5 cups (1.2 L)
Salt	¼ teaspoon	½ teaspoon
Pan size	2-quart (2-L)	3-quart (2.8-L)
Yield	2½ to 3 cups (400 to 480 g)	5 cups (800 g)

In a heavy saucepan, combine the barley, water, and salt. Cover, bring to a boil, then lower the heat and simmer until the barley is tender and no trace of bright white is visible at the center when a grain is cut in half, about 40 minutes. Drain well. If not using right away, rinse the grains under cold water to cool, drain well, then transfer to an airtight container and refrigerate or freeze. To reheat, see page 15.

BUCKWHEAT
Fagopyrum esculentum Moench,
fam. Polygonaceae | gluten free

Buckwheat kasha / Buckwheat groats

Buckwheat is a gluten-free pseudograin from the knotweed family of dicots—the same family as tangy rhubarb and tangy garden sorrel—and thus, despite the name, is not related to wheat at all. The plant is native to southern China and was likely first domesticated in China in the second or first century B.C.E; it has been cultivated extensively in Russia (the plant does well in the cold) only since the fifteenth century. The multisided, funny-looking, almost-pyramidal seed of the plant is contained in a hard shell or hull that's removed in processing. The pale, green-brown hulled seeds are called buckwheat groats, and the dark-brown roasted seeds are called kasha.

Buckwheat is a complete protein, containing all of the essential amino acids—including the elusive lysine, which is not commonly found in grains—and is high in blood-improving magnesium. It's also been proven useful in controlling blood sugar levels, due partly to its high dietary fiber content.

Despite all that good news, buckwheat groats and kasha were a tough sell for me, an acquired taste. But I did acquire it. The distinctive flavor of the grains—earthy, nutty, dark—can easily wipe out more delicate ingredients like fresh vegetables and herbs, and so work best with other deep, rich flavors. Pairing the groats with smoky flavors, as in the smoked fish cakes on page 74, or setting the richness off with a brightly dressed salad of sharp greens, say, lets them shine in a way that they don't in the common kasha varnishkes preparation, where kasha is tossed with farfalle pasta, mushrooms, and little else to counterbalance its earthiness.

Cooking buckwheat groats or kasha in simmering water like any other grain tends to yield grains that stick together and can't easily be tossed with other ingredients (though it's perfectly fine if you're shaping them into griddle cakes or the like). The best solution is odd yet traditional: Beat a whole egg or an egg white and stir in the raw groats to coat them well, cook the groats in a dry saucepan until the grains separate and appear dry, then add water and continue to cook until tender. The coating (butter or oil can be used instead of the egg but they don't coat the buckwheat quite as well) keeps the grains pleasantly fluffy and separate.

BUCKWHEAT FLOUR
Buckwheat flour, which is always whole grain even if the label doesn't specify so, is an excellent option for those who may not want to bother with whole groats but wish to reap their benefits. Buckwheat flour is a form in which the grain's earthiness is tamer and possibly more welcome anyway—it is absolutely delightful, and a great addition to quickbread recipes. I like to add a few cupped handfuls of it to whatever bread dough I'm kneading at the moment for extra flavor and richness—don't add too much of this flour, though, or the dough won't be stretchy enough to rise properly. (Since it doesn't contain gluten, use it judiciously in yeasted breads, with plenty of gluten-containing flour such as wheat.) All-buckwheat crêpes and pancakes are subtle enough to serve as bases for sweet dishes. Soba noodles made entirely with buckwheat flour are rare, but even those with wheat flour as the main ingredient and some buckwheat are more healthful than all-wheat noodles.

As much as I've learned about whole grains, it's still a mystery to me why buckwheat flour, even though it's made from whole buckwheat groats, results in crêpes, pancakes, and breads that do not end up tasting remotely like the cooked groats do. So even if you've been scarred by a poorly made kasha varnishkes at some point in your life, do not rule out using buckwheat flour.

TO COOK BUCKWHEAT GROATS OR KASHA (ROASTED BUCKWHEAT)

Grain	1 cup (165 g)	2 cups (330 g)
Egg, butter or oil	1 large egg white, or 1 tablespoon butter or oil	1 whole large egg, or 2 tablespoons butter or oil
Water	1½ cups (360 ml)	3 cups (720 ml)
Salt (opt.)	¼ teaspoon	½ teaspoon
Pan size	2-quart (2-L)	3-quart (2.8-L)
Yield	3½ cups (600 g)	7 cups (1.2 kg)

If using egg, beat the egg in a bowl and add the buckwheat; toss to coat well. Heat a heavy saucepan over medium heat, then add the egg-coated buckwheat and cook, stirring constantly, until the grains are dry and no longer clumping together, about 3 minutes. Add the water and salt. Cover, bring to a boil over high heat, then lower the heat and simmer until the water is absorbed and the buckwheat is tender, about 10 minutes. Remove from the heat and let stand, covered, for 5 minutes.

If using butter or oil, heat the butter or oil in a heavy saucepan over medium heat, then add the buckwheat and cook, stirring constantly, until fragrant, about 3 minutes. Add the water and salt. Cover, bring to a boil over high heat, then lower the heat and simmer until the water is absorbed and the buckwheat is tender, about 10 minutes. Remove from the heat and let stand, covered, for 5 minutes.

If not using right away, spread on a large plate to cool, then transfer to an airtight container and refrigerate or freeze. To reheat, see page 15.

CORN
Zea mays, fam. Poaceae
gluten free

Popcorn / Cornmeal

It appears from recent genetic research and archeological excavations that corn, or maize, is a descendant of a wild grass called teosinte, which is native to the Rio Balsas river valley in Mexico; corn was first domesticated in the region sometime around 8700 B.C.E. And as every schoolchild knows (or used to know), Columbus took the popular maize from the New World back to Europe, and it spread from there, quickly becoming the most-cultivated grain crop in the world, as it was both plentiful and cheap.

But problems arose with corn when grown and consumed in its new locations. In Latin America, corn kernels were commonly soaked in an alkaline lime solution in a process called nixtamalization, probably first developed around 1500 B.C.E.; this removed some of the tough outer layers so it would be easier to grind into a paste to make the region's staples: tortillas, tamales, and so on. It's unclear whether it was known then that nixtamalization brings with it a beneficial side effect—the release of niacin and amino acids in the grain that would otherwise be unavailable to the body—but either way, when corn was introduced to Europe, the concept of nixtamalization was unfortunately left behind. In addition, the Central and South Americans knew to combine corn, an incomplete protein, with local squash and legumes, which made up for its nutritional shortcomings (the Three Sisters, as they were called, also have complementary growing patterns and so were planted together), but that habit didn't make the trip either. As corn's popularity increased and its use spread, so did a horrible and often deadly condition called pellagra, which we now know is a result of niacin deficiency. As recently as the early twentieth century, pellagra could still be found among patients in mental institutions in the United States (particularly in the South) who were fed diets consisting mainly of corn products, and it slowly dawned on scientists and doctors studying the problem that diet rather than contagion might be to blame.

Corn, nixtamalized or not, has a reputation as a relatively poor nutrition source, and when compared to other whole grains, the rap is not entirely undeserved. It's at the bottom of the protein-content list, along with rice, but has high levels of vitamins A and B_1 (thiamin). It's also high in fiber, of course, and is a pretty decent source of calcium for a grain, especially when nixtamalized.

So is corn always whole grain? Though nixtamalization removes much of the grain's bran, enough of the outer layer remains—and the nutritional benefits of the process are great enough—that the USDA and the Whole Grains Council consider hominy, known as posole in the Southwest, and its derivatives (*masa harina* for tamales and tortillas, for example) to be whole grain products.

Cornmeal is trickier. A large percentage of the cornmeal sold in supermarkets has been degerminated (it should say so on the package), which means the germ of the grain has been removed. This improves shelf life, but renders the cornmeal nutritionally inferior. Some cornmeal is actually labeled "whole corn" or "whole grain"; however, when it is not labeled as such, sometimes it *is* actually made from whole corn, especially if it is "stone ground," but it's hard to tell without seeing the meal itself. If you see lots of dark specks, it's probably whole grain cornmeal; otherwise it's likely not.

Grits and polenta are similarly confusing, as the grinds differ dramatically from brand to brand, and often the labeling is unhelpful or unclear about whether the product was made from whole corn or degerminated corn. In general, though, fine cornmeal will look and feel like very coarse flour (look for brown specks to determine whether it's whole grain); "polenta" is a medium grind (and very often is not whole grain); "old-fashioned grits," "hominy grits," "speckled grits," and "corn grits" are all fairly coarse (and are usually whole grain). If you're lucky, you may also come across roasted cornmeal, a hyper-regional Pennsylvania Dutch product, which is whole grain. Roasting the whole corn before grinding it not only imparts a deep, toasty flavor but also improves the cornmeal's shelf life without the need to remove the germ.

Uncooked and canned cooked whole hominy can be found with the Mexican foods in better supermarkets, and of course in Mexican grocery stores. The uncooked grains, sold in bags like dried beans, look like small (1/8-inch / 3 mm), off-white or pale yellow, irregularly shaped chunks of gravel; on closer inspection, you'll be able to recognize their corn-kernel provenance. Canned hominy can be white or yellow, and while some people express strong preferences for one or the other, I myself can't detect any difference whatsoever between them beyond the color.

TO SOFT-COOK CORNMEAL, POLENTA, OR GRITS

Grain	1 cup (160 g)	1½ cups (240 g)
Water	4 cups (960 ml)	6 cups (1.4 L)
Salt	½ teaspoon	1 teaspoon
Pan size	2-quart (2-L)	3-quart (2.8-L)
Yield	4 cups (960 g)	6 cups (1.4 kg)

In a heavy saucepan, combine the water and salt. Bring to a boil, then gradually whisk in the cornmeal. Lower the heat and simmer (it should plop and bubble just once every few seconds), whisking frequently and stirring with a silicone spatula to prevent it from sticking to the pan, until the cornmeal is thick but still pourable and the individual granules are tender, about 35 minutes for coarse, 15 minutes for medium, or 5 to 10 minutes for fine cornmeal; add another ½ cup (120 ml) water if the mixture becomes thick before the granules are tender. Serve hot, or let cool and refrigerate in an airtight container.

TO REHEAT: Scrape it into a saucepan and add a little water. Heat over medium heat, stirring to incorporate the water and prevent the cornmeal from sticking, until smooth and hot.

TO PREPARE FIRM CORNMEAL, POLENTA, OR GRITS

Prepare the cornmeal, polenta, or grits using the soft-cooked method above, then pour into an airtight container or in a ½-inch-thick (12-mm-thick) layer in a lightly oiled pan, let cool, then cover and chill in the refrigerator until firm. A 9-inch (23-cm) square pan is just right for 4 cups (960 g) of cooked cornmeal.

Cut the firm cornmeal into squares, rectangles, the Empire State Building, or whatever shape you want. In a well-seasoned or nonstick skillet, heat some olive oil, butter, lard, or bacon grease over medium-high heat. Add the cornmeal shapes in one layer and cook without disturbing them until well browned on the bottom, 5 to 6 minutes. Flip and brown the other side. To minimize spattering, pat the bottom of each shape dry with a paper towel before adding it to the pan. Alternatively, heat a charcoal grill. Lightly brush the cornmeal shapes on either side with oil and grill until well marked. Pan-fried or grilled cornmeal shapes can be made a day in advance, covered, and refrigerated.

TO REHEAT: Place shapes on a wire rack set on a baking sheet and reheat in a 350°F (175°C) oven for about 15 minutes.

TO COOK WHOLE HOMINY OR POSOLE

Grain	1 cup (160 g)	2 cups (320 g)
Water	3 cups (720 ml)	6 cups (1.4 L)
Salt (opt.)	½ teaspoon	1 teaspoon
Pan size	2-quart (2-L)	3-quart (2.8-L)
Yield	2½ cups (600 g)	5 cups (1.2 kg)

In a heavy saucepan, combine the hominy, water, and salt. Cover, bring to a boil, then lower the heat and simmer until the hominy is tender and no trace of bright white is visible at the center when a grain is cut in half, about 40 minutes. Drain well. If not using right away, rinse under cold water to cool, drain well, then transfer to an airtight container and refrigerate or freeze. To reheat, see page 15.

MILLET

Pennisetum glaucum, fam. Poaceae
gluten free

Millet / Puffed millet

Yes, the pale tan spherical grain that bulks out birdseed is millet—and delicious, nutritious birdseed it is, too. Most of the crop grown in the United States is used for animal feed, but as its popularity here grows, that may change. Pearl millet is the most common variety grown for food in the United States, but don't be fooled by its name into thinking it's been "pearled," or had its nutritients processed out; it is whole. This gluten-free true grain has been a staple for vegetarian and health-conscious cooks for decades, but it really does deserve a wider audience. Millet is more common in the Indian subcontinent than it is in the West, and for centuries, before rice rose to dominance, it was the staple grain of China. In the northern regions, it is still used much as rice is in the rest of the country; it is usually cooked to a soft gruel similar to rice-based congee or jook rather than a fluffy pilaf. It is also available puffed, sold in the cereal aisle of the grocery store. Millet, which by some estimates serves as the main source of nutrition for a third of the world's population, contains several important nutrients, including magnesium, phosphorous, and vitamin B_3 (niacin).

The grain is practically foolproof, cooking up into a fluffy pilaf-type texture with very little effort. Toasting the raw grains, either in a dry pan or in a little fat, deepens and intensifies millet's otherwise fairly mild flavor, but has no effect on the cooked millet's finished texture; it's up to you whether you toast or not. Millet tastes a lot like corn to me and works very well in spicy, highly seasoned, cumin-scented dishes—Mexican- and Indian-style ones especially. It's also perfect for thickening liquidy stews and dals, and can also be molded into little timbales for fussy-fancy serving presentations or mixed with a little egg to bind it into patties for pan-frying.

MILLET FLOUR

Mild, easygoing millet flour (aka bajra flour) is used extensively in India, particularly with fresh fenugreek leaves (methi) in the Gujarati snack pancakes called dhebra, and in parathas, rotis, dosas, and other flatbreads, where it's often combined with wheat flour.

TO COOK MILLET

Grain	1 cup (200 g)	2 cups (400 g)
Water	2 cups (480 ml)	4 cups (960 ml)
Salt (opt.)	¼ teaspoon	½ teaspoon
Pan size	2-quart (2-L)	3-quart (2.8-L)
Yield	4 cups (700 g)	8 cups (1.4 kg)

In a heavy saucepan over medium-high heat, toast the millet, stirring constantly, until fragrant, 3 to 4 minutes. Add the water and salt, cover, bring to a boil, then lower the heat and simmer until the millet is tender and the liquid is absorbed, 20 to 25 minutes. If not using right away, spread on a large plate to cool, then transfer to an airtight container and refrigerate or freeze. To reheat, see page 15.

OATS

Avena sativa, fam. Poaceae
sometimes gluten free

Top: Oat groats / Steel-cut oats
Bottom: Scottish (pinhead) oats / Rolled oats

World peace and prosperity! Lions and lambs, dogs and cats, left and right, all lie down together and cuddle! Single-payer health care for everyone! There's really nothing a well-cooked pot of the great *Avena sativa* isn't capable of achieving for humankind if only we'd let it—well, maybe not universal health care . . . though we might need it less if we all ate more oats.

I suppose I do tend to go over-board declaring my love of oats, but even if they weren't arguably one of the most healthful foods on the planet (proven beyond a doubt to decrease the risk of heart disease, for example), easy to prepare, easy to shop for (oat products are always whole grain), I'd still be in their thrall simply because they're delicious and easily changed up from bowl to bowl. You can do pretty much anything with well-cooked oats.

But I wasn't always this way: Like many Americans who grew up on quick-cooking oatmeal or even, God forbid, the flavored instant stuff in the single-serving envelopes (which I actually kinda liked as a kid), I had no idea what pleasures awaited me in the form of chewy steel-cut oats (which are, as the name suggests, whole oat groats that have been cut into pieces with a steel blade), creamy Scottish or pinhead oats (which are cut oats that have been ground to a finer consis-tency and contain more floury bits), and hearty "old-fashioned" rolled oats (which are oat groats that have been briefly steamed and then flattened between metal rollers to different de-grees of thinness). There's a long-lived thread on Chowhound asking folks what popular foods they can't seem to bring themselves to appreciate, and oatmeal has come up more times than I'm comfortable reporting. Most detractors admit to the grain's mildly sweet and pleasant flavor but blame its consistency for their unreasonably hysterical revulsion. Cooking oatmeal isn't rocket science, but too often, I think, oats, whether rolled or steel-cut, are simply overcooked, in too much liquid. The porridge should be creamy and thick, but the individual pieces of grain should remain texturally distinct, even a little chewy. Try oats again, cooking them less—a revelation may be in the offing for you as well.

The other issue people seem to have with oatmeal is that bowl after bowl of the stuff, day after day, can get old quick. However, oats are endlessly adaptable to all sorts of dishes and flavor combinations, and it is a shame not to take advantage of the grain's versatility. The list of crazy ideas I offer on pages 48 to 51 is a start.

In addition to fantastic rolled and cut oats, whole oat grains, unfortu-nately called oat groats, should not be neglected. They cook up more quickly than you might expect—in just about 20 minutes—and are a pleasant, slightly sweet, easygoing grain to use in salads, in pilafs with beans or lentils, in homey stews, or as a comforting plain side dish.

Oats themselves are gluten free, but it's important to note that most are grown or processed in such close proximity to gluten-containing grains that they may contain or be contami-nated with gluten. If you have celiac disease or are very sensitive to gluten, stay away from the bulk bins and check the package's label to be sure your oats are gluten free.

OAT FLOUR

Very fine, lovely oat flour is light and delicate and a little sweet, perfect for tender cookies and cakes, or for dredging food to be pan-fried or baked, or for mixing into granola or fruit-crisp toppings. It is always whole grain and is available in many grocery stores or easily made at home—though my oat flour never gets quite as fluffy as store-bought. Simply grind rolled oats (the thinner the better) to a powder in a spice mill or food proces-sor. If you like, you can then sift it to remove larger bits; I don't bother.

TO COOK OAT GROATS

Grain	1 cup (180 g)
Water	3 cups (720 ml)
Salt (opt.)	¼ teaspoon
Pan size	2-quart (2-L)
Yield	2½ cups (560 g)

In a heavy saucepan, combine the oat groats, water, and salt. Cover, bring to a boil, then lower the heat and simmer until the oats are tender and no trace of bright white is visible at the center when a grain is cut in half, about 20 minutes. Drain well. If not using right away, rinse under cold water to cool, drain well, then transfer to an airtight container and refrigerate or freeze. To reheat, see page 15.

TO COOK STEEL-CUT OR SCOTTISH (PINHEAD) OATS

Grain	½ cup (90 g)	1 cup (180 g)
Water	2 cups (480 ml)	4 cups (960 ml)
Salt (opt.)	Pinch	¼ teaspoon
Pan size	2-quart (2-L)	2-quart (2-L)
Yield	1½ to 1¾ cups (370 to 430 g)	3 to 3½ cups (740 to 860 g)

In a heavy saucepan, combine the oats, water, and salt. Bring to a boil, then lower the heat and simmer, stirring frequently, until the mixture is thick and the oats are tender but still a little chewy, 20 to 25 minutes for steel-cut oats, 10 minutes for Scottish. If not using right away, scrape into an airtight container, let cool, and refrigerate. To reheat, see page 15.

TO COOK REGULAR OR EXTRA-THICK ROLLED OATS

Grain	½ cup (80 g)	1 cup (160 g)
Water	1 cup (240 ml) for regular oats, or 1¼ cups (300 ml) for extra-thick oats	2 cups (480 ml) for regular oats, or 2½ cups (600 ml) for extra-thick oats
Salt (opt.)	Pinch	¼ teaspoon
Pan size	2-quart (2-L)	2-quart (2-L)
Yield	1 cup (240 g)	2 cups (480 g)

In a heavy saucepan, combine the oats, water, and salt. Bring to a boil, then lower the heat and simmer, stirring frequently, until the mixture is thick and the oats are tender but still a little chewy, 6 to 8 minutes for regular rolled oats, 10 to 15 minutes for extra-thick. If not using right away, scrape into an airtight container, let cool, and refrigerate. To reheat, see page 15.

ALL HAIL THE SPURTLE

The traditional stirring implement for oatmeal porridge in Scotland is a long, round wooden stick with a tapered rounded or slightly angled end. My mom, when she heard I was going to be writing a book about whole grains, got to work whittling a quiverful of spurtles from mountain alder branches she cut from around the house in the Scotia Valley, north of Spokane, where she and my dad apparently enjoy making work for their retired selves. The spurtles are beautiful, of course, but also, surprisingly, much better for stirring oatmeal—especially the steel-cut variety—than my usual standby for such tasks, the heatproof silicone spatula. A spurtle can get into the corners of the pot and move through the mass of oatmeal without pushing it around too much. Or something. It's hard to explain why these spurtles work so well, but if you make a lot of oatmeal, I'd suggest whittling yourself a stick for stirring it, or have my mom or someone like her whittle one for you.

QUINOA

Chenopodium quinoa,
fam. Amaranthaceae | gluten free

Ivory quinoa / Red quinoa

An ancient pseudograin in the same family as amaranth, and closely related to the edible weed lamb's quarters, quinoa is native to the Andes and has been cultivated in high-altitude Peru since about 3000 B.C.E. The Incas called it *chisiya mama,* or the mother grain, and it's not hard to understand why: The seeds offer a well-balanced complete protein and high levels of calcium, phosphorus, and iron, and the plants grow well in the cold, dry climate of the Andes, where few other crops can survive. Quinoa does, however, require labor-intensive processing to remove the bitter saponin that coats each seed to protect it from birds and insects; these days, most modern quinoa producers employ extensive washing and abrasion to remove it. But since some of the powdery coating may remain even if it's not immediately visible, I still rinse all quinoa well before cooking, having been scarred by my first experience with quinoa a decade and a half or so ago: I'd cooked it myself, never having eaten it before (why not, right?) and had no idea it was supposed to be rinsed first. It was many years before I decided to try it again. Later I read that when the Spanish arrived in South America, they might have rejected quinoa for the same reason, as they declined to send any back to the motherland with shipments of potatoes and corn.

I'm glad I did try it again, because it's quite possibly the most versatile, easy-to-prepare whole grain there is. It's awfully hard to mess up quinoa, which is quite forgiving to the inattentive cook: It never really gets mushy, as the germ, which unfurls from the grain as it cooks, remains a little crunchy (pleasantly so!) even when simmered much longer or in more water than recommended. The flavor is mild, nutty, slightly sweet; the texture is light and fluffy.

Quinoa seeds are a touch smaller than those of millet, but are flat and disk-shaped rather than perfect spheres. If you look closely, you can see the germ (which makes up a whopping 60 percent of the grain), a bright white strand surrounding the edge of the disk. There are three main varieties of quinoa that are readily available in good supermarkets and health food stores: ivory or white, red, and black. Red and black quinoa retain a bit more texture when cooked, and their grains don't clump together as much. In all of the recipes in this book, the three are pretty much interchangeable (like I said, quinoa forgives all), but I do make suggestions when the color or consistency of one would be preferable to another. Quinoa is also available as flakes, which resemble very thin, translucent rolled oats—check the gluten-free section of the store for them. They can be used as a very-quick-cooking hot cereal, or added to baked goods or blended drinks, or ground into flour.

QUINOA FLOUR

You can easily make your own quinoa flour by whirring ivory quinoa to a powder in a spice mill (a mini food processor might work if yours is more powerful than mine seems to be), but it's also available in health food stores—it's always whole grain, even if it doesn't say so on the label. It has a mild, grassy flavor that dissipates a bit as it bakes. I'd add it in small doses to baked goods to up the protein value, but remember that its lack of gluten means it needs to be paired with high-gluten flours in yeast breads.

TO COOK WHOLE IVORY, RED, OR BLACK QUINOA

Grain	1 cup (170 g)	2 cups (340 g)
Water	1½ cups (360 ml)	3 cups (720 ml)
Salt (opt.)	¼ teaspoon	½ teaspoon
Pan size	2-quart (2-L)	3-quart (2.8-L)
Yield	3 cups (560 g)	6 cups (1.1 kg)

Rinse the quinoa well in a fine-mesh sieve; drain well. Put it in a heavy saucepan with the water and salt. Cover and bring to a boil over medium-high heat, then lower the heat and simmer until the quinoa is tender and the liquid is absorbed, 15 to 20 minutes. Fluff with a rubber spatula. If not using right away, transfer to a sieve or spread on a large plate to cool, then transfer to an airtight container and refrigerate or freeze. To reheat or thaw, see page 15.

SPROUTING GRAINS

There aren't huge health benefits to be found in sprouted grains unless you have something against cooked foods and need the additional protein that results from sprouting or if you find cooked grains difficult to digest—sprouting the grain to eat it raw (or simply soaking overnight and draining them before cooking them in the usual way) removes some of the acids present in some grains that can upset the stomach. I like to sprout grains every once in a while for no better reason than that I enjoy the crunchy-chewy texture of raw grains in some dishes, like the salads on pages 107 and 109. Millet, quinoa, hard red wheat berries, and rye berries are the easiest to sprout.

TO SPROUT MILLET, QUINOA, HARD RED WHEAT BERRIES, OR RYE BERRIES

Put 1 cup (200 g) raw millet, quinoa, hard red wheat berries, or rye berries in a fine-mesh sieve and rinse well under cool running water; drain. Transfer to a quart-size (960-ml) container (a glass canning jar with a wide mouth is perfect) and cover with at least 3 cups (720 ml) cool water (enough to fill the jar). Cover loosely with the lid and let soak at room temperature for about 8 hours. Drain by holding an upside-down fine-mesh sieve flush against the mouth of the jar and flipping over; once drained, tip the grains back into the jar. Cover with water again to rinse the grains, drain them well, put the lid on loosely or cover the jar with a piece of cheesecloth secured with a rubber band, and set aside at room temperature for 4 to 8 hours. Continue to rinse and drain like this about twice a day, until the grains are sprouted—the sprouts will be very small but tender-crunchy, with just the barest hint of pale green. Note that sprouted grains don't look like sprouted beans—the sprout part is much shorter and smaller. Tighten the lid on the jar and refrigerate. Eat the sprouts raw (in a salad, for example, or on a sandwich), or knead them into bread dough for extra texture, within 2 days.

RICE

Oryza sativa, fam. Poaceae
gluten free

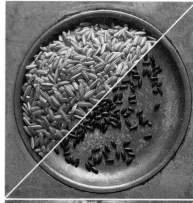

Top: Wehani rice / Chinese black rice
Bottom: Short-grain brown rice / Brown basmati rice

Rice is one of the earliest domesticated grains, first cultivated in the Yangtze River Valley in China at least eight thousand years ago (probably much earlier), and the staple food of more than half the world's population. Rice is more important to Asian food cultures than any one food is to American food culture. You likely already have a sense of the centrality of rice in Asia, and have read that in many Asian languages the words that refer to generalized eating and to rice in particular are similar, if not the same (kind of how in my mom's family the word for dessert was "pie"). If you need a more commercial-minded illustration of rice's wide-ranging importance, you might be interested to know that the word *Toyota* means "rich rice field," and *Honda* means something like "main rice field."

Most rice consumed today is white rice, which has been milled to such an extent that the bran and germ have been polished off to reveal the pearly white, starchy endosperm; in the process, rice loses most of its B vitamin and iron content, as well as most of the fiber. Brown rice, our focus here, is the whole grain: rice with its bran and germ and all its nutrients intact. Replacing white rice with brown rice—or red or Chinese black rice, which are also whole—can have significant health benefits. Chinese black rice, or gao den, a medium-grain nonglutinous rice, is worth seeking out in particular—it's available in any Asian grocery store and many supermarkets—for its iron content as well as its gorgeous color. Sure, whole grain rice is nuttier tasting than white rice, but what's wrong with nutty? Like other nonprocessed grains, it takes a bit longer to cook (though there are ways you might get around that) and does have a shorter shelf life, but unless you're stocking up for the end times, as an average consumer you won't need to worry too much about brown rice going rancid.

There are countless varieties of rice, but since as yet only a few of them are very readily available here in their unpolished, whole grain form, the recipes in this book represent those few general types, and you can adapt them to whatever new variety of rice you might find in specialty stores. The most common whole grain rices are:

- **Brown basmati rice:** long grain, aromatic, fluffy with separate grains when cooked
- **Long-grain or Carolina brown rice:** relatively fluffy when cooked
- **Short-grain brown rice or brown sweet rice:** stickier or creamier when cooked
- **Chinese black or "forbidden" rice:** medium grain, relatively sticky and creamy when cooked
- **Wehani or red rice:** medium grain, separate when cooked

There are entire books devoted to determining the very best way to cook different kinds of rice, and no matter what method you use, you should be aware that every bag or container of rice will be a little bit different from the last. One particular brand and variety of rice had been cooking up perfectly for me for so long that I thought I'd finally cracked the rice-cooking code. My hubris was rewarded with a couple miserable months of slogging my way through a huge bag of the same rice that absolutely refused to become tender at the center no matter how long it was cooked or in how much water or how much the rest of it disintegrated into mush in the pan. I'll provide some simple and usually very effective stovetop saucepan methods below, but with rice more than any other grain you'll probably have to experiment to figure out what works best for you and your rice. If you have a rice cooker—which I do not, since I have a couple of good heavy saucepans and, usually, the time to employ them to cook grains—rices and other whole grains like millet, quinoa, wheat berries, rye berries, even cornmeal can all be cooked in one, though you will probably have to experiment a bit to find the right setting

and grain-to-water ratio for each grain and for your particular model of rice cooker.

BROWN RICE FLOUR
I thought brown rice flour was an affront to humanity—it was coarse and produced dry and unpalatable baked goods—until I discovered the extra-super-fine variety made by Bob's Red Mill and the stuff that's now available in bulk at my local specialty food store. These more sophisticated flours make tender, crumbly butter cookies, and are eminently useful in gluten-free baked goods.

TO COOK BROWN BASMATI, LONG-GRAIN BROWN RICE, OR WEHANI OR OTHER RED RICES, TWO-STAGE METHOD
The best way I've found to cook long-grain brown rices so the grains stay relatively separate and don't become mushy is fairly simple and requires no fussy measurements.

Rinse the rice in at least three changes of cool water, then put it in a heavy saucepan (for about a cup of rice use a 1½- to 2-quart / 1.4- to 2-L pot; for a larger batch use a 3-quart / 2.8-L pot) and add water to just cover it. Bring to a boil, then lower the heat and simmer for 15 minutes. The rice will be tender but not cooked all the way through. Drain in a deep sieve and rinse gently under running water. (If you like, transfer all or some of the rice to freezer bags and refrigerate or freeze to steam later.) To continue to cook the rice, put about 1 inch of water in the saucepan and set the sieve over the pan with the lid nestled down over the rice. (Even better, especially if you're making a large-ish batch, consider putting the rice in a collapsible steamer basket and setting it down inside the pan and then covering the pan.) Bring to a boil and steam the rice until tender and cooked all the way through, 15 to 20 minutes.

If you eat a lot of rice, it might make sense to parboil a couple cups of it at a time, dividing it into batches and refrigerating or freezing it for later. To thaw frozen parboiled rice, dump it out of the bag or other container into a sieve or steamer basket and rinse under cool running water for a minute or so, using your fingers to separate the grains; it's now ready to steam and serve.

TO COOK BROWN BASMATI, OR OTHER LONG-GRAIN OR SHORT-GRAIN BROWN RICE, SIMPLE ABSORPTION METHOD

If you prefer to cook your rice in one stage, you can either simmer any amount of rice in lots of salted water (like pasta) and drain it well in a sieve, or use the absorption method below. If you use the absorption method, cook in small batches of no more than 1 cup to keep it from becoming mushy.

Grain	1 cup (190 g)
Water	2 cups (480 ml)
Salt (opt.)	¼ teaspoon
Pan size	2-quart (2-L)
Yield	3 to 4 cups (600 to 800 g)

Rinse the rice in at least three changes of cool water; drain well. In a heavy saucepan, combine the rice, water, and salt. Bring to a boil over medium-high heat, then cover, reduce the heat to low, and simmer until the rice is tender and most of the liquid is absorbed, about 30 minutes. Drain if necessary.

Cover and let stand for 5 to 10 minutes before fluffing and serving. If not using right away, spread on a large plate and let cool, then transfer to an airtight container and refrigerate or freeze. To reheat or thaw, see page 15.

TO COOK WEHANI OR OTHER RED RICE, SIMPLE ABSORPTION METHOD

Grain	1 cup (190 g)
Water	2 cups (480 ml)
Salt (opt.)	¼ teaspoon
Pan size	2-quart (2-L)
Yield	2½ cups (500 g)

Rinse the rice in at least three changes of cool water; drain well. In a heavy saucepan, combine the rice, water, and salt. Bring to a boil over medium-high heat, then cover, reduce the heat to low, and simmer until the rice is tender and most of the liquid is absorbed, about 30 minutes. Drain if necessary. Cover and let stand for 5 to 10 minutes before fluffing and serving. If not using right away, spread on a large plate and let cool, then transfer to an airtight container and refrigerate or freeze. To reheat or thaw, see page 15.

TO COOK CHINESE BLACK RICE

This rice cooks up deep purple, with a risotto-like consistency rather than dry, separate grains. In my experience the cheaper rice labeled "gao den" and sold in Asian food shops needs to be soaked in advance so it cooks evenly; more expensive—perhaps fresher?—rice labeled "forbidden rice" doesn't need a soak.

Grain	1 cup (190 g)
Water	2 cups (480 ml)
Salt (opt.)	¼ teaspoon
Pan size	2-quart (2-L)
Yield	2½ cups (500 g)

Rinse the rice in a sieve under cool running water. If soaking, put the rice in a container and cover with cold water by 1 inch (2.5 cm); set aside to soak for 4 hours. Drain well. In a heavy saucepan, combine the rice, water, and salt. Bring to a boil over medium-high heat, then cover, reduce the heat to low, and simmer until the rice is tender and most of the liquid is absorbed, about 40 minutes. Drain if desired. Cover and let stand for 5 to 10 minutes before stirring gently and serving. If not using right away, spread on a large plate and let cool, then transfer to an airtight container and refrigerate or freeze. To reheat or thaw, see page 15.

RYE

Secale cereale, fam. Poaceae
contains gluten

Rye berries

The species of rye that is cultivated is not too distantly descended from a wild grass native to the mountainous area around Turkey, northern Iran, and Caucasus. Because it can germinate at lower temperatures than can other cereals like wheat, it has long been a staple crop of eastern Europe and Russia, otherwise known as the land of pumpernickel, a deliciously dark, dense bread made of varying shades of low-gluten rye flour.

Whole rye berries do appear to be seeds of a fairly wild plant. They're probably the most intimidating-looking of the true grains you'll see in the bulk bins at the local co-op or grocery store: Long, rough, with a greenish tint, they look like they were just harvested yesterday, and they'll take ages to cook into something palatable—if they ever do. I'm here to tell you that they are absolutely worth using regularly. They indeed take about 50 minutes to cook, but like all large-ish grains, they freeze exceptionally well and can be taken right out of the freezer and run under cool water for just a minute to thaw

before being used in salads or added to hearty soups or even kneaded into a bread dough. The flavor of rye berries is often described as tangy, but I detect something more like green-ness, and I will admit that I find it difficult to separate the flavor of rye from that of its fragrant and near-constant companion, caraway. To me, rye tastes like "whatever it is that goes so well with caraway."

WHOLE RYE FLOUR

Whole rye flour is also sometimes called dark rye flour, and this—as opposed to light rye flour, which has the bran and germ removed and is good for Jewish rye bread—is what I use in the recipes in this book. Its low gluten content means that when it's used in yeast breads, it's usually combined with wheat flour; it makes a great, dense, pumpernickel-type bread. Dark rye meal, or pumpernickel flour, is very coarse and is best suited to real wild-fermented German-style breads.

TO COOK RYE BERRIES

Grain	1 cup (180 g)
Water	3 cups (720 ml)
Salt (opt.)	¼ teaspoon
Pan size	2-quart (2-L)
Yield	2½ cups (440 g)

In a heavy saucepan, combine the rye berries and water. Cover, bring to a boil, then lower the heat and simmer until the rye berries are tender and no trace of bright white is visible at the center when a grain is cut in half, about 50 minutes. Add the salt toward the end. Drain well. If not using right away, rinse

under cold running water until cool, drain well, then transfer to an airtight container and refrigerate or freeze. To reheat or thaw, see page 15.

SORGHUM

Sorghum bicolor, fam. Poaceae
gluten free

Sorghum

Sorghum is believed to have originated in Africa and then migrated to India, though it's not clear in which region it was domesticated. It was most likely brought to America from Africa by slaves, and is now grown in dry areas of Texas, Oklahoma, and Kansas, as well as along the muddy Mississippi. Ben Franklin himself was the first in this country to grow a type of sorghum now known here as "broomcorn," whose stiff tassels were used to make broom bristles—the admirably curious fellow had plucked a few stray sorghum seeds from an imported broom and planted them.

For the last few centuries, sorghum has been saddled with a reputation as "poor-folks' food," but as gluten-free eating has become more popular (or more necessary, depending on your situation), once-lowly sorghum is finally starting to gain some major culinary cred. In the South, sorghum syrup, also known as sorghum molasses, which is extracted from the stalks like sugar from sugar cane, was once a common drizzling sweetener for pancakes, biscuits, and cornbread (too common, according to my late Kentucky-raised grandmother, who wouldn't touch the stuff later in life, as it reminded her of poor times); now it's practically a boutique ingredient. Most sorghum used for food in this country is in the form of whole grain flour, which is almost ubiquitous in gluten-free bakery-made goods and baking mixes.

Though sorghum is widely used as a whole grain in Africa and the Indian subcontinent, I'd never seen whole sorghum grains for sale until white sorghum berries turned up recently in one of my regular bulk-purchase haunts. I tried 'em, liked 'em, and so decided to include a few recipes using them here, in the hopes that you'll be able to obtain them as well. Round and irregularly pale tan and dark brown, sorghum grains are about as big as . . . well, as big as the shot we used to bite down on when dining on one of the geese that flew over my parents' house in Virginia and got unlucky just before Thanksgiving or Christmas, or ball bearings, or BBs. They are just slightly sweet, and mild, not nutty like other true grains, and when cooked they have a consistency similar to that of Israeli couscous—that is, a bit chewy, like tiny balls of pasta. You could certainly use cooked sorghum in any recipe to replace Israeli couscous.

To my delight, at least some varieties of sorghum, including the white sorghum I use, can be popped in a little oil like popcorn (or even in a dry pan with no oil at all, like amaranth). The puffs are Lilliputian, but look like popcorn and are deeply toasted in flavor. Not all of the grains will pop in the pan, but the ones that don't are not dangerously hard like popcorn "old maids." Rather, they are crunchy and totally edible like the half-popped popcorn kernels that I and I'm sure many other people so adore. (Incidentally, if you know how to deliberately half-pop popcorn, please contact me posthaste via this book's publisher with that information.) They're so small that eating them out of hand is a bit tiresome unless you're of the scoop-and-pour-into-the-mouth school of popcorn eating rather than the dainty pluck-and-nibble, but I happily use it as a cold breakfast cereal, and it would be beautiful in something like the fool on page 52 or stirred into a granola.

TO COOK WHOLE SORGHUM

Grain	1 cup (190 g)	2 cups (380 g)
Water	2 cups (480 ml)	4 cups (960 ml)
Salt (opt.)	Pinch	¼ teaspoon
Pan size	2-quart (2-L)	3-quart (2.8-L)
Yield	3 cups (480 g)	6 cups (960 g)

Rinse the sorghum well in a fine-mesh sieve; drain well. In a heavy saucepan, combine the sorghum and water. Cover, bring to a boil, then lower the heat and simmer until the sorghum is tender and almost all of the grains have revealed at least some of the translucent grayish germ, 45 to 50 minutes. Add the salt toward the end. Drain well. If not using right away, rinse under cold water to cool, then transfer to an airtight container and refrigerate or freeze. To reheat or thaw, see page 15.

TO POP SORGHUM

In a large heavy saucepan with a lid, heat about 2 teaspoons vegetable oil over high heat until it shimmers. Add ⅓ cup (65 g) raw sorghum, cover, and cook, shaking the pan frequently, until the popping sounds taper off, about 2 minutes. Immediately turn out into a large bowl and serve. Makes about 1 cup (20 g), with some unpopped but perfectly munchable kernels.

TEFF
Eragrostis tef, fam. Poaceae
gluten free

Brown teff / Ivory teff flour

Teff originated in Ethiopia and, for whatever reason, stayed there for many millennia. In Ethiopia it's the main grain used to make the ubiquitous flatbread injera: The grains are coated with a symbiotic yeast, much like the bloom on wine grapes, which aids natural fermentation of the teff-flour batter. (The injera recipe on page 180 also contains some commercial yeast to speed up and standardize the process a bit.) Very little teff is grown outside of Ethiopia, but because of the increasing popularity of the gluten-free grain and the flour made from it, that has been changing in recent years.

Teff and teff flour is always whole grain, as the individual grains are so exceptionally tiny (the word *tef*, in fact, comes from the Amharic for "lost") that it's impossible to remove the bran. There are three main varieties of teff: ivory (or white), brown, and red. I've only ever seen whole brown teff and ivory or brown teff flour for sale; apparently, the red variety, while the easiest and cheapest to grow, is less desirable. Whole teff grains cook into a porridge about the consistency of soft polenta or Cream of Wheat cereal, which is why I like to use it in a spicy breakfast upma (page 62) in place of soji (a refined wheat farina similar to Cream of Wheat).

TO COOK TEFF

Grain	½ cup (100 g)	1 cup (200 g)
Water	1½ cups (360 ml)	3 cups (720 g)
Salt (opt.)	Pinch	¼ teaspoon
Pan size	2-quart (2-L)	2-quart (2-L)
Yield	1 cup (250 g)	2 cups (500 g)

In a heavy saucepan over medium-high heat, toast the teff, stirring constantly, until fragrant and beginning to crackle, 3 to 4 minutes. Add the water and salt, bring to a boil, then lower the heat and simmer, stirring occasionally, until the mixture is thick and the individual grains are slightly swollen, about 20 minutes. If not using right away, let cool, then transfer to an airtight container and refrigerate or freeze. To reheat, see page 15.

TRITICALE
Triticosecale, fam. Poaceae
contains gluten

Triticale berries

As its name implies, triticale (pronounced "trit-i-KAY-lee") is a hybrid cross between wheat (*Triticum*), specifically hard winter wheat, and rye (*Secale*). It was first grown in the 1870s, but it wasn't until the 1950s that breeders began seriously trying to develop the grain for full-scale production. The idea was that the hybrid would be as productive and disease resistant as wheat, and as hardy as cold-loving rye. The crops were relatively successful, and continue to improve as breeding practices are refined, but consumers have for the most part failed to notice that a new grain is among us. The main benefit of triticale is that it can be more successfully grown organically—or at least with fewer pesticides and synthetic fertilizers than wheat requires. Triticale is low in gluten, so its flour isn't ideal for making yeast breads, but it may be useful to people who are sensitive to gluten but do not have celiac disease. Its rye heritage makes triticale flour a natural addition to rye breads if you want to lighten the distinctive rye flavor a bit; try adding cooked triticale berries to the bread dough for more texture.

In its whole grain form, triticale is very similar to the more readily available hard red wheat berries, and so objectively speaking, it may not be worth seeking out unless you need an organic and lower-gluten grain. You can substitute triticale berries for wheat berries in any recipe in this book.

TO COOK WHOLE TRITICALE BERRIES

Grain	½ cup (180 g)	2 cups (360 g)
Water	3 cups (720 ml)	6 cups (1.4-L)
Salt (opt.)	¼ teaspoon	½ teaspoon
Pan size	2-quart (2-L)	3-quart (2.8-L)
Yield	2 cups (320 g)	4 cups (640 g)

In a heavy saucepan, combine the triticale berries and water. Cover, bring to a boil, then lower the heat and simmer until the triticale berries are tender and no trace of bright white is visible at the center when a grain is cut in half, about 40 minutes, adding the salt toward the end. Drain well. If not using right away, run under cold water to cool, drain well, then transfer to an airtight container and refrigerate or freeze. To reheat, see page 15.

WHEAT

Triticum aestivum, fam. Poaceae
contains gluten

Top: Kamut / Soft white wheat berries
Middle: Freekeh / Cracked wheat
Bottom: Farro / Bulgur

Triticum is the grandfather of the true grains and arguably the most versatile in its whole grain form—from a multitude of varieties of wheat berries, to cracked wheat, couscous, bulgur, and, of course, whole wheat flour. According to the Whole Grains Council, about two-thirds of the grain consumed in the United States is wheat. It's high in gluten, which is what makes yeasted bread doughs stretchy and able to rise as carbon dioxide forms through the activity of yeast. Of course, most of the wheat consumed here and around the world is in the form of highly processed white flour. In the States and some other countries, white flour is almost always enriched, meaning that some of the nutrients lost when the bran is removed are added back (and folic acid is also added for good measure). But enriched flour is nutritionally inferior to flour made from whole wheat: Whole wheat flour, whether white whole wheat or regular, contains more protein and much more fiber.

But there's a world of wheat out there beyond flour—wheat has more forms than many other grains. Chewy, nutty wheat berries have been a favorite of mine since my mom cooked them up for my brother and me as a special breakfast treat with a sprinkle of sugar and plenty of cold milk to cool the grains down. Wheat berries can be used in countless other ways as well: in soups and Indian-style stews like dals, in cold salads, and warm as a plain side dish. Cracked wheat, whether made from regular wheat berries or still slightly green ones (in which case it is sold as freekeh), is whole wheat that has been coarsely crushed; it can be made into sweet puddings or hearty side dishes, and can be soaked in water until soft and added to bread doughs

for texture. Whole wheat farina—a whole grain version of my beloved childhood Cream of Wheat cereal, aka wheat farina or, in India, soji—is still pretty tough to find in retail markets, but you can make something like it using cracked wheat: Just blitz it in a good spice grinder until it's a couple shades finer, and it'll cook into a nice soft porridge. Bulgur is whole wheat that has been partially cooked, dried, and broken into fine pieces for quick cooking—it's an important form of the grain, especially in the Middle East, where it appears in salads like tabbouleh and is used to stretch more valuable (or at least more expensive) meat. Whole wheat couscous is another quick-cooking form of the grain; it's made by a laborious process of moistening ground wheat (specifically the hard durum variety) and rubbing and rolling the pieces together until they clump into little pellets, then steaming them in specialized vessels. The whole wheat couscous available in stores needs only a brief soak in boiling water to reconstitute it.

Besides all the different forms whole wheat can take, there are the many different varieties of *Triticum* that are readily available in supermarkets and health food stores. Two types of whole wheat berries are commonly available: hard red wheat and soft white wheat. Hard red wheat berries are higher in protein and cook up firmer than soft white wheat berries.

In Italy, *farro* is the common name for einkorn, emmer, and spelt, which are unique but similar species of wheat:

- einkorn:
  Triticum monococcum or *farro piccolo*
- emmer:
  Triticum dicoccon or *farro medio*
- spelt:
  Triticum spelta or *farro grande*

Despite my personal resistance to understanding the Italian language (which probably dates back to college years marred by eight A.M. Latin classes), I use the word *farro* to refer to what I am pretty sure is specifically emmer because most often it is labeled "farro" in retail settings, it is indeed smaller and more delicate in texture than spelt (hence *farro medio*), and because some sources identify both farro and emmer as *Triticum dicoccon*. In other words, when you buy something in this country that's labeled "farro," it's almost certainly emmer. Almost always "semi-pearled," meaning that some of the bran has been removed in processing, farro/emmer berries cook into very tender, almost creamy grains and, because they release a fair amount of starch when stirred during cooking, are commonly used in risotto-like preparations. Spelt is firmer, with larger berries, and is more appropriate for use in composed salads or hearty stews. Einkorn, a small variety of wheat berry, is still pretty hard to find in this country, and I haven't had much need to seek it out when very similar alternatives are so readily available just down the street at the local grocery store.

Another heirloom species of wheat, Kamut is the trademarked brand name for a grain "owned" by one Bob Quinn, a Montana farmer who was the first to successfully market it, beginning in the 1980s. Legend—and Kamut International, Inc., natch—has it that after World War II, an airman stationed in Egypt somehow obtained thirty-six grains of wheat that had been found in a tomb (not King Tut's, but it might as well have been—this is legend after all). The airman gave them to a farm-boy friend of his, the farm boy mailed them to his farmer father in Montana, the grains were planted, the grains grew, and the species, untouched by modern biotechnology for thousands of years, was revived. The common name for the species is khorasan wheat, an ancient ancestor of durum wheat that boasts more protein and vitamins and minerals than common wheat. Its grains are much larger and more elongated than those of common wheat, and are a beautiful golden color. Some people claim that Kamut tastes buttery; I find it mild and slightly sweet, appealingly firm and chewy when cooked. There's also some early evidence that Kamut may be more tolerable than common wheat to people with gluten or wheat sensitivities.

WHOLE WHEAT, WHITE WHOLE WHEAT, AND WHOLE WHEAT PASTRY FLOURS

White whole wheat flour is made from a hard white wheat variety, so it's lighter in color and milder in flavor than regular whole wheat flour made from hard red wheat, and can easily be substituted for all or part of the all-purpose (white, refined) flour in just about any recipe. Plus, it offers the same nutritional advantages over refined white flour as the darker, hard red wheat variety, bringing more protein, slightly fewer carbohydrates, and of course *tons* more fiber:

- **100 g white or regular whole wheat flour:**
  13.2 g protein, 72 g carbohydrate, 10.7 g fiber
- **100 g all-purpose (white, refined) flour:**
  10.3 g protein, 76.3 g carbohydrate, 2.7 g fiber

Whole wheat pastry flour is made from a soft white wheat and has a nutritional profile similar to regular whole wheat flour, but because it is slightly lower in protein and gluten, it won't make for a stretchy, high-rising yeast dough; use it instead for short pastries, cookies, or crackers.

WHOLE SPELT FLOUR

Spelt is a kind of wheat, but since it contains considerably less gluten than other wheat flours, it gets its own paragraph. It has just enough gluten that you can successfully use only spelt flour in yeasted breads, though they'll be denser and heavier than regular-wheat-flour goods. Some people who are sensitive to the gluten in more common wheat varieties can tolerate spelt, but those with celiac disease should avoid it completely.

TO COOK HARD RED OR WHITE WHEAT BERRIES, SOFT WHITE WHEAT BERRIES, SPELT BERRIES, OR KAMUT BERRIES

Grain	1 cup (175 g)	2 cups (350 g)
Water	3 cups (720 ml)	6 cups (1.4 L)
Salt (opt.)	¼ teaspoon	½ teaspoon
Pan size	2-quart (2-L)	3-quart (2.8-L)
Yield	2½ cups (475 g)	5 cups (950 g)

In a heavy saucepan, combine the wheat berries and water. Cover, bring to a boil, then lower the heat and simmer until the wheat berries are tender and no trace of bright white is visible at the center when a grain is cut in half, about 30 minutes for soft white wheat, 35 minutes for spelt, 40 minutes for Kamut, 50 minutes for hard red or white wheat. Add the salt toward the end. Drain well. If not using right away, spread on a large plate to cool, then transfer to an airtight container and refrigerate or freeze. To reheat or thaw, see page 15.

TO COOK FARRO (EMMER)

Grain	1 cup (180 g)	2 cups (360 g)
Water	1½ cups (360 ml)	3 cups (720 ml)
Salt (opt.)	Pinch	¼ teaspoon
Pan size	2-quart (2-L)	3-quart (2.8-L)
Yield	2½ cups (420 g)	5 cups (840 g)

In a heavy saucepan over medium-high heat, toast the farro, stirring frequently, until fragrant, about 4 minutes. Stir in the water and salt, cover, bring to a boil, then lower the heat and simmer until the grains are tender and most of the water is absorbed, 15 to 20 minutes. Dump the farro into a fine-mesh sieve to drain, then fluff and serve. If not using right away, run under cold water to cool, then transfer to an airtight container and refrigerate or freeze. To reheat or thaw, see page 15.

TO COOK FINE- OR MEDIUM-GRIND (no. 1 or 2) BULGUR

Grain	1 cup (140 g)	2 cups (280 g)
Water	1¼ cups (300 ml)	2½ cups (600 ml)
Salt (opt.)	¼ teaspoon	½ teaspoon
Pan size	2-quart (2-L)	3-quart (2.8-L)
Yield	3 cups (540 g)	6 cups (1 kg)

In a heavy saucepan, bring the water to a boil. Stir in the bulgur and salt, cover, and remove from the heat. Let stand until the bulgur is tender and the water is absorbed, about 10 minutes for fine, 15 minutes for medium. If the bulgur is tender and there is still a little water remaining in the pan, drain the bulgur in a fine-mesh sieve. Fluff with a spatula. If not using right away, spread on a large plate to cool, then transfer to an airtight container and refrigerate or freeze. To reheat or thaw, see page 15.

TO COOK COARSE-GRIND (no. 3) BULGUR

Grain	1 cup (140 g)	2 cups (280 g)
Water	2 cups (480 ml)	4 cups (960 ml)
Salt (opt.)	¼ teaspoon	½ teaspoon
Pan size	2-quart (2-L)	3-quart (2.8-L)
Yield	3 cups (540 g)	6 cups (1 kg)

In a heavy saucepan, bring the water to a boil. Stir in the bulgur and salt, cover, and lower the heat. Simmer until the bulgur is tender and the water is absorbed, about 15 minutes. If the bulgur is tender and there is still a little water remaining in the pan, drain the bulgur in a fine-mesh sieve. Fluff with a spatula. If not using right away, spread on a large plate to cool, then transfer to an airtight container and refrigerate or freeze. To reheat or thaw, see page 15.

TO COOK CRACKED WHEAT OR FREEKEH

Grain	1 cup (160 g)	2 cups (320 g)
Water	1½ cups (360 ml)	2½ cups (570 ml)
Salt (opt.)	¼ teaspoon	½ teaspoon
Oil	2 teaspoons	1 tablespoon
Pan size	2-quart (2-L)	3-quart (2.8-L)
Yield	2 cups (360 g)	4 cups (720 g)

In a heavy saucepan, heat the oil over medium-high heat and add the cracked wheat or freekeh. Cook, stirring, until fragrant, about 2 minutes. Add the water and salt, cover, bring to a boil, then lower the heat and simmer until the water is absorbed and the cracked wheat is tender, 10 to 12 minutes. If the cracked wheat is too soupy at this point, uncover and cook until the excess water has evaporated. Remove from the heat, fluff with a spatula, cover, and let stand for 5 minutes. If not using right away, spread on a large plate to cool, then transfer to an airtight container and refrigerate or freeze. To reheat or thaw, see page 15.

TO COOK WHOLE WHEAT COUSCOUS

Grain	1 cup (170 g)	2 cups (340 g)
Water	1½ cups (360 ml)	3 cups (720 ml)
Salt (opt.)	¼ teaspoon	½ teaspoon
Oil	2 teaspoons	1 tablespoon
Pan size	2-quart (2-L)	3-quart (2.8-L)
Yield	3 cups (480 g)	6 cups (960 g)

In a heavy saucepan, bring the water and oil to a boil. Stir in the couscous and salt, cover, and remove from the heat. Let stand until the couscous is tender and the water is absorbed, about 5 minutes. Fluff with a spatula. If not using right away, spread on a large plate to cool, then transfer to an airtight container and refrigerate or freeze. To reheat or thaw, see page 15.

WILD RICE

Zizania palustris, fam. Poaceae
gluten free

Wild rice

Wild rice is misleadingly named in two ways. *Zizania palustris* is a true grain, an aquatic grass, but is not a member of the rice genus and so, despite name and appearance, is not actually a rice. In addition, most of the wild rice sold commercially outside the upper Midwest is not wild at all, but cultivated in paddies.

Dark black wild rice has most of the bran layer intact; brown wild rice, which cooks a little more quickly, has been partly scarified (that is, some of the bran has been removed), though the scarification process apparently doesn't result in much nutrient loss. The labeling should tell you where and how the wild rice was harvested, whether by hand, using traditional Ojibwe Indian methods, or by machine. In general, wild rice grown in lakes and rivers in the Midwest (Minnesota and Michigan are the main producers) is thin and short; wild rices from Canada usually have thin, long grains; and cultivated wild rice (such as that grown in California) is often thick and short.

Each variety from each producer or harvester is slightly different in flavor, color, and texture. As with true rices, it may take some experimenting and label reading to determine the best way to cook the one you have on hand.

TO COOK BLACK OR BROWN WILD RICE

Grain	½ cup (80 g)	1 cup (160 g)
Water	1½ cups (360 g)	3 cups (720 g)
Salt (opt.)	Pinch	¼ teaspoon
Pan size	2-quart (2-L)	2-quart (2-L)
Yield	1½ cups (240 g)	3 cups (480 g)

Rinse the wild rice in a sieve; drain well. In a heavy saucepan, combine the rice, water, and salt and bring to a boil. Reduce the heat to low, cover, and simmer until the wild rice is tender but still chewy and most of the grains have split, about 50 minutes for black or 35 minutes for brown; some of the grains may have butterflied all the way open to reveal the pale interior. Drain if necessary, then cover and let stand for 5 minutes. Fluff with a rubber spatula. If not using right away, spread on a large plate to cool, then transfer to an airtight container and refrigerate or freeze. To reheat, see page 15.

1

Breakfast and Brunch

Whole grains for breakfast is a no-brainer. If you're going to eat a meal that's centered on grains, morning is a fine time to do it, when the energy provided by their good carbohydrates will benefit you most. Porridge-style steel-cut or old-fashioned rolled oats are popular choices, and there are approximately sixty thousand ways to make oatmeal more interesting from one day to the next (see pages 48 to 51 for but a few of them). And remember that anything you can do to oatmeal you can do to other grains, including quinoa, amaranth, teff, cracked wheat, corn or hominy grits, and flakes made from rolled barley, wheat, or rye berries (these are sold as "flakes" but are just like rolled oats). Griddle cakes, crêpes, and waffles, too, are quick to mix up for a brunch party or even on a weekday; all it takes is overcoming the resistance to using, say, a whisk that early in the morning. I know that can be a high mountain to climb, depending on the strength of your caffeinated beverage, so I've also included plenty of make-ahead and take-and-go options here.

PURE MUESLI

Makes about 10 servings | vegan, gluten free*

This makes a batch big enough to prepare in a large sauté pan and store in a quart-size canning jar, with about two servings' worth of overage for enjoying right away. The following is my go-to combination, but obviously you should feel free to use whatever you have on hand. I like a mixture of nuts and seeds for crunch (and together they make a complete protein)—try sunflower seeds, chia seeds, chopped pecans, walnuts, hazelnuts. Good-quality dark dried apricots are dense and almost fudgy, and I love how their sticky edges gather up the little bits of muesli, hiding the treat inside. Any and all dried fruit like cranberries, cherries, diced apples, peaches, nectarines, raisins, or currants would be delicious too. Be sparing with dried tropical fruits, however, which often are highly sugared.

To serve, mix equal parts muesli and plain yogurt or milk (or even the whey from draining yogurt) and let the muesli soften in the fridge overnight—the classic Swiss way, though not vegan. Or simply pour milk, nut milk, or juice over the muesli and eat it unsoaked. Sweeten each serving to taste, if you'd like, but with the dried fruit, it really doesn't need extra sweetener. You could also sprinkle ground cinnamon or cardamom over the bowl, or cocoa powder if you're so inclined.

- **2 tablespoons flax seeds**
- **4 cups (640 g) rolled oats**
- **¼ cup (15 g) pepitas**
- **¼ cup (30 g) sliced almonds**
- **2 tablespoons sesame seeds**
- **2 tablespoons shredded unsweetened coconut**
- **⅓ cup (45 g) diced dried apricots, preferably unsulphured**

In a food processor or spice grinder, coarsely crack the flax seeds and put them in a large bowl.

In a large, deep sauté pan over medium heat, toast the oats, tossing or stirring constantly, until some of the oats are golden and they're very hot to the touch, 3 to 5 minutes (depending on the size of the pan). Pour into the bowl with the flax and let cool slightly, then scoop about half of the oats into a food processor and pulse 4 or 5 times to roughly chop; return the chopped oats to the bowl.

In the same pan over medium heat, toast the pepitas and almonds together until the pepitas are swollen and the almonds are lightly browned. Scrape into the bowl with the oats. In the still-hot pan, off the heat, toast the sesame seeds for just a few seconds, until shiny and golden, scrape them into the oats, then toast the coconut, again off the heat for just a few seconds. Add to the oats and toss well to combine. Add the apricots and toss. Let cool completely, then transfer to an airtight container, where the muesli will keep at room temperature for up to several weeks.

* See page 25.

BARELY SWEET GRANOLA

Makes about 14 servings | vegan, gluten free*

I find store-bought granola somewhat repulsive: teeth-achingly sweet and teeth-breakingly hard. Artisanal versions from farmers' markets and the like are a little better, but I simply can't justify the expense when it's so easy to hit the bulk bins and mix up a huge batch of my own slightly sweet and crisp-rather-than-hard version with almost no effort. There are endless possibilities for variety within the following ratio: For every 5 cups (800 g) rolled oats (thick or thin—doesn't matter), use about 1¼ cups (280 g) nutty/seedy add-ins, ⅓ cup (80 ml) oil, ⅓ cup (65 g / 80 ml) sweetener, and any sort of dried fruit you like. Some people say that the granola will stay crisp longer if you keep the dried fruit separate and mix it in just before serving, but I can't say I've noticed a difference.

- ¼ cup (45 g) flax seeds
- 5 cups (800 g) rolled oats
- ½ cup (50 g) sliced almonds
- ¼ cup (15 g) pepitas
- ¼ cup (35 g) sesame seeds
- ¼ cup (20 g) shredded unsweetened coconut
- ¼ cup (15 g) popped amaranth (page 20)
- ½ teaspoon ground cinnamon (optional)
- ⅓ cup (80 ml) olive oil, vegetable oil, or a combination
- ⅓ cup (80 ml) agave nectar or maple syrup
- 1 teaspoon pure vanilla extract
- 1 cup (225 g) dried fruit

Preheat the oven to 250°F (120°C). Spray a 9-by-13-inch (23-by-33-cm) baking dish with nonstick cooking spray or lightly oil it.

In a food processor or spice grinder, coarsely crack the flax-seeds. In a large bowl, combine the oats, almonds, pepitas, sesame seeds, flax seeds, coconut, amaranth, and cinnamon, if using. In a small bowl, combine the oil, agave nectar, and vanilla extract. Drizzle the wet ingredients into the dry ingredients and stir to coat. Scrape the mixture into the prepared baking dish. Bake, turning and stirring occasionally, until evenly golden brown, 1½ to 2 hours. Transfer the dish to a wire rack and let cool to room temperature, stirring occasionally; the granola will get crisp and crunchy as it cools. Stir in the dried fruit and serve. The granola will keep in an airtight container (a half-gallon glass canning jar works well) at room temperature for at least 3 weeks.

VARIATIONS

★ To use honey (not vegan) or barley malt syrup (not gluten free) as a sweetener, first warm it in a small saucepan over low heat and then stir in the oil and vanilla. To use a nonliquid sweetener like granulated sugar or brown sugar, warm it in a small saucepan with 1 tablespoon water until dissolved.

★ To make a sweeter granola that holds together in larger lumps, increase the sweetener and oil to ½ cup (120 ml) each. You might also wish to add a few tablespoons of oat or other flour to help bind the bits. This is good as an ice cream or yogurt topping—more of a treat than an every-morning cereal.

★ Try a mixture of wheat flakes, barley flakes, rye flakes, and rolled oats for a deeper-flavored (though not gluten-free) granola.

* See page 25.

QUINOA BREAKFAST PORRIDGE
WITH VANILLA AND ALMOND MILK

Serves 2 | vegan, gluten free

I love the different kinds of crunch in this porridge: the toothsome quality of the spiraled outer germ of each quinoa grain, the tiny vanilla-bean seeds, the sweet crunch of coarse sugar, and the toasty crispness of sliced almonds.

- **1 cup (170 g) raw quinoa, well rinsed**
- **3 cups (720 ml) almond milk, homemade if possible (page 71)**
- **1/2 vanilla bean, split lengthwise**
- **1/4 cup (25 g) dried cranberries or cherries**
- **2 tablespoons turbinado sugar, or to taste**
- **2 tablespoons sliced almonds, toasted**

In a heavy 2-quart (2-L) saucepan, combine the quinoa and 2 cups (480 ml) of the almond milk. Scrape in the vanilla bean seeds and add the pods as well. Bring to a simmer and cook, stirring occasionally, until the quinoa is tender, about 20 minutes. Stir in the cranberries and cook until softened, about 3 minutes. Stir in most of the sugar and stir until dissolved. Scoop into serving bowls (reserve the vanilla bean pods; rinse and dry, then bury in a container of sugar to make vanilla sugar). Serve with the remaining almond milk, the almonds, and a little more sugar.

SPICY STEEL-CUT OATMEAL
WITH GARLIC CHIPS

Serves 2 | vegan, gluten free*

I often crave a spicy breakfast—chorizo and egg tacos, skillet-crisped sweet potatoes with liberally applied Cajun spices, leftover kung pao chicken—and I also believe that nothing can beat a bowl of steel-cut oatmeal in the morning, so I make this meal to satisfy both cravings at once.

You might think of hot cereal as a wintertime dish, a prelude to shoveling out the car or leaping over slush lakes in the crosswalks on your hike to work, but this savory version, with crisp scallions, bright cilantro, and vinegary heat from the chile paste, is invigorating all year round. If you'd like some (nonvegan) protein in your bowl, fry an egg (or shredded cooked chicken or firm tofu) in the oil leftover from frying the garlic and set it on top of the oatmeal.

- **1/2 cup (125 g) raw steel-cut oats**
- **2 tablespoons olive oil**
- **4 cloves garlic, very thinly sliced**
- **About 1 tablespoon tamari**
- **Chinese chile paste (sambal oelek) to taste**
- **2 scallions, thinly sliced on a bias**
- **2 tablespoons chopped fresh cilantro**

In a heavy 1 1/2- to 2-quart (1.4- to 2-L) saucepan, combine the oats and 2 cups (480 ml) water. Bring to a boil, then lower the heat and simmer, stirring occasionally, until creamy and tender, about 25 minutes.

Meanwhile, in a small sauté pan, heat the oil over medium-high heat and add the garlic, tilting the pan so the oil is deeper at the edge and the garlic floats as it fries. Fry, stirring, until crisp and golden, about 1 minute. Remove the garlic to a paper towel to drain.

Spoon the oatmeal into two small bowls. Drizzle with tamari and dollop with chile paste. Sprinkle the scallions, cilantro, and garlic chips over the top and serve.

* See page 25.

BAKED OATMEAL
WITH DRIED CRANBERRIES

Serves 4 to 6 | gluten free*

Baked oatmeal was a revelation to me the first time I made it. You basically just mix everything together and stick it in the oven; it's the ideal dish to serve when you have house guests (better than making that one omelet or waffle at a time). By the time you've had a cup of coffee and washed up the two bowls and the whisk, breakfast is ready. While there's no flour in the dish, the finished texture is light and cakelike—add some whipped cream or a drizzle of honey-sweetened whisked yogurt, and it could be mistaken for dessert. Or just serve with cold milk or a bit of half-and-half poured over it in a bowl.

- **1 tablespoon unsalted butter, plus more for the pan**
- **2½ cups (400 g) raw rolled oats**
- **½ cup (110 g) brown sugar**
- **1½ teaspoons ground cinnamon**
- **1 teaspoon baking powder**
- **Pinch of salt**
- **⅓ cup (35 g) dried cranberries**
- **1 cup (240 ml) milk, plus more for serving if desired**
- **½ cup (120 ml) plain Greek yogurt**
- **1 large egg**
- **1 teaspoon pure vanilla extract**

Preheat the oven to 350°F (175°C). Butter a 9-inch (23-cm) square baking pan.

In a large bowl, combine the oats, brown sugar, cinnamon, baking powder, and salt. Toss in the cranberries.

In a medium bowl, whisk together the milk, yogurt, egg, and vanilla. Add to the oat mixture and stir to combine. Transfer to the prepared pan and dot the top with the butter. Bake until golden brown on top and firm throughout, 25 to 30 minutes. Scoop portions into serving bowls and serve hot.

VARIATIONS

★ Use any dried fruit instead of the cranberries. Diced dried apricots, nectarines, and apples all work well—and with these, try adding 1 to 2 tablespoons minced crystallized ginger.

★ Use 1½ cups (360 ml) buttermilk instead of the regular milk and yogurt.

* See page 25.

HOT CEREAL TOPPINGS AND EMBELLISHMENTS
Ideas for Experimentation

Every time I hear about some centenarian or other who has survived on the same breakfast every day for eighty-three years (a slice of dry toast and coffee with cream, perhaps, followed by a cigarette), I cringe. I just cannot imagine a life of such utter dullness. But if the breakfast in question were nutty, chewy, creamy steel-cut oatmeal, one of my absolute favorites and one of the most healthful breakfast foods known to man, and I were allowed to put anything at all in or on top of it, I could certainly handle the repetition. If you enjoy oatmeal but find yourself in a rut, read on and fall back in love.

If you're making a savory oatmeal, consider cooking it in good chicken or beef broth instead of water or milk. For a jook- or congee-type breakfast, cook it in about twice as much liquid, so it remains soupy, and top with shredded or diced cooked meat, sliced scallions, fried shallots, chopped peanuts or roasted sesame seeds, and soy sauce or tamari.

For further variation, try using other quicker-cooking whole grains for breakfast: Quinoa (page 27), soft-cooked amaranth (page 19), millet (page 24; stir a few times while cooking to make it smoother), farro (page 36), and cracked wheat (page 37) all make excellent breakfast grains. Long-cooking grains like wheat berries and spelt berries (page 36) or farro (page 36) can be made in a big batch and kept in the refrigerator or freezer so you can pull out a bit as you need it.

INSPIRATIONAL COMBINATIONS

Following are some super-simple and highly accessible ways to serve oatmeal—classic combinations suitable for those whose prior experience might be limited but who'd like to move a bit beyond cinnamon and milk. Add any dried fruit to the oatmeal while it's cooking, for at least the last few minutes, so it has time to soften and plump up, and serve with milk, almond or rice milk, soy milk, plain yogurt, or none of the above.

- Dried apples, ground cinnamon, maple syrup
- Dried figs, honey, toasted pine nuts
- Dried apricots, ground cinnamon, toasted sliced or slivered almonds
- Dried cherries, toasted hazelnuts, shaved dark chocolate
- Crumbled goat cheese or cream cheese, honey, torn fresh basil or mint leaves
- Fresh sliced peaches or nectarines, ground cardamom, a drizzle of half-and-half
- Fresh diced mango, toasted unsweetened coconut flakes, raw sugar
- Fresh banana, toasted walnuts, turbinado sugar
- Sliced avocado, segmented orange, toasted pepitas

ASPIRATIONAL COMBINATIONS

For the advanced connoisseur, these are some of the most unusual oatmeal-based concoctions I've come across. I've tried each, and I wouldn't have included them here if they weren't totally worthwhile.

- **Whiskey porridge:** Demerara sugar, a pat of butter, and a splash of Johnny Walker Red (apparently a standard offering on the Dubai British expat brunch circuit)
- **Jake's oatmeal:** blue cheese and soy sauce (much, much more delicious than it sounds; I also like a few plump raisins thrown in as the oatmeal cooks, for a sort of Stilton-and-Port effect)
- **Chile oatmeal, à la Edward Lee (as told to *Esquire*):** dried ancho chile (snipped in as the oats are cooking), almond butter, mashed banana, honey and brown sugar, a drizzle of coconut milk, cinnamon and paprika, and minced fresh jalapeño
- **Kedgeree porridge, from a Golden Spurtle championship contestant:** oats cooked with butter-sautéed onion, curry powder, and nutmeg, smoked mackerel, and a little heavy cream, topped with hard-cooked egg wedges and fresh parsley

From top left: Rolled oats, vanilla bean, dried cherries; steel-cut oats, blue cheese, fig preserves; millet, cardamom, dates, orange segments, honey; steel-cut oats, lox, cream cheese, scallions; steel-cut oats, gjetost cheese, dark muscovado sugar, crushed pistachios; steel-cut oats, roasted and crisped pork belly, cracked black pepper, toasted sesame seeds, scallions, maple syrup

ADDITIONAL TOPPINGS AND STIR-INS

Mix and match away! Most mornings I like to choose a variety of toppings with different textures and complementary flavors, but sometimes it's comfort that I want (or want for my daughter)—in that case, I'll keep things traditional and stir in a few bits of soft juicy peach and a drizzle of honey, leaving the crunchy nuts and seeds for another day.

CRUNCHY OR CRISP:

- Toasted pepitas, sesame seeds, sunflower seeds
- Sliced or slivered almonds
- Walnuts, pecans, hazelnuts, cashews
- Toasted pine nuts
- Popped amaranth or toasted wheat berries (pages 20 and 52)
- Poppy seeds
- Fried thinly sliced garlic or shallots
- Sliced scallions, tender cilantro stems
- Toasted coconut shavings
- Packaged Indian snacks such as sev (fried chickpea-flour vermicelli), crushed puri (wheat-flour wafers), boondi (chickpea- or lentil-flour balls)
- Granola (page 45)
- Gingersnap crumbs
- Cacao nibs

FRUITY:

- Chopped or mashed banana
- Diced, grated, or butter-sautéed apple
- Fresh or frozen strawberries, blueberries, blackberries, raspberries, grapes, chopped pineapple
- Pomegranate seeds or pomegranate molasses
- Orange or grapefruit segments
- Dried cranberries, cherries, apricots, apple, papaya, guava, pineapple, currants, raisins, figs, chopped dates
- Apple or pear butter, applesauce
- Pumpkin butter
- Diced fresh tomatoes
- Tamarind-date chutney (page 90)

From top left: Rolled oats, smooshed banana, toasted coconut, agave nectar, raw cacao beans; steel-cut oats, dried gooseberries, pecans, cinnamon, sourwood honey; steel-cut oats, fried egg, olive oil–fried garlic chips, cilantro, soy sauce, sambal oelek; rolled oats, dried mango, almond butter, avocado, coconut milk, honey; steel-cut oats, country ham, fig syrup, popped sorghum; steel-cut oats, peach, basil, dark muscovado sugar

CREAMY:

- Milk, half-and-half, buttermilk
- Fresh sweet or cultured cream, crème fraîche (page 74), mascarpone, bits of cream cheese or Brie, clotted cream
- Shredded extra-sharp cheddar cheese, crumbled goat cheese or blue cheese
- Plain yogurt
- Almond milk (page 71), soy milk, rice milk
- Coconut milk
- Butter
- Fried or poached egg, or stir an egg into the oats as they're cooking
- Sliced or mashed avocado
- Almond butter, cashew butter, natural peanut butter
- Leftover canned pumpkin (freeze in little mounds on a sheet of waxed paper, then toss in a freezer bag and add straight to cereal as it cooks)
- Diced sweet potato (add at the beginning of cooking)

SPICY:

- Cinnamon, cardamom, nutmeg, ginger
- Chai masala
- Hot or sweet paprika, smoked paprika, chile powder
- Curry powder, garam masala, chaat masala (page 233)
- Granulated garlic, dried onion flakes
- Fresh jalapeño or serrano chiles
- Snipped dried chiles, chipotle chile flakes
- Chile paste (sambal oelek) or hot sauce (such as Sriracha, or a habanero-based sauce)
- Mint and cilantro chutney

SWEET:

- Honey, agave nectar, maple syrup, cane syrup, sorghum syrup, golden syrup, malted barley syrup
- Demerara, turbinado, or other coarse raw sugar
- Brown sugar
- Vanilla sugar or a few drops of pure vanilla extract
- Jam or preserves
- Marmalade
- Sorghum-plum compote (page 55)
- Apple cider
- Dark chocolate chips

OTHER ENRICHMENTS, HEALTHFUL AND NOT SO MUCH:

- Crushed or ground flax seeds
- Chia seeds, hemp seeds
- Toasted wheat germ
- Wheat bran
- Crumbled bacon, crisped braised pork belly, pan-fried country ham
- Whiskey, Scotch
- Amaretto

POPPED AMARANTH AND TOASTED WHEAT BERRY FOOL

Serves 3 to 4 | vegetarian

Here, tiny puffs of amaranth and crunchy, nutty toasted wheat berries are suspended in lightly sweetened, tangy whipped cream and yogurt, along with whatever fresh fruit you have on hand. Serve it as a special breakfast treat, or add a little more sugar and call it dessert.

- ¼ cup (45 g) raw wheat berries
- ¼ cup (50 g) raw amaranth
- 1 cup (240 ml) heavy cream
- Sugar or vanilla sugar to taste (about 1½ teaspoons)
- 1 cup (240 ml) plain yogurt
- 1½ cups (340 g) fresh berries, pitted cherries, or diced cantaloupe or honeydew melon

Heat a small, heavy stainless-steel sauté pan over high heat. Add the wheat berries and cook, shaking the pan frequently, until they crackle and swell up and are just starting to color, about 2 minutes. Remove to a bowl.

To the same pan over high heat, add half of the amaranth, cover immediately, and cook until the grains are all popped, no longer than 30 seconds. Immediately dump them in the bowl with the wheat berries and repeat with the remaining amaranth. Toss to combine the grains, then divide them among serving bowls.

Whip the cream with about ¾ teaspoon sugar until soft peaks form. In a separate bowl, whisk the yogurt together with about ¾ teaspoon sugar until smooth. Gently fold the cream into the yogurt, then dollop the mixture onto the grains and cover the top with fruit. Serve, or gently fold the grains, cream, and fruit together before serving.

FLUFFY BUCKWHEAT PANCAKES

Makes about 12 (4-inch / 10-cm) pancakes; serves 3 to 4 | vegetarian, gluten free

Buckwheat pancakes are a stone-cold classic, but they're often heavy and a little too buckwheaty for my taste, so I cut the buckwheat flour with neutral brown rice flour to lighten them. Folding beaten egg white into the batter makes these totally whole grain pancakes beautifully fluffy, but don't think you have to haul out the electric mixer first thing in the morning: It's just one egg white, and it can easily be whipped to a foam in a small bowl with a whisk. You could also, of course, skip the egg-separating altogether; the pancakes will still be delicious, just a bit denser. Serve them with maple syrup or runny sour cherry preserves, or make tiny pancakes and serve them blini style, with salty lox and a dollop of sour cream or crème fraîche (and a glass of Champagne).

- ½ cup (65 g) buckwheat flour
- ½ cup (70 g) extra-fine brown rice flour
- ½ teaspoon baking powder
- ¼ teaspoon baking soda
- ¼ teaspoon salt
- 1 large egg, separated
- About ¾ cup (180 ml) milk
- 1 tablespoon unsalted butter, melted, or olive oil, plus more for the pan
- ½ tablespoon agave nectar or maple syrup

Preheat the oven to 250°F (120°C). Line a baking sheet with aluminum foil or parchment paper.

In a large bowl, whisk together the flours, baking powder, baking soda, and salt. Put the egg white in a small bowl and whisk until bright white and foamy—there's no need for it to be stiff; just whisk as enthusiastically as you can for a minute. Put the egg yolk in a glass measuring cup, add milk to make 1 cup (240 ml), add the melted butter and agave nectar, and whisk.

Pour the milk mixture into the flour mixture and stir with a spatula until just combined; it will be a little lumpy. Fold in the egg white.

Melt some butter in a heavy skillet or griddle over medium heat. Ladle in scant ¼-cupfuls (60-ml measures) of batter. Cook until dry at the edges and well browned on the bottom, about 1½ minutes, then flip and cook the other side until done. Transfer to a plate in the warm oven and repeat with the remaining batter. Serve hot.

VARIATIONS

★ To make these pancakes vegan: Use a nondairy milk such as soymilk or almond milk. Omit the egg and use flax instead: Grind 1 tablespoon flax seeds to a powder and whisk with ¼ cup (60 ml) water; add to the flour mixture with the milk mixture. Use olive oil instead of butter.

★ Use white whole wheat flour (not gluten free) instead of the brown rice flour.

★ Right after you ladle the batter into the skillet, sprinkle the pancakes with chopped pecans.

CORNMEAL PANCAKES WITH SORGHUM-PLUM COMPOTE

Makes about 24 small pancakes and 1 quart (960 ml) compote; serves 4 to 6 | vegetarian, gluten free

Sorghum syrup, made from the sorghum grain (see page 31), is a Southern staple, but it can be a little hard to find even here in Georgia. It has a dark, almost bitter edge that goes particularly well with tart black-skinned, red-fleshed plums, but feel free to use a milder fruit (like peaches or nectarines) and substitute maple syrup, golden syrup (such as Lyle's, the British import), agave nectar, or honey.

FOR THE COMPOTE

- **1 pound (455 g) plums, pitted and diced**
- **¼ cup (60 ml) sorghum syrup, or more to taste**
- **1 tablespoon freshly squeezed lemon juice**

FOR THE PANCAKES

- **1¼ cups (200 g) raw fine-grind cornmeal**
- **¾ teaspoon salt**
- **1 teaspoon sugar**
- **1 teaspoon baking powder**
- **1 cup (240 ml) buttermilk or plain yogurt thinned with water to the consistency of buttermilk**
- **2 large eggs, beaten**
- **Unsalted butter for the pan**

MAKE THE COMPOTE

In a heavy 2-quart (2-L) saucepan, combine the plums, sorghum syrup, and lemon juice. Bring to a boil, stirring frequently, then lower the heat and simmer briskly until the plums are very soft and broken down, 20 to 30 minutes. The compote will keep, covered, in a clean glass jar in the refrigerator for at least 3 weeks. Reheat before serving, if desired.

MAKE THE PANCAKES

Sift the cornmeal, salt, sugar, and baking powder into a large bowl. Stir in the buttermilk and eggs.

In a large sauté pan or on a griddle, melt a little butter over medium-high heat. When the foam dies down, working in batches, spoon in ¼-cup (60-ml) puddles of the batter. Cook without disturbing until you can see that the edges are browned and bubbles appear at the center of the pancake, about 2 minutes; use a metal spatula to turn and cook the other side until browned, about 2 minutes. Serve immediately with the compote, or cover loosely with aluminum foil to keep warm while you melt a little more butter and cook the remaining pancakes.

BUTTERMILK OATCAKES
Makes about 15 cakes | vegetarian, gluten free*

Not really like traditional pancakes, these are toothsome, nutty, and hearty "pan cakes" that would make a good winter breakfast before a long hike in the woods, or carried along on a predawn outing. Cooled and wrapped in plastic (or thrown in a sandwich bag), they can be kept in the refrigerator for several days to be warmed up in a warm skillet or a toaster oven (or eaten cold or at room temperature out of a lunch box); they can also be frozen in a freezer bag for several months.

- 1½ cups (360 ml) milk or water
- 2½ cups (400 g) raw rolled oats
- ½ cup (120 ml) buttermilk
- 2 large eggs
- 2 tablespoons unsalted butter, melted, plus more for the pan
- 1 tablespoon agave nectar or honey
- 1 teaspoon pure vanilla extract
- ½ teaspoon salt
- 2 teaspoons baking powder

In a small heavy saucepan, combine the milk and 1½ cups (240 g) rolled oats. Bring to a simmer over medium heat and cook, stirring frequently, until the oats are tender and the mixture is very thick (when you drag a heatproof spatula along the bottom of the pan, no liquid should show at the edge of its path), 3 to 8 minutes depending on the thickness of the oats. Let cool to lukewarm.

Meanwhile, in a large bowl, stir together the buttermilk, eggs, butter, agave nectar, and vanilla. In a blender or small food processor, combine the remaining 1 cup (160 g) of oats, the salt, and baking powder and blend to a fine flour. Stir the cooked and cooled oatmeal into the buttermilk mixture, then stir in the oat flour mixture until thoroughly incorporated.

Preheat the oven to 250°F (120°C). Line a baking sheet with foil or parchment paper.

On a large griddle or in a large well-seasoned skillet, melt a bit of butter over medium heat. Ladle in ¼-cupfuls (60-ml measures) of batter and cook until bubbles appear on the surface, 4 to 5 minutes, then flip and cook until the other side is browned, 4 to 5 minutes; lower the heat if the cakes are browning too quickly. Transfer to the baking sheet and keep warm in the oven while you cook the rest of the batter, adding more butter to the griddle if needed. Serve warm.

VARIATIONS

★ To make apple or pear oat cakes: Core and dice 2 small apples or pears (peeling is optional) and cook them in 1 tablespoon unsalted butter in a large sauté pan over medium heat, stirring frequently, until golden brown and soft, about 10 minutes. Let cool, then stir the fruit into the batter, along with ½ teaspoon ground cinnamon.

★ Gently fold about 1 cup (150 g) pitted and diced peaches, plums, or nectarines into the batter. You could also use fresh or frozen (not thawed) blueberries, raspberries, blackberries, or diced strawberries.

★ Add 1 cup (150 g) diced banana and 3 tablespoons shredded unsweetened coconut to the batter, along with 1 tablespoon coarsely ground flax seeds.

★ Instead of making oat flour in a blender, replace those extra oats with any whole grain flour—wheat, buckwheat, rye, quinoa, amaranth, teff, brown rice, whatever—and just whisk it with the baking powder and salt before adding to the batter.

* See page 25.

WALNUT WAFFLES

Makes 3 or 4 Belgian waffles, or more thin waffles; serves 3 or 4 | vegetarian, gluten free

My daughter, Thalia, who at five whole years knows her sweet treats, eats wedges of these waffles straight out of the freezer, frost and all, and indeed they freeze very well. If you're more discerning than a kindergartner, and you should be, put frozen waffles on a baking sheet and heat at 350°F (175°C) for 15 minutes, or pop them in a toaster. These are dark, crisp, and so deeply flavorful (and filling) you might want, as Thalia does, to forgo toppings altogether.

Beating the egg whites together with the sugar is a trick I learned from a Pamela Anderson recipe in *Fine Cooking*. The technique not only strengthens the batter's structure so it doesn't collapse while you cook one waffle at a time; it also helps make the waffles nice and crisp. Because the batter is so sturdy, you can double this recipe if you'd like. Just be sure you have a very large bowl in which to fold all the elements together.

- **2 large eggs, separated**
- **¼ cup (50 g) sugar**
- **3 tablespoons light molasses**
- **1½ cups (360 ml) milk**
- **½ cup (1 stick / 110 g) unsalted butter, melted and cooled for a few minutes, or vegetable oil**
- **1 cup (100 g) raw quinoa flakes or quinoa flour**
- **1 cup (130 g) buckwheat flour**
- **¼ cup (30 g) cornstarch**
- **2 teaspoons baking powder**
- **Pinch of salt**
- **½ cup (60 g) walnuts**

Preheat the oven to 200°F (90°C) and put a cooling rack on a baking sheet in the oven. Preheat a waffle iron; lightly grease the iron if necessary.

In a medium bowl, with a whisk or a handheld electric mixer, beat the egg whites and sugar until thick, glossy, and bright white.

Put the egg yolks in a large bowl and whisk in the molasses, milk, and butter until smooth.

In a mini food processor or blender, put the quinoa flakes, buckwheat flour, cornstarch, baking powder, salt, and walnuts and pulse to combine and chop the walnuts. Add to the egg-yolk mixture and stir with a rubber spatula to just combine—the batter will be lumpy. Quickly and gently fold in the egg-white mixture. Scoop ¾ to 1 cup (180 to 240 ml) of the batter onto the hot waffle iron, close, and cook according to the manufacturer's instructions, or until the steam issuing from the sides dissipates. Remove the waffle to the rack in the oven and repeat with the remaining batter. Serve hot.

VARIATIONS

★ For malted whole wheat waffles (not gluten free): Omit the walnuts and replace the molasses with 2 tablespoons malted barley syrup; warm the syrup with the melted butter to soften it before attempting to whisk it into the egg yolk and milk.

★ Instead of quinoa flakes and buckwheat flour, use 2 cups (225 g) whole wheat flour, or 1 cup (200 g) quinoa flour and 1 cup (115 g) whole wheat flour.

BUCKWHEAT CRÊPES FILLED WITH BUTTERED FRUIT AND SWEET RICOTTA

Makes about 24 (6-inch/15-cm) crêpes | vegetarian

These simple-to-make whole grain crêpes are perfect for serving to company. The batter needs to be made at least 2 hours in advance so the flour granules have time to absorb some of the liquid, but you can do this the night before. You can even fill the crêpes and put the packets (shaped like blintzes) on a baking sheet, cover them with plastic, and refrigerate for several hours before warming them in the oven for 20 minutes. Freeze half of the plain crêpes for another time (the recipe makes double the amount needed for the filling), or, for a crowd, serve some of the crêpes filled with this sweet filling and some with the savory ham-and-cheese variation on page 59. These are quite versatile; use your imagination.

FOR THE CRÊPES

- 1 cup (130 g) buckwheat flour
- 1/2 cup (70 g) white whole wheat flour
- 1/2 teaspoon salt
- 1 1/2 (360 ml) cups milk
- 3 tablespoons unsalted butter, melted, or vegetable oil
- 3 large eggs

FOR THE FILLING (FOR ABOUT 12 CRÊPES)

- 15 ounces (425 g) ricotta (about 1 1/2 cups)
- 3 tablespoons agave nectar or honey
- 1/2 teaspoon ground cardamom
- 2 tablespoons unsalted butter, plus 1 tablespoon softened butter
- 2 cups (285 g) thinly sliced nectarines, apricots, plums, or peaches
- 1 teaspoon sugar

MAKE THE CRÊPES

In a large bowl, whisk all the ingredients together until very smooth and transfer to a 4-cup (960-ml) measuring cup. (Alternatively, blend them in a blender.) Refrigerate the batter for at least 2 hours or overnight. The batter should be the consistency of heavy cream; thin it with a little water if necessary.

Heat a well-seasoned 9-inch (23-cm) crêpe pan or nonstick sauté pan over medium heat. Pour about 3 tablespoons of the batter into the center of the pan, tilting the pan to spread the batter into a thin round. Cook for 1 minute, or until the crêpe is lightly browned on the bottom and the edges begin to lift from the pan, then flip and cook the other side for 30 seconds. Remove to a piece of waxed paper and repeat with the remaining batter. The crêpes can be stacked, slipped into a gallon-size (3.8-L) freezer bag, and kept for up to 3 days in the refrigerator or up to 1 month in the freezer (thaw overnight in the refrigerator before using).

FILL AND WARM THE CRÊPES

Preheat the oven to 400°F (205°C). Line a baking sheet with parchment paper. In a medium bowl, whisk together the ricotta, agave nectar, and cardamom; set aside.

In a large sauté pan, melt the 2 tablespoons butter over medium heat and add the nectarines. Cook, stirring frequently, until just tender, about 5 minutes.

Lay 6 crêpes, pretty side down, on the counter and spread the center of each with some of the ricotta mixture, then top with some of the nectarines. Fold in the sides to cover the filling, then fold the bottom up to the center of the crêpe, then fold the top down over the center to make a little square package. Arrange seam side down on the prepared baking sheet. Repeat with the remaining 6 crêpes and filling. Spread the tops of the crêpe packages with the softened butter and sprinkle with sugar. Bake for 15 minutes and serve.

VARIATIONS

★ For a savory ham-and-cheese filling: Blanch 8 cups (240 g) fresh spinach leaves in 1 inch (2.5 cm) boiling water for 1 minute, drain, and squeeze dry. Chop and season with salt and pepper. Spread each crêpe with about ½ tablespoon Nicole's Spicy Tomato Chutney (page 255) or other tart-sweet preserve, top with shredded Gruyère or Swiss cheese (about ¾ cup / 115 g total), and cover with a slice of good-quality Black Forest ham. Fold up, brush with butter (omit the sugar topping), and bake until heated through.

★ For a dosa-style curried potato filling (for 6 meal-size crêpes): Whisk ¼ cup (60 ml) plain Greek yogurt, ½ teaspoon turmeric, ½ teaspoon ground coriander, 1 teaspoon grated fresh ginger, and 1 minced hot green chile together; set aside. In a large heavy skillet or sauté pan, heat 2 tablespoons olive oil until hot, then add 1 teaspoon cumin seeds, 3 cups (480 g) chopped cooked potatoes, and 1 (15-ounce / 430-g) can chickpeas (drained and rinsed). Cook over medium heat until the potatoes and chickpeas are heated through, then stir in the yogurt mixture and add salt to taste; cook for 2 minutes, stirring constantly. Fill the crêpes with the mixture (no need to warm the crêpes first, and no need to wrap up like a package—just fill them like tacos) and top with more plain yogurt, ½ cup (10 g) torn fresh cilantro, and thinly sliced hot green chile, if desired.

GRITS WITH QUICK HOMEMADE SAUSAGE AND CRISPED SAGE

Serves 4 | gluten free

An egg or a fluffy biscuit would not be out of place next to a little mound of these savory sausage grits, and if a little syrup from the biscuit—maple or sorghum, depending on where in the country you are—happened to seep into the grits' personal space, well, so much the better.

- **Salt**
- **½ cup (80 g) raw corn grits or hominy grits**
- **2 tablespoons olive oil**
- **12 fresh sage leaves**
- **⅓ pound (150 g) Quick Homemade Sausage (see below)**
- **Freshly ground black pepper to taste**

In a heavy 2-quart (2-L) saucepan, bring 3 cups (720 ml) water and a pinch of salt to a boil. Gradually, 1 tablespoon at a time, add the grits, stirring constantly. Cook until the grits are thick and each grain is tender, 15 to 20 minutes, stirring frequently (especially toward the end of the cooking) and turning down the heat to medium-low when the grits start to bubble and plop out of the pan.

Meanwhile, in a large sauté pan or skillet, heat the oil over medium-high heat. Add the sage and cook until crisp and just starting to color, about 1 minute, then remove with a slotted spoon to a paper towel to drain. Return the pan and oil to the heat and add the sausage. Cook, breaking up the meat into pieces with a spatula, until well browned and cooked through, 5 to 6 minutes. Drain off any excess fat if necessary, then return the pan to the heat and add about 2 tablespoons water. Stir to scrape up the browned bits, then remove from the heat and set aside.

When the grits are tender, scrape the sausage into them. Cook until just heated through, about 1 minute, then season with salt and pepper to taste. Spoon onto plates or into a serving bowl and scatter the sage over the top. Grind some pepper on top if desired, and serve.

QUICK HOMEMADE SAUSAGE

Makes 1⅓ pounds (600 g) | gluten free

- **1⅓ pounds (600 g) ground turkey (not too lean) or pork**
- **1 clove garlic, grated**
- **¾ teaspoon salt**
- **½ teaspoon freshly ground black pepper**
- **1 teaspoon minced fresh sage**
- **1 teaspoon minced fresh marjoram (optional)**
- **1 teaspoon maple syrup or brown sugar**

Combine all the ingredients in a large bowl and beat vigorously with a rubber spatula or wooden spoon until thoroughly combined, sticky, and sort of emulsified. Divide into four ⅓-pound (150-g) portions, wrap each tightly in plastic wrap, and put in a resealable plastic freezer bag and refrigerate or freeze until needed. The sausage can be refrigerated for up to 2 days, or frozen for at least 1 month (thaw in the refrigerator before using).

DAVE'S GOETTA
(CINCINNATI-STYLE PORK LOAF WITH PINHEAD OATS)
Makes 1 large loaf or 4 mini loaves; serves dozens | gluten free*

Goetta ("GET-uh") is one of those only-in-Cincinnati dishes, like cinnamon-spiced chili on top of spaghetti, that you just will not see anywhere else (unless you travel the Midwest or cook from cookbooks by me). My husband, Derek, and our endlessly game daughter, Thalia, and I had it for the first time on a splendid fall road trip (Georgia–New York–New Orleans–Georgia), at a down-at-the-heels but incredibly welcoming breakfast counter in Over-the-Rhine, Cincinnati, called Tucker's. Goetta is much like my family's beloved cornmeal-based pork loaf, paan hass (and Derek's family's beloved scrapple), but has no offal and is made with pinhead or steel-cut oats rather than cornmeal and buckwheat flour. The oats firm up so the loaf can be thinly sliced and pan-fried until crisp-crunchy. Go ahead and make the whole batch and wrap up and freeze what you don't use. This recipe is from my dad.

- **1 pound (455 g) Quick Homemade Sausage (page 60) or 1 pound (455 g) bulk breakfast sausage**
- **1 large onion, diced (about 2 cups / 320 g)**
- **1 rib celery with leaves, finely diced**
- **1 bay leaf**
- **2 cups (360 g) raw pinhead (Scottish) oats or steel-cut oats**
- **1½ teaspoons salt, or more to taste**
- **2 teaspoons freshly ground black pepper**
- **Bacon grease, butter, or olive or vegetable oil for frying**
- **Maple syrup for serving (optional)**

Put 5 cups (1.2 L) of water in a large heavy pot or Dutch oven. Add the sausage in little chickpea-size bits, then add the onion, celery, and bay leaf. Bring to a boil, then lower the heat and simmer for 10 minutes, breaking the sausage bits up with a spoon. Add the oats, salt, and pepper, bring to a boil, then lower the heat and cook, stirring frequently, for 50 minutes. The oats will be very soft and very thick, and they'll start to stick to the bottom of the pan; don't worry about that, just keep stirring frequently, and lower the heat if necessary to keep the mixture from burning. Taste and season with more salt if necessary.

Spoon the mixture into 1 large or 4 mini loaf pans and smooth the top. Let cool to room temperature, then cover with plastic wrap and refrigerate until firm, about 2 hours. (The goetta can be kept in the refrigerator for up to 4 days; to freeze, turn the loaf out onto a large piece of plastic wrap and wrap tightly, then put the loaf in a freezer bag, suck out the excess air, seal, and freeze for up to 6 months. Thaw in the refrigerator before slicing and frying. You can cut the loaf into 3 or 4 sections for easier freezing and thawing, if you like.)

Turn the goetta loaf out onto a cutting board and cut it into ¼-inch-thick (6-mm-thick) slabs. Heat a little bacon grease on a large griddle or in a large sauté pan or skillet over medium heat. When it's hot, add a few slices of the goetta and cook until nicely browned, at least 5 minutes on each side. Serve hot, with maple syrup, if you like.

* See page 25.

TEFF UPMA
(SPICY INDIAN MUSH)

Serves 2 or 3 | vegan, gluten free

My friend and cookbook author Leda Scheintaub introduced me to a south Indian way of cooking soji a few years ago, and breakfast hasn't been the same for me since. Usually this dish is made with refined wheat farina (labeled soji or rava in Indian grocery stores; it's basically Cream of Wheat cereal), but it's just as good or better made with whole teff grains, whole wheat farina, or even cracked whole wheat that's been ground a little finer in a spice mill. This is a spicy, intensely aromatic, filling dish. I like to make it extremely hot and serve it with a dollop of cooling plain yogurt or a tall cucumber smoothie. Fresh curry leaves (Murraya koenigii, or sweet neem) are available at Indian and some Asian grocery stores.

- **1 tablespoon olive or canola oil**
- **1 onion, diced**
- **1 fresh hot red or green chile, seeded and diced, or more if you want it hotter**
- **1 teaspoon ginger-garlic paste (see Note) or minced fresh ginger and garlic**
- **10 fresh curry leaves**
- **1 teaspoon brown mustard seeds**
- **1 teaspoon curry power**
- **1/4 teaspoon ground cayenne**
- **2 dried red chiles (optional)**
- **1/2 teaspoon salt, or more to taste**
- **3/4 cup (150 g) raw teff**

In a large sauté pan, heat the oil over medium-high heat. Add the onion and fresh chile and cook, stirring frequently, until well browned and caramelized, about 8 minutes. Add the ginger-garlic paste and cook, stirring, for 30 seconds. Add the curry leaves, mustard seeds, curry powder, cayenne, dried chiles, if using, and salt and cook, stirring, for 15 seconds.

Add the teff and 2 1/2 cups (570 ml) water and bring to a boil, stirring constantly. Lower the heat and simmer about 20 minutes, continuing to stir frequently, especially toward the end, to keep the mixture from sticking; add a little more water if necessary. When it's done, it should be very thick—not porridgy, almost solid—and will hold its shape. Taste and add more salt if necessary. Serve hot.

VARIATION

★ Instead of teff, use amaranth, or for a couple of not-gluten-free options, 1 cup (180 g) whole wheat farina, or 1 cup (160 g) cracked wheat that has been ground more finely in a spice mill. Add 1/2 teaspoon turmeric with the rest of the spices. For farina or cracked wheat, reduce the simmering time to about 10 minutes.

NOTE: To make ginger-garlic paste, combine two parts chopped ginger and one part chopped garlic in a mini food processor, adding only as much water as you need to process to a finely ground but dry-ish paste.

HUEVOS RANCHEROS WITH GRIDDLED CORNMEAL

Serves 2 or 3 | vegetarian, gluten free

Cornmeal huevos rancheros may be as good an excuse as you'll ever need to host a brunch. Most of the elements can be prepared well in advance, so all you'll have to do at the last minute is reheat, fry up the eggs, and put everything on plates—or, of course, you can just set out big bowls of black beans and salsa, and a warm platter of cornmeal squares and have guests assemble their own breakfasts.

FOR THE BEANS

- 1 tablespoon olive or vegetable oil
- ½ large onion, diced
- 1 clove garlic, minced
- 1 bay leaf
- Generous pinch of ground cayenne
- 1 pound (455 g) dried black beans, rinsed
- 2 teaspoons salt

FOR THE SALSA

- 1½ pounds (680 g) ripe tomatoes (about 3 large), diced
- 1 small sweet onion, diced
- 2 hot green chiles, seeded and minced
- ½ bunch fresh cilantro, chopped
- Juice of 1 to 2 limes
- Salt to taste

FOR THE CORNMEAL

- 1 cup (160 g) raw cornmeal (any kind), cooked and spread in an oiled 9-inch (23-cm) square pan, refrigerated until cooled and solidified (page 23)
- Salt and freshly ground black pepper
- 2 tablespoons olive or vegetable oil

TO SERVE

- 2 tablespoons olive or vegetable oil
- 6 large eggs
- Salt and freshly ground black pepper
- Lime wedges

MAKE THE BEANS

In a large, heavy pot or Dutch oven, heat the oil over medium-high heat. Add the onion and garlic and cook, stirring frequently, until the onion is translucent, about 5 minutes. Add the bay leaf, cayenne, beans, and 6 cups (1.4 L) water. Cover and bring to a boil, then lower the heat and simmer for 45 minutes. Add the salt, then cook until the beans are tender but still hold their shape, about 30 minutes longer. With a slotted spoon, remove 1½ cups (330 g) of the beans to a sealable container; refrigerate or freeze for another use (for example, in the burgers on page 164). Remove and discard some of the remaining cooking liquid from the pot and crush some of the beans to thicken the mixture (or hit it with an immersion blender for a few seconds). Cover and keep warm.

MAKE THE SALSA

While the beans are cooking, in a large bowl, combine the tomatoes, onion, chiles, and cilantro, and add lime juice and salt to taste. Let stand at room temperature for 1 hour, then taste and season again.

MAKE THE GRIDDLED CORNMEAL

Preheat the oven to 250°F (120°C). Line a baking sheet with paper towels.

Cut the cooled cornmeal into 12 squares and sprinkle with salt and pepper. In a large sauté pan, heat a little of the oil over medium-high heat. Working in batches, add the cornmeal squares and cook without disturbing until you can see that they are browned at the edges, 5 to 7 minutes. Using a metal spatula, turn them over and cook until the second side is browned. Transfer to the prepared baking sheet and keep warm in the oven.

ASSEMBLE THE HUEVOS RANCHEROS

Wipe out the pan and add a little more oil to it. Place over medium-low heat and crack in the eggs. Sprinkle with salt and pepper, then cook until the eggs are the way you like them (partly cover the pan for sunny-side up; flip for over-easy or medium). Arrange the cornmeal squares on serving plates and spoon some of the beans over them. Top each serving with an egg, and top the egg with salsa.

KINCHE (ETHIOPIAN CRACKED WHEAT) WITH SPICED BUTTER AND FRESH TOMATOES

Serves 4 | vegetarian

My daughter and our friend and I had the most amazing breakfast at a restaurant in the Ethiopian neighborhood near Decatur, Georgia, last summer. Among the other offerings piled on the injera in front of us—eggs soft-scrambled with tomatoes and green chiles, berbere-spiced shards of torn French bread, beef tibs (lightly stewed cubes of tender beef)—was a mound of mild, comforting, buttery cracked wheat. If you want more heat, add ½ teaspoon of berbere spice (page 181) to ¼ cup (25 g) of sambal oelek and serve alongside.

- **4 tablespoons (55 g) Niter Qibe (spiced butter; see recipe below)**
- **1 large sweet onion, sliced**
- **2 plum tomatoes, diced**
- **Salt**
- **1½ cups (240 g) raw cracked wheat**
- **Scrambled eggs for serving (optional)**
- **1 recipe Injera (page 180), for serving (optional)**

In a large sauté pan, heat 3 tablespoons of the spiced butter over medium heat. Add the onion and cook, stirring occasionally, until well browned and caramelized, about 20 minutes. Add the tomatoes and a couple pinches of salt and cook until soft, about 5 minutes.

Meanwhile, in a heavy 2-quart (2-L) saucepan, heat the remaining 1 tablespoon of spiced butter and add the cracked wheat; cook over medium heat, stirring, until fragrant, about 2 minutes. Add 2 cups (480 ml) water and 1 teaspoon salt. Cover, bring to a boil, then lower the heat and simmer until the water is absorbed and the cracked wheat is tender, about 10 minutes. Dump the cracked wheat into the pan with the onion mixture and gently fold all the ingredients together with a spatula over medium-high heat until heated through and well combined. Add more salt to taste if needed. Serve hot with scrambled eggs and injera, if desired.

NITER QIBE (SPICED BUTTER)

Makes about ¾ cup (170 g) | vegetarian

- **1 cup (2 sticks / 225 g) unsalted butter (see Note)**
- **4 green cardamom pods, lightly crushed**
- **1 teaspoon fenugreek seeds**
- **½ teaspoon cumin seeds**
- **⅛ teaspoon turmeric**
- **1 teaspoon minced fresh ginger**
- **1 clove garlic, minced**
- **¼ small onion, diced**

NOTE: Vegans may feel free to substitute margarine or even vegetable oil and skip the skimming and straining.

Put all the ingredients in a heavy saucepan and cook over low heat until the butter is no longer bubbling, which means that the excess water has cooked out, about 1 hour. Skim off and discard the foam on the surface, then pour the clear butter through a fine-mesh sieve into a clean container, leaving the milky solids at the bottom behind. Discard the solids in the sieve. The butter can be made weeks in advance and refrigerated or frozen in airtight containers. It will keep for at least 6 months in the refrigerator, and I suppose indefinitely in the freezer.

YAM KAI (THAI EGGS) WITH LEFTOVER GRAINS

Serves 2 | gluten free

Thai-style eggs, most commonly made with softened glass noodles rather than a whole grain, are incredibly versatile, appealing to me as a quick but fun and satisfying breakfast or lunch or supper because I usually have everything I need on hand. In fact, every time I make this—and I make it often—I'm amazed that such a dish essentially just came out of my fridge. It's even easier if you have a little bag of cooked rice or other grains in the freezer: Just break off a chunk, put it in a sieve, and rinse under cool water until the grains separate. If you don't have fish sauce, you can use 1 tablespoon soy sauce instead, and if you don't have chile paste, use a couple good pinches of crushed red chiles.

The one secret to good yam kai, in my experience, is that you must cook the shallots until they're almost burned. And the more of them you use, the better—as many as you can stand to peel and slice in the morning as you down your first cup of coffee; four is my limit.

- 1½ tablespoons freshly squeezed lime juice (from ½ lime)
- 1½ tablespoons fish sauce
- 1½ teaspoons chile paste (sambal oelek), or to taste
- 1 cup (190 g) cooked barley, sorghum, quinoa, millet, or brown rice (pages 20, 32, 27, 24, or 29–30), cooled
- 4 large eggs
- 1 tablespoon vegetable oil
- 4 shallots, thinly sliced
- 4 scallions, cut into 2-inch (5-cm) lengths, green and white parts separated
- 1 leftover cooked pork chop, meat removed from the bone and thinly sliced (optional)

In a medium bowl, stir together the lime juice, fish sauce, 1 teaspoon of the chile paste, and the cooked grain of your choice; set aside.

Put the eggs and the remaining ½ teaspoon of chile paste in a small bowl and beat with a fork to combine; set aside.

In a large heavy sauté pan, heat ½ tablespoon of the oil over medium-high heat. Add the shallots, the white sections of the scallions, and the pork, if using, and cook, stirring occasionally, until the shallots are very dark brown and shriveled, about 4 minutes. Add the scallion greens and the remaining ½ tablespoon of oil and cook for 1 minute. Pour in the egg mixture and cook without disturbing for 30 seconds, then turn and stir, breaking it up a little but keeping good-size pieces together, cooking until just set, about 45 seconds. Pour in the grain mixture and cook, turning with a spatula, until heated through, about 1 minute. Serve.

CEREAL BARS WITH YOGURT

Makes 8 large bars | vegetarian, gluten free*

Some days you need to just pull something out of the fridge and run out the door; these soft, not-too-sweet bars are a satisfying substitute for a sit-down breakfast. They boast all the goodness of whole grains, of course, but also provide protein, an important but often overlooked component in a morning meal, from the custardy egg and yogurt topping, the nuts, and the quinoa flakes.

- ¼ cup (½ stick / 55 g) unsalted butter, melted, plus more for the pan
- 1 ¾ cups (280 g) raw rolled oats
- 1 cup (100 g) raw quinoa flakes or 1½ cups (25 g) puffed millet
- ½ teaspoon ground cinnamon
- Pinch of salt
- ⅓ cup (75 g) packed brown sugar
- ¾ cup (185 g) unsweetened applesauce
- 1 cup (240 ml) plain Greek yogurt
- 1 large egg
- ¼ cup (60 ml) honey, agave nectar, fruit preserves, jam, or other sweetener
- ½ cup (55 g) finely chopped nuts

Preheat the oven to 350°F (175°C). Lightly butter a 9-inch (23-cm) square baking pan.

In a small food processor, combine 1½ cups (240 g) of the oats, the quinoa flakes (or puffed millet), cinnamon, and salt; process until the oats are finely ground. Transfer to a medium bowl and stir in the butter, brown sugar, and applesauce. Spread in the prepared baking pan.

In the food processor (no need to clean it first), combine the yogurt, egg, and honey until smooth. Spread the mixture over the batter in the pan, then sprinkle evenly with the nuts and remaining ¼ cup (40 g) oats.

Bake until the yogurt topping is set, about 30 minutes. Let cool on a wire rack, then cut into 8 rectangles. Store in the refrigerator in an airtight container in two layers separated by waxed paper for up to 5 days. Wrap each bar individually in waxed paper to take-and-go or to pack into wintertime lunch boxes.

* See page 25.

BATIDO DE TRIGO
(LATIN AMERICAN PUFFED-WHEAT DRINK)
Serves 1 | vegan

I admit to having fond memories of that oversweetened puffed-wheat boxed cereal I loved as a kid (though my mom invariably cut the good stuff with the unsweetened kind as soon as she brought it home from the grocery store), especially the way it made the milk taste cloying and wheaty by the time the last few puffs in the bowl had gone soggy. So I was positively transported the first time I had an icy, thick batido de trigo, a shake made with puffed wheat at a Mexican place in Jackson Heights, Queens, after a Mets game at Shea Stadium. I'm sure that one was loaded with sweetened condensed milk, but it's just as delightful with no more than a couple squeezes of agave nectar. To boost the nutritional content, sprinkle in some toasted wheat germ, wheat bran, and/or ground flax seeds.

- **1 cup (240 ml) cold almond (see below), rice, or soy milk**
- **1½ cups (15 g) unsweetened puffed wheat**
- **Dash of ground cinnamon**
- **Agave nectar or other sweetener to taste**
- **4 ice cubes**

Combine the almond milk, puffed wheat, cinnamon, and agave nectar in a blender and let soak for 5 minutes. Add the ice and blend until smooth. Serve immediately.

VARIATIONS

★ For an extra-rich (nonvegan) drink, use regular milk plus 2 tablespoons sweetened condensed milk (or to taste) and omit the agave nectar.

★ Use any puffed whole grain instead of or in combination with the wheat: Puffed millet, spelt, and brown rice all work well.

★ Instead of puffed wheat, use 1 cup (170 g) cooked and cooled farro (you can use it straight from the freezer) or leftover cooked oatmeal. Or soak uncooked rolled oats in the milk mixture overnight and blend with ice in the morning. Note that firmer cooked grains—wheat berries, rye, and the like—don't work so well: They tend to just bounce around in the blender.

★ Vary the flavorings: Add a dash of vanilla or almond extract, or replace the cinnamon with cardamom or nutmeg (for a nog effect).

ALMOND MILK
Makes a scant 4 cups (900 ml) | vegan, gluten free

- **1 cup (110 g) whole raw or roasted almonds**
- **½ teaspoon pure vanilla extract (optional)**

Put the almonds in a container with 4 cups (960 ml) cold water. Cover and refrigerate for at least 4 hours and up to overnight. Puree in a blender until very smooth, then pour through a fine-mesh sieve into a clean container, pushing on the almond pulp to extract as much of the liquid as possible. Stir the vanilla extract into the almond milk, if desired, then cover and store in the refrigerator, where it will keep for at least 5 days.

2

Appetizers and Small Bites

I guess I thought it was cute the first time my daughter requested an "appetizer" while I was laboring over a supper that was taking too many darn hours to make (this might very well have been during my several-days-long marathon of Thai street food cooking that was so authentic a mysterious grit appeared in one dish). But now she expects them every evening, the little scamp. I often think ahead enough to set out an appealing platter of cut raw vegetables and a little ramekin of hummus, or a bowl of nuts, or a cut-up piece of fruit (my mom was right all along: Put beautiful whole fruit in a centerpiece-worthy bowl on the table and it will rot there, but *cut up* that shriveled old apple and it'll be gone in seconds). Usually this keeps us all satisfied until the main dish is ready. But hosting a dinner party, or serving hors d'oeuvres with drinks requires something a little more sophisticated, and those are the kinds of recipes you'll find here. Obviously many of these would also make a lovely light lunch or brunch, or even a summer supper. They're all intensely flavorful, as small bites should be.

SMOKED FISH AND KASHA CAKES
WITH WATERCRESS SALAD AND CRÈME FRAÎCHE
Serves 8 | gluten free

A very elegant way to serve hearty kasha, these delicate pan-fried cakes are studded with pieces of oil-rich smoked fish, which I've found to be a perfect foil for the distinctly flavored roasted buckwheat groats. Paired with a dollop of cream and a small, sharp-tasting watercress salad, they make a lovely appetizer. You could also make half-size cakes and serve them with drinks at a cocktail party: spoon a tiny bit of crème fraîche or sour cream on top, and garnish with a sprig of watercress or dill.

To make this especially fancy, use 4 ounces (115 g) flaked smoked trout (pick out any bones and skin) instead of the kippers and tuna.

FOR THE KASHA CAKES
- **2 cups cooked kasha (page 22), cooled**
- **1 (3.25-ounce / 90-g) can kippered (smoked) herring, drained and flaked**
- **1 (4.5-ounce / 130-g) can light tuna in olive oil, drained and flaked**
- **2 teaspoons minced fresh dill**
- **Salt and freshly ground black pepper**
- **1 large egg, lightly beaten**
- **About 1/4 cup (60 ml) olive oil**

FOR THE SALAD AND TO SERVE
- **3 tablespoons Champagne vinegar or white-wine vinegar**
- **1/2 teaspoon salt**
- **1/4 teaspoon freshly ground black pepper**
- **1/2 teaspoon grainy mustard**
- **3 tablespoons olive oil**
- **4 ounces (about 4 cups / 115 g) watercress, washed and spun dry**
- **8 teaspoons crème fraîche (see Note)**
- **8 sprigs fresh dill**

MAKE THE KASHA CAKES
In a large bowl, combine the kasha, kippered herring, tuna, and dill. Taste and season with salt and pepper. Stir in the egg. Divide the mixture into 8 portions in the bowl.

In a large sauté pan, heat half of the oil over medium-high heat until it shimmers. Shape 4 portions of the kasha mixture into tightly packed 3-inch (7.5-cm) round patties and add them to the pan. (Don't worry if the mixture doesn't hold together well: Form them on a spatula and gently slide them into the hot oil as you make them; the patties will firm up as they cook.) Cook until nicely browned on the bottom, about 6 minutes. Turn and brown the other side, then remove to a large plate and cover loosely with aluminum foil to keep warm. Repeat with the remaining oil and patties.

MAKE THE SALAD
In a large bowl, whisk together the vinegar, salt, pepper, and mustard, then gradually whisk in the oil. Add the watercress and toss to coat. Pile some of the salad on each of 8 serving plates and top with a kasha patty. Dollop each patty with crème fraîche and top with a dill sprig. Serve.

NOTE: To make about 2 cups (480 ml) homemade crème fraîche: In a heavy saucepan, combine 2 cups (480 ml) heavy cream (preferably 36 percent butterfat or more) and 1/4 cup (60 ml) cultured buttermilk. Place over medium heat and bring just to 100°F (38°C) on a candy thermometer, stirring. Immediately pour into a nonreactive bowl, cover, and set aside at room temperature for 24 hours; don't stir. Transfer the bowl to the refrigerator for 8 hours or overnight, then leave it out at room temperature again for 24 hours. Store in an airtight container (pouring off runny liquid if there is any) in the fridge until ready to use; it will keep for up to 2 weeks.

PAN-FRIED SMELT WITH TAMARI-CITRUS DIPPING SAUCE
Serves 4

When I was living alone in Hell's Kitchen as a freelancer (i.e., when I didn't have a lot of money to spend on fancy fish fillets), I'd go to the seafood market down by the Port Authority near my apartment and buy small handfuls of smelt, just six or eight at a time, annoying the hell out of the fish guy, who was clearly used to selling to customers with larger appetites (and, probably, more generous budgets). I came to truly love these cheap—and, I later learned, sustainably correct—little freshwater fishes, simply coated in cornmeal and quickly fried in a skillet until the coating is crunchy and the tails are crisp as potato chips. There's no need to remove the bones: they're delicate and pleasantly crunchy, and are an excellent source of calcium.

One pound of them makes a light appetizer for four people, but you could easily fry up several pounds' worth—what's known in the upper Midwest as a mess o' smelt—cut a few lemons into wedges, maybe mix up some homemade tartar sauce (try plain Greek yogurt whisked with a blob of good-quality mayonnaise, some freshly squeezed lemon juice, and a spoonful of the tomato chutney on page 255), and invite some friends over for smelt and ice-cold beer.

Look for bags of frozen cleaned smelt in the dark, infrequently visited corners of the frozen foods section of the supermarket, and in Asian markets. To thaw them quickly, submerge the unopened bag in a container of cold water and set it in the sink under a barely dripping faucet for 15 minutes or so.

FOR THE DIPPING SAUCE
- **2 tablespoons tamari**
- **3 tablespoons freshly squeezed lime juice**
- **1 tablespoon freshly squeezed lemon juice**
- **2 tablespoons thinly sliced scallion**
- **Pinch of crushed red pepper**
- **Pinch of toasted sesame seeds**

FOR THE SMELT
- **½ cup (85 g) raw fine-grind cornmeal**
- **¼ cup (30 g) white whole wheat flour**
- **½ teaspoon salt**
- **¼ teaspoon freshly ground black pepper**
- **1 large egg**
- **2 tablespoons milk**
- **1 pound (455 g) cleaned smelt (gutted, heads and fins cut off)**
- **About ½ cup (120 ml) vegetable oil**

MAKE THE DIPPING SAUCE
Combine all the ingredients together in a small bowl with 1 tablespoon water.

MAKE THE SMELT
Preheat the oven to 250°F (120°C). Put a wire rack over a baking sheet in the oven.

In a medium bowl, whisk together the cornmeal, flour, salt, and pepper. In a separate medium bowl, whisk together the egg and milk. Rinse and drain the fish in a colander, then dump them into the bowl with the egg mixture.

In a large heavy sauté pan, heat about ¼ cup (60 ml) of the oil (about ⅛ inch / 3 mm deep) over medium heat until it shimmers and a bit of the cornmeal mixture sizzles when you drop it into the oil. Lift a fish from the egg mixture, letting the excess drain off, then dredge in the cornmeal mixture. Carefully lower it into the oil and repeat until you've added six or seven fish to the oil—don't crowd them in the pan. Cook, turning with tongs, until deeply browned and crisp, 5 to 6 minutes total. Using the tongs, remove the fish to the rack in the oven to keep warm. Repeat with the remaining fish, pouring out the oil and replacing it with fresh oil about halfway through. Serve hot, with the dipping sauce.

VARIATION
★ For a gluten-free version, use cornstarch instead of the wheat flour.

POLENTA TART WITH SWISS CHARD, GRUYÈRE, AND CRÈME FRAÎCHE

Serves 6 | vegetarian, gluten free

This "tart" has a baked polenta round as its base and a creamy, cheesy Swiss chard topping that bubbles and browns lightly in the oven. Cut thin wedges to serve with a pile of salad for a light brunch, or serve on little plates with drinks in the evening.

- **Olive oil, for greasing the pan**
- **Salt**
- **1 cup (160 g) raw medium- or coarse-ground cornmeal or polenta**
- **½ small bunch (about 4 ounces / 115 g) Swiss chard, washed and coarsely chopped**
- **2 tablespoons crème fraîche (see Note on page 74)**
- **½ cup (110 g) shredded Gruyère cheese**
- **2 large eggs, lightly beaten**
- **Pinch of freshly ground black pepper**
- **Pinch of freshly grated nutmeg**

Lightly oil a 9-inch (23-cm) tart pan with removable bottom and set it on a parchment paper–lined baking sheet.

In a heavy 2-quart (2-L) saucepan, combine 4 cups (960 ml) water and ½ teaspoon salt. Bring to a boil, then gradually whisk in the cornmeal. Lower the heat and simmer (it should plop and bubble just once every few seconds), whisking frequently and stirring with a silicone spatula to prevent it from sticking to the pan, until the cornmeal is thick but still pourable and the individual granules are tender, about 35 minutes for coarse-grind cornmeal or 15 minutes for medium-grind cornmeal; add another ½ cup (120 ml) water if the mixture becomes thick before the granules are tender. Spread the hot polenta to an even, ½ inch (12 mm) thickness in the tart pan. Let cool completely to set. If making in advance, cover with plastic wrap and store in the refrigerator for up to 1 day.

Preheat the oven to 425°F (220°C).

Bake the polenta round on the prepared baking sheet until dry on top, about 25 minutes. Turn it out of the pan onto the baking sheet and remove the pan bottom (now on top); bake until dry on the exposed side, about 25 minutes. Turn the polenta back over into the tart pan and set on the baking sheet. Set aside.

While the polenta round is baking, bring 1 inch (2.5 cm) of water to a boil in a large saucepan. Add the chard, cover, and cook until tender, about 5 minutes. Drain and plunge the greens into a bowl of ice water to stop the cooking, then drain well again, squeezing out any excess water.

In a medium bowl, stir together the crème fraîche, cheese, eggs, ¼ teaspoon salt, the pepper, and nutmeg. Stir in the chard. Spread the mixture over the warm polenta round (if it's very runny, use a slotted spoon and leave some of the liquid in the bowl). Immediately return the baking sheet with the pan to the oven and bake until the topping is set, about 25 minutes. Let cool for at least 10 minutes before cutting into wedges and serving warm or serve at room temperature. Store leftovers, covered, in the refrigerator for up to 2 days.

> NOTE: If you don't have a tart pan, draw a 9-inch (23 - cm) circle on a piece of parchment and flip it over, penciled side down, onto a baking sheet. Let the cooked polenta cool for 5 minutes in the saucepan, then spread it ½ inch (12 mm) thick over the circle. Let cool, then bake as above. When topping the polenta round with the filling, some filling may run off the edge a little and bake onto the parchment; just trim those bits off post-baking, before cutting and serving (they make a tasty snack in themselves).

SHREDDED PORK WITH SMOKY FRUIT SAUCE ON MINI CORN CAKES

Makes about 48 assembled mini corn cakes; serves 12 as an hors d'oeuvre | gluten free

I may live in Georgia, but I'm close enough to Ayden and Lexington, North Carolina, to know what real barbecue is, and you'll notice I didn't presume to call this pulled pork or barbecue or anything of the sort. When you can't have the real thing, when you've run out of hickory or the morning is too long gone or you're just too lazy to tend a whole hog in an open pit for eighteen hours, there's nothing wrong with subtly hinting in the general direction of barbecue. Throw some lesser cuts of pork in the oven, mix up a quick chipotle-vinegar sauce, and pan-fry a few dozen little corn cakes to go with, and you've got yourself a homey, fun hors d'oeuvre or party dish. And everything can be made in advance and reheated just before serving.

FOR THE PORK

- **2 pounds (910 g) boneless pork shoulder, cut into 1-inch-thick (2.5-cm-thick) slices, or country-style ribs**
- **¹⁄₂ teaspoon salt**
- **¹⁄₄ teaspoon freshly ground black pepper**
- **¹⁄₄ teaspoon hot paprika**
- **1 tablespoon olive oil**

FOR THE SAUCE

- **¹⁄₂ cup (120 ml) peach or nectarine jam or preserves, pureed if very chunky**
- **1 cup (240 ml) cider vinegar**
- **¹⁄₂ teaspoon chipotle chile flakes or ¹⁄₂ chipotle chile in adobo, minced**
- **Salt to taste**

FOR THE CORN CAKES

- **1¹⁄₄ cups (200 g) raw fine-grind cornmeal**
- **³⁄₄ teaspoon salt**
- **1 teaspoon sugar**
- **1 teaspoon baking powder**
- **1 cup (240 ml) buttermilk or plain yogurt thinned with water to the consistency of buttermilk**
- **2 large eggs, beaten**
- **1 cup (170 g) fresh or frozen (thawed) sweet corn kernels (from 1 large ear)**
- **1 scallion, thinly sliced on the bias**
- **Unsalted butter**

MAKE THE PORK

Preheat the oven to 300°F (150°C).

Put the pork in a baking dish or pan in a single layer and sprinkle with the salt, pepper, and paprika; drizzle with the oil. Cover the dish with aluminum foil and roast for 1 hour, then uncover the dish and roast for 30 minutes longer, until the meat is tender and easily pulled apart. When cool enough to handle, shred the meat, discarding any large pieces of fat (your hands work best for this, but you can also use two forks). Set aside in a medium bowl.

MAKE THE SAUCE

Simmer all the ingredients in a small saucepan for 15 minutes. Pour enough over the meat, to just coat it; toss well, and add more to taste as necessary. The meat and sauce can be made up to 2 days in advance and refrigerated; warm in a saucepan over low heat when ready to use.

MAKE THE CORN CAKES

Preheat the oven to 250°F (120°C).

In a large bowl, whisk together the cornmeal, salt, sugar, and baking powder. In a separate medium bowl, whisk together the buttermilk and eggs. Pour the buttermilk mixture into the cornmeal mixture and fold with a rubber spatula until just combined; the batter will be lumpy. Stir in the corn and scallion (reserve a handful of green scallion slices for garnish).

In a large sauté pan or on a griddle, melt a little butter over medium-high heat. When the foam dies down, working in batches, spoon in 2-tablespoon puddles of the batter. Cook without disturbing until you can see that the edges are browned and bubbles appear at the center of the corn cake, about 2 minutes; use a metal spatula to turn and cook the other side until browned, about 2 minutes. Transfer to a baking sheet and keep warm in the oven. (Alternatively, let cool, then cover and refrigerate for up to 1 day; reheat on a baking sheet in the oven before serving.)

Top each cake with a bit of the shredded pork and garnish with scallion. Serve warm or at room temperature.

SWEET POTATO AND MILLET CAKES WITH POBLANO CREAM

Makes 14 (3-inch / 7.5-cm) or 34 (1½-inch / 4-cm) cakes; serves 4 or 5 as an appetizer | vegetarian, gluten free

Millet, especially when it's been toasted in the pan before being cooked in water or broth, has a faint cornlike aroma, and despite its long history as a staple of Chinese cuisine to rival rice, I've always thought it's best when paired with Latin American flavors like cumin and chiles. Here you cook the millet right in the same pan with diced sweet potatoes and onion, then shape the mixture into patties and bake them until browned and crisp on the outside. Top each with a little dollop of spicy, tangy chile cream, or serve them plain alongside a brothy soup or roast chicken or pork. If you don't want to go to the trouble of roasting fresh chiles for the cream, use 1 (7-ounce / 198-g) can of mild (Hatch-style) diced green chiles, drained, or ½ cup (70 g) diced jarred roasted red peppers.

FOR THE POBLANO CREAM

- ½ cup (200 g) diced roasted poblano or other mild green chiles (about 3 large poblanos; see Note)
- 1 fresh serrano or jalapeño chile, seeded and diced
- 2 scallions, chopped
- 4 ounces cream cheese
- ½ cup (120 ml) plain Greek yogurt
- ¼ teaspoon salt, or more to taste

FOR THE SWEET POTATO AND MILLET CAKES

- 1 tablespoon olive oil, plus more for the baking sheet
- 1 onion, diced
- Salt
- ½ teaspoon ground cumin
- ¼ teaspoon ground cayenne
- ½ cup (100 g) raw millet, rinsed and drained
- 2 small peeled sweet potatoes (1 pound / 455 g), diced (about 2½ cups)
- 1 large egg, beaten
- 1 scallion, thinly sliced on a bias

MAKE THE POBLANO CREAM

In a mini food processor, combine all the ingredients and process until smooth. Transfer to an airtight container and refrigerate for at least 2 hours.

MAKE THE SWEET POTATO AND MILLET CAKES

Heat the oil in a heavy 2-quart (2-L) saucepan over medium-high heat. Add the onion and a pinch of salt and cook, stirring occasionally, until translucent, about 5 minutes. Add the cumin, cayenne, and millet and cook, stirring, until the onion is starting to brown, 3 to 5 minutes. Add ¾ cup (180 ml) water, ½ teaspoon salt, and the sweet potatoes. Cover, bring to a boil, then lower the heat and simmer until the sweet potatoes and millet are tender and all of the liquid is absorbed, about 25 minutes; if the millet is tender but liquid still pools in the pan, uncover and cook for another 5 minutes. Turn out into a large bowl and let cool to room temperature, fluffing and turning occasionally.

Preheat the oven to 450°F (230°C). Generously oil a baking sheet.

Add the egg to the cooled millet mixture and stir to thoroughly incorporate it. Spoon ¼-cup (60-ml) mounds of the mixture on the prepared baking sheet and spread them into 3-inch (7.5-cm) diameter cakes ½ inch (12 mm) thick. To make smaller cakes, spoon out heaping tablespoon mounds and shape them into 1½-inch (4-cm) rounds. Bake on the lower rack of the oven for 20 minutes, then flip the cakes over with a metal spatula and bake until golden brown on both sides, 10 to 15 minutes longer.

Arrange on individual serving plates or a platter, dollop with the poblano cream, and garnish with the scallion. Serve warm or at room temperature.

NOTE: To roast chiles, put them on a baking sheet under the broiler or set the peppers directly on a gas burner and roast, turning, until blistered and blackened all over. Put in a bowl, cover, and set aside until cool enough to handle. Slip off the skin, then cut out the stem and remove the seeds.

STUFFED SWEET PEPPERS WITH MILLET, MONTEREY JACK, AND BASIL

Makes about 42; serves 8 to 10 | vegetarian, gluten free

These addictive little bombs of flavor and contrasting textures—creamy, crunchy, sweet, salty—are easy to mix, stuff, and broil quickly for an informal get-together or just as something for the famished family to nosh on while, say, the pot of chili is taking forever to simmer to perfection on the stovetop. The peppers can be stuffed, covered on a baking sheet, and refrigerated up to 1 day before broiling and serving.

- 2 cups (350 g) cooked millet (page 24)
- 4 ounces (115 g) shredded Monterey Jack cheese
- 6 tablespoons (40 g) freshly grated Parmesan cheese
- ½ cup (40 g) chopped fresh basil
- Salt and freshly ground black pepper
- 8 ounces (225 g) sweet mini bell peppers (20 to 22 peppers; 2 to 3 inches / 5 to 7.5 cm long each)
- 2 teaspoons olive oil

Preheat the broiler to high and place a rack about 6 inches (15 cm) underneath the heat source. Line a rimmed baking sheet (or two quarter sheet pans) with aluminum foil.

In a medium bowl, combine the millet, cheeses, basil, 1 teaspoon salt, and ½ teaspoon black pepper, or more to taste—the mixture should be quite salty and flavorful. Stir gently to incorporate the cheese without mushing up the millet grains.

Cut the stem end off each sweet pepper, then cut in half lengthwise; pull out and discard any seeds. Fill each half with millet mixture, mounding it up a bit, and arrange stuffing side up on the prepared baking sheet. Drizzle with the oil. Broil, rotating the baking sheet halfway through, until the filling is a little bubbly and lightly browned, 6 to 8 minutes. Serve warm.

VARIATION

✳ Instead of small sweet bell peppers, you can use mild jalapeños—they may not be as kid friendly, but they'll be good!

SHRIMP AND QUINOA SPRING ROLLS
Serves 6 | gluten free

These pretty, pink-and-green translucent rolls don't really need a dipping sauce, but if you like you can serve them with little bowls of the tamari-citrus one on page 76. Feel free to vary the filling ingredients to suit your tastes, using shreds of roast pork or strips of firm tofu or flaked white fish instead of the shrimp. You can even make it more of a fresh salad and fill each rice paper wrapper with just raw grated carrots, sliced scallions, a lightly steamed asparagus spear, maybe some crunchy sprouts, and a sprinkle of tamari.

- **12 large shrimp, peeled and deveined**
- **1 tablespoon vegetable oil**
- **1 shallot, thinly sliced lengthwise**
- **2 teaspoons minced fresh ginger**
- **1 teaspoon minced garlic**
- **2 medium carrots, peeled and cut into matchsticks**
- **1 tablespoon tamari**
- **12 (8- to 9-inch / 20- to 23-cm) rice-paper spring roll wrappers**
- **1½ cups (275 g) cooked ivory quinoa (page 27), chilled**
- **12 fresh cilantro leaves**
- **12 fresh mint leaves, plus 12 whole sprigs**
- **12 small leaves Bibb or Boston lettuce, washed and patted dry**

In the bottom of a steamer, bring 1 inch (2.5 cm) water to a boil. Add the shrimp to the steamer basket, cover, and steam until opaque and cooked through, about 4 minutes. Transfer the shrimp to a bowl of ice water to cool, then halve each shrimp lengthwise. Put in an airtight container and chill in the refrigerator.

In a small sauté pan, heat the oil over medium-high heat. Add the shallot, ginger, and garlic and cook, stirring frequently, until the shallot is translucent, about 3 minutes. Add the carrots and cook, stirring, until they are just tender, 1 to 2 minutes. Stir in the tamari. Remove to a plate and let cool, then put in an airtight container and chill in the refrigerator. (The shrimp and the carrot mixtures can be prepared up to 1 day in advance—and can be stored in the same container.)

Fill a wide bowl or pan with hot water. Add 1 spring roll wrapper and let soak until pliable and tender, about 1 minute. Remove it from the water and lay it out on a clean work surface. Place 2 shrimp halves, pink side down, on the wrapper, in the center of the end closest to you. Cover the shrimp with about 2 tablespoons of the quinoa. Top the quinoa with a pinch of the carrot mixture (about one-twelfth of it), then set a cilantro leaf and a mint leaf on top. Fold the two sides of the wrapper over the filling, then roll up like a burrito, enclosing the filling. Nestle the spring roll in a lettuce leaf with a sprig of mint and set on a serving platter. Repeat with the remaining wrappers, filling, lettuce, and mint sprigs. The spring rolls can be made up to 1 hour in advance and the platter covered tightly with plastic wrap and refrigerated. Serve cold.

CHICKPEA-FLOUR CRÊPES WITH QUINOA, MELTED PEPPERS, AND GOAT CHEESE
Serves 8 | vegetarian, gluten free

Socca, a specialty of Nice and similar to the farinata of north-western Italy, is traditionally made in enormous paella-type pans in a very hot oven—wood-fired, preferably—and poured thick enough that the finished pancake can be cut into wedges and served like pizza. I like to make a similar batter but make thin crêpes of it on the stovetop rather than under the broiler as most recipes tell you do to (with the notable exception of Daniel Boulud's recipe, which I was happy to see also suggested the stovetop-only method). I then stack the crêpes on a tin plate and set out bowls of fluffy quinoa with super-sweet, slowly caramelized peppers and shallots, a bit of goat cheese, and fresh thyme sprigs for self-service filling. Serve with a salad of greens in a simple vinaigrette and a glass of cold rosé for a beautiful late-summer, early-fall supper.

- **1 cup (130 g) chickpea flour (besan)**
- **Salt**
- **3 tablespoons olive oil**
- **4 shallots, thinly sliced**
- **8 ounces (225 g) mini sweet peppers or red, yellow, or orange bell peppers, seeded and cut into 1/4-inch (6-mm) strips**
- **1/2 teaspoon fresh thyme leaves, plus whole sprigs for garnish**
- **Freshly ground black pepper**
- **1 1/2 cups (275 g) cooked quinoa (page 27)**
- **3 ounces (85 g) goat cheese**

Sift the chickpea flour and 1/2 teaspoon salt into a medium bowl. Whisk in 1 cup (240 ml) water and 1 tablespoon of the oil. Let the batter stand at room temperature for 1 to 2 hours.

In a large sauté pan, heat 1 tablespoon of the oil over medium heat. Add the shallots, sweet peppers, thyme leaves, and a pinch of salt and black pepper and cook, stirring occasionally and lowering the heat if the vegetables brown too quickly, until very soft and caramelized, about 20 minutes. Add 2 tablespoons water and scrape up any browned bits on the bottom of the pan. Add the quinoa and salt to taste and cook, turning to combine and heat through, about

5 minutes. Cover to keep warm and set aside in a serving bowl. Put the cheese on a serving plate with a serving knife and garnish with some whole thyme sprigs.

Heat a large, well-seasoned cast-iron or nonstick griddle or skillet over medium-high heat until a drop of water splashed onto it dances across the surface. Pour a little bit of the remaining 1 tablespoon of oil onto a paper towel and use it to grease the griddle. Whisk the batter again, then ladle a scant 1/4 cup (60 ml) of batter onto the griddle so it spreads into a thin shape approximating a round. Cook until all of the top surface appears dry, 20 to 30 seconds, then use a thin spatula or your fingers to lift one side of the crêpe and gently fold it in half. Remove to a serving plate. Repeat with the remaining batter, oiling the skillet between each crêpe. Serve the crêpes with the quinoa and peppers, and cheese so your guests can fill them to their liking themselves.

BROWN-RICE ONIGIRI (JAPANESE-STYLE RICE BALLS) WITH SEAWEED AND QUICK-PICKLED FENNEL

Makes about 10 small balls | vegan, gluten free

Using this recipe as a starting point, you can make onigiri ("ah-NEE-gree") with just about any ingredients folded into the rice or stuffed into the center. The more intensely flavored, the better: umeboshi (pickled) plums (available in Asian stores and good supermarkets), other seaweeds such as hijiki or crumbled nori, gomashio (page 248), bits of salty-sweet Chinese-style broiled or roasted pork, soy-marinated teriyaki chicken or beef, and so on. Or you can just use plain rice with vinegar and sugar, and sprinkle with toasted sesame seeds and salt. If you like, you can also shape them into pyramids, logs, or more exotic forms—whatever fits well in your lunch box or looks attractive on your plate.

- **1 cup (190 g) raw short-grain brown rice**
- **2 teaspoons rice vinegar or brine from the pickled fennel**
- **Pinch of sugar**
- **1/2 cup (50 g) chopped Quick-Pickled Fennel (recipe follows)**
- **8 g mixed dried seaweed (I like a ready-mixed combination of wakame, agar, suginori, tsunomata, and mafunori), soaked in warm water for 5 minutes**

Rinse the rice in a fine-mesh sieve; drain well. Put it in a heavy 2-quart (2-L) saucepan with 1 1/2 cups (360 ml) water. Cover and bring to a boil over medium-high heat, then lower the heat and simmer until the rice is tender and most of the liquid is absorbed, about 30 minutes. Drain in the sieve if necessary. Turn out into a large bowl and sprinkle with the vinegar, sugar, pickled fennel, and seaweed. Use a rubber spatula to gently stir and fold the hot rice until the other ingredients are evenly incorporated.

While the rice is still warm, drape a piece of plastic wrap over your hand and scoop in a golf-ball-size mound of the rice mixture. Use the plastic to help you shape it into a sphere, then turn it out of the plastic and set it on a plate or in a sealable container. Repeat with the remaining rice mixture. Serve warm or at room temperature, or cover and refrigerate until cold, then pack into a bento or lunch box.

QUICK-PICKLED FENNEL
Makes about 1 pint (200 g) | vegan, gluten free

Keep a little jar of this in the refrigerator to add to green salads or to fold into any cooked grains where a hit of anise and orange will be welcome— I like to dice a few slices of fennel and fold it into cooked bulgur with a few pitted black olives and a handful of white beans for a quick lunch.

- **1 large fennel bulb, stalks cut off**
- **1 teaspoon salt**
- **1½ cups (360 ml) rice vinegar**
- **1 teaspoon finely grated orange zest**
- **1 teaspoon agave nectar**

Trim the root end off the fennel bulb and cut the bulb lengthwise into quarters. Cut the fennel into ¼-inch (6-mm) slices and put them in a colander. Toss with ½ teaspoon of the salt and let stand for 30 minutes; the fennel will release some of its liquid and become a bit limp. Rinse under cold water, drain well, and transfer to a heatproof container (such as a pint-size glass canning jar).

In a small saucepan, combine the vinegar, ¾ cup (180 ml) water, the orange zest, agave nectar, and the remaining ½ teaspoon of salt. Bring to a boil, stirring to dissolve the salt, then pour over the fennel to cover. Let cool, then cover and refrigerate until very cold, at least 2 hours. The fennel will keep in the refrigerator for at least 1 month.

OVEN-BAKED BROWN-RICE SUPPLÌ
(ITALIAN STUFFED RICE BALLS)
Makes 10 to 12 small balls | vegetarian, gluten free

What is it about rice shaped into little balls that's so end-lessly appealing? They're truly comfort food. These supplì are baked rather than fried, but are still crisp on the outside, with the typical mild fresh mozzarella treat in the center. They can be served with a quick tomato sauce, of course, or a simple salad of greens tossed with freshly squeezed lemon juice, olive oil, and a little salt and pepper.

- **5 to 6 cups (1.2 to 1.4 L) vegetable stock or water**
- **1 tablespoon olive oil**
- **½ onion, diced**
- **Salt**
- **1 cup (190 g) raw short-grain brown rice**
- **½ cup (120 ml) white wine**
- **½ teaspoon freshly ground black pepper**
- **1½ tablespoons unsalted butter**
- **⅓ cup (35 g) plus ¼ cup (25 g) fresh whole wheat bread crumbs**
- **1 large egg, beaten**
- **1 tablespoon chopped fresh parsley or basil**
- **About 4 ounces (115 g) fresh mozzarella, cut into ½-inch (12-mm) pieces, or 10 to 12 bocconcini**

Put the stock in a saucepan and bring to a simmer.

Meanwhile, in a large deep sauté pan, heat the oil over me-dium heat. Add the onion and a pinch of salt and cook, stirring occasionally, until soft and golden brown, about 8 minutes. Add the rice and stir to coat with the oil. Add the wine and cook, stirring frequently, until it is almost all evaporated and absorbed, about 3 minutes. Ladle in about half of the sim-mering stock, to just cover the rice. Add ½ teaspoon salt and the pepper, cover the sauté pan, and simmer, stirring occa-sionally and adding more simmering stock if needed to keep the rice just covered, for 30 minutes.

Uncover the pan and add stock to cover if necessary. Cook uncovered, stirring the risotto more frequently now, until the rice is tender and most of the liquid has evaporated and what remains is more opaque and slightly thickened, 10 to 15 minutes. Stir in 1 tablespoon of the butter until it melts. Scrape the risotto into a large bowl and set aside to cool to room temperature.

Preheat the oven to 450°F (230°C). Line a baking sheet with parchment paper.

In a small sauté pan, melt the remaining ½ tablespoon of but-ter over medium-high heat and add the ⅓ cup (35 g) of bread crumbs. Cook, stirring, until darkened a shade and toasty smelling, about 4 minutes. Scrape onto a plate and set aside.

Stir the egg, parsley, and remaining ¼ cup (25 g) of bread crumbs into the cooled risotto. Gently shape into spheres about the size of golf balls, pushing a piece of the cheese into the center of each, being sure to completely cover the cheese with the risotto mixture. Roll in the toasted bread crumbs and arrange on the prepared baking sheet. Bake until golden brown, about 45 minutes, turning the balls over halfway through. Serve hot.

VARIATION

✱ For quicker cooking, you can shallow-fry the balls in a large heavy sauté pan in ⅛ inch (3 mm) of olive oil over medium heat (no need to toast the bread crumbs in butter first, as they'll crisp and brown in the pan). Cook for 4 to 5 minutes on each side, turning the balls frequently with tongs, until the cheese is completely melted—cut one open to check.

BROILED FIGS WITH COUSCOUS, FETA, MINT, AND BALSAMIC SYRUP

Serves 6 | vegetarian

I love the way figs look when slit partway through the stem end and eased open into a blossom shape, the dark or bright green outer skin highlighting the pink flesh within. Topped with a little mound of couscous, creamy feta, and mint, and drizzled with an inky balsamic syrup, these figs make an impressive but super-easy first course.

FOR THE BALSAMIC SYRUP
- **¹⁄₂ cup (120 ml) balsamic vinegar**
- **2 teaspoons agave nectar or honey**

FOR THE FIGS
- **1¹⁄₂ cups (240 g) cooked whole wheat couscous (page 37), warm**
- **¹⁄₂ cup crumbed feta cheese (about 2 ounces / 55 g)**
- **¹⁄₄ cup (20 g) chopped fresh mint, plus 6 sprigs for garnish**
- **6 large fresh figs, such as Brown Turkey**
- **1 tablespoon olive oil**
- **Freshly ground black pepper**

MAKE THE BALSAMIC SYRUP
In a wide skillet or sauté pan, bring the vinegar to a boil; cook until reduced to about 3 tablespoons, about 3 minutes. Stir in the agave nectar and set the syrup aside.

MAKE THE FIGS
Preheat the broiler to high. Line a rimmed baking sheet with aluminum foil.

In a medium bowl, toss together the couscous, cheese, and chopped mint. Set aside.

Cut the stems off the figs. Set a fig on a cutting board stem end up. Using a sharp knife, cut into quarters lengthwise without cutting all the way through the bottom. Place on the prepared baking sheet and gently spread the quarters apart into a flat-ish flower shape. Broil, 6 inches (15 cm) from the heat source, until just beginning to brown at the tips, 4 to 5 minutes. Remove from the oven and leave the broiler on.

Using a large spoon, scoop up a portion of the couscous mixture and lightly pack it into a mound in the spoon, then set it in the center of a fig. Repeat with the remaining figs. Drizzle with the oil and grind some pepper over the figs. Return to the oven and broil until sizzling and heated through, 4 to 5 minutes. Use a metal spatula to transfer each fig to a serving plate. Drizzle lightly with the balsamic syrup (you won't use it all), garnish with a mint sprig, and serve hot.

PUFFED-GRAIN AND GREEN-TOMATO CHAAT (INDIAN STREET-FOOD SNACK)

Serves 2 or 3 | vegetarian

Yes, it's a lot of ingredients, but feel free to omit vegetables at will, or just use a good curry powder instead of the individual spices. Also, while the puffed grains should be sautéed and tossed with the vegetables just before serving, most of the elements can be prepared days in advance. If you love this as much as I do, you might consider keeping a chaat kit in a corner of the fridge that consists of little containers of the chutney-yogurt mixture, tamarind chutney, and plain yogurt, plus a larger container of the vegetable mixture (tomato, cucumber, onion, chickpeas, cilantro, chile), so it's a snap to make this perfect snack any time.

- **1 teaspoon mint-cilantro chutney (see Notes)**
- **2 tablespoons plus ¹⁄₃ cup (80 ml) plain yogurt**
- **¹⁄₂ cup (90 g) diced green tomato**
- **¹⁄₂ cup (75 g) diced cucumber**
- **¹⁄₂ cup (80 g) diced sweet onion**
- **¹⁄₂ cup (80 g) cooked chickpeas**
- **¹⁄₄ cup (20 g) chopped fresh cilantro**
- **1 tablespoon minced serrano or jalapeño chile**
- **¹⁄₄ cup (40 g) rolled oats**
- **1 tablespoon vegetable oil**
- **¹⁄₂ teaspoon cumin seeds**
- **¹⁄₄ teaspoon paprika, plus more for garnish**
- **¹⁄₄ teaspoon turmeric**
- **Pinch of salt**
- **2 cups (20 g) unsweetened puffed whole grains, such as brown rice, wheat, spelt, or millet**
- **¹⁄₃ cup (80 ml) tamarind chutney (see Notes)**
- **¹⁄₄ teaspoon ground cumin**
- **Lime wedges**
- **Chopped pitted dates (optional)**

In a small bowl, stir together the mint-cilantro chutney and 2 tablespoons yogurt; set aside. In a large bowl, toss together the green tomato, cucumber, onion, chickpeas, cilantro, and chile; set aside.

In a large sauté pan over medium-high heat, toast the oats, tossing frequently, until deeply browned and crisp, about 5 minutes; transfer to a plate and set aside.

Return the pan to medium-high heat and add the oil, cumin seeds, paprika, turmeric, and salt. Cook, stirring, until fragrant and sizzling, about 1 minute. Add the puffed grains and stir to coat with the spiced oil as well as you can. Scrape into the bowl with the vegetables, along with the oats, and toss to combine. Scoop the mixture into serving bowls and dollop with the chutney-yogurt mixture, the tamarind chutney, and remaining ¹⁄₃ cup (80 ml) plain yogurt. Sprinkle with the ground cumin and a little paprika and serve immediately, with lime wedges for squeezing over the top and chopped dates, if desired.

VARIATION

❋ Try adding some popped amaranth or sorghum (pages 20 or 32) to the puffed grain mixture.

NOTES: Bright green mint-cilantro chutney is available in Indian grocery stores and in the international section of many regular supermarkets; the tall glass jars are usually just labeled "mint chutney." It's spicy, salty, and vinegary and will keep almost indefinitely in the refrigerator.

You can find tamarind chutney in Indian markets as well, but it is easy to whip up at home. To make tamarind chutney, which will also keep pretty much forever in a clean glass jar in the fridge, coarsely chop about 14 dates (or use about ¹⁄₃ cup / 55 g raisins) and put them in a small saucepan with 2 tablespoons tamarind concentrate and enough water to cover them. Simmer until the dates are very soft, then puree in a mini food processor or blender until very smooth, adding water if necessary to make a thick but pourable sauce. Season with a couple pinches of salt. This makes about 1 cup (240 ml).

3

Salads

It couldn't be easier to make a salad with whole grains—to the point that it's almost embarrassing to have written the recipes in this chapter down. Think of them as starting points, or ideas for those times when your own power of invention is flagging (I have those often myself). Here's how you make a whole-grain salad: Pull some cooked grains—leftovers—out of the refrigerator, toss with a dressing and whatever fresh vegetables you have on hand, spoon onto a pretty plate, and you've got an elegant lunch or the start of a splendid supper. Or pack it in a bento box, maybe with a waxed-paper packet containing a few pinches of something crisp or crunchy for sprinkling on top (the nut-and-seed topping on page 249, for example). Most of these salads can easily double as main courses; if they're lacking protein as they are and you want more heft to your meal, here are a few easy solutions:

- Add a can's worth of white beans, red beans, or chickpeas, well rinsed and drained.
- Crisp some cubes of extra-firm tofu in a little oil in a sauté pan and toss them with the salad.
- Add a generous dollop of plain yogurt or scatter shaved hard cheese, cubes of feta, or crumbles of goat cheese or blue cheese on top.
- Cut up a hard-cooked egg (see Note, page 117) or two and toss it in.
- Flake in some olive oil–packed canned tuna.
- Thinly slice a leftover grilled chicken breast or pork chop and toss it with the salad.

CATFISH AND BARLEY LARB
(SPICY, SOUR THAI SALAD WITH CRUSHED RICE)

Serves 4

Larb, the warm or room-temperature Thai salad seasoned with crushed toasted raw rice, is one of my all-time favorite dishes. It has everything I love in a summertime meal in darn-near-equatorial Georgia: tart lime juice and fragrant kaffir lime leaves, sweat-inducing chiles and cooling mint, plenty of salty fish sauce, and loads of cilantro. You can find kaffir lime leaves in some supermarkets these days, and in any Asian market. With a few pantry staples on hand and a stash of kaffir leaves in the freezer, where they'll keep for months, larb is a possibility any day. It also makes a fine packed lunch, since it's just as good cool or at room temperature as warm.

- **1 tablespoon raw brown rice**
- **$\frac{1}{2}$ to 1 teaspoon crushed red pepper, or to taste**
- **Juice of 3 limes**
- **$1\frac{1}{2}$ tablespoons fish sauce**
- **4 kaffir lime leaves, very thinly sliced**
- **$\frac{1}{4}$ cup (20 g) chopped fresh mint**
- **$\frac{1}{2}$ cup (40 g) chopped fresh cilantro**
- **4 shallots, thinly sliced**
- **2 tablespoons vegetable oil**
- **10 ounces (280 g) skinless catfish fillets or other white fish, such as wild cod or tilapia**
- **4 large Bibb or Boston lettuce leaves, washed and patted dry (optional)**
- **$2\frac{1}{2}$ cups (400 g) warm cooked hulled brown or purple barley (page 20)**

In a large sauté pan over medium-high heat, toast the rice, tossing frequently, until deeply browned, about 3 minutes. Remove to a spice grinder or mortar and let cool for a few minutes; process or pound with a pestle until finely ground. Transfer to a large bowl and add the crushed red pepper, lime juice, fish sauce, kaffir lime leaves, mint, cilantro, and shallots; set the dressing aside.

Return the sauté pan to medium-high heat and add the oil. When it shimmers, add the fish and cook, turning once with a metal spatula, until golden and lightly crisped on each side and opaque throughout, 6 to 8 minutes total depending on the thickness of the fillet. Remove to paper towels to drain. If the fish sticks to the pan a little, so much the better: Scrape up those bits and drain them on the towels too. Let cool to warm, then coarsely chop the fish and add it and any browned bits to the bowl with the dressing. Toss to combine. If you'd like, arrange lettuce leaves on a platter and scoop in the barley, then the fish mixture. Serve warm or at room temperature.

VARIATIONS

★ To make this vegan, make the dressing with soy sauce instead of fish sauce, using a little less lime juice. Omit the fish, and instead sauté the barley in 1 tablespoon oil, turning frequently with a metal spatula, until crisp-chewy, 8 to 10 minutes. Scrape into the bowl with the dressing and toss to combine. Serve warm or at room temperature in lettuce leaves.

★ The fish sauce dressing is great spooned generously over hot pan-roasted pork chops; serve with a side of Chinese broccoli or other greens sautéed with garlic.

★ Use 1 pound (455 g) ground pork instead of the fish; cook it until nicely browned and crisped, and drain off any excess fat before you mix it with the dressing.

COWBOY SALAD
(BARELY STEAMED BROCCOLI AND BARLEY SALAD)
Serves 2 | vegetarian

Raw broccoli salad or slaw is a worthy thing, but it's a well-known fact that people under the age of six tend to prefer their broccoli cooked, and the quick steaming here could make the difference between love and hate at the supper table. If you have a microwave oven, you can just put the broccoli in a bowl with a splash of water, cover with a paper towel, and hit it for 33 or 44 seconds (those numbers being quicker to punch in than even ones, and it's all about speed, isn't it?).

My mom has been making this salad for years and years, and I've asked but I still don't understand why she calls it "cowboy." Some long-winded story about a rancher in Montana. Call it whatever you want, as long as it's mysterious.

This recipe contains an example of one of those fussy steps that seem unnecessary but that if taken will subtly elevate a dish to something a bit more pleasing and refined than it might otherwise be: covering the onion with ice water while you prepare the rest of the salad. This crisps, chills, and mellows it a little, so it contrasts nicely but doesn't overpower them with oniony bite.

- ½ small sweet onion, diced
- Ice water
- 1 small head broccoli
- ¼ cup (60 ml) plain Greek yogurt
- Juice of ½ lemon
- 1 teaspoon salt, or more to taste
- Several grinds black pepper
- 2 cups (320 g) cooked hulled or hull-less barley (page 20), cooled
- 1 rib celery, diced
- 2 tablespoons dried cranberries (optional)

Put the onion in a bowl and cover with ice water; set aside.

Cut the broccoli into tiny florets; dice the stems and peel and dice the main stalk. Put in a sieve and set the sieve over a pot with a little boiling water in the bottom. Put the pot lid over the sieve and steam the broccoli for 2 minutes. Transfer to a bowl of cold water to stop the cooking. Drain well.

In a large bowl, whisk together the yogurt, lemon juice, salt, and pepper. Add the broccoli, barley, celery, and cranberries, if using. Drain and add the onion and toss to combine. Taste and add more salt and pepper if necessary. Serve at room temperature or chill in the refrigerator and serve cold. The salad can be prepared up to 1 day in advance.

GREEN LENTIL, WEHANI RICE, AND ARTICHOKE HEART SALAD

Serves 4 | vegan, gluten free

I'm not big on rice salads, unless the rice in question is nutty, beautiful red Wehani, which to me is less like rice than a firmer, more substantial grain in the wheat family. Here it's paired with green lentils (my favorite kind), which cook right in the same saucepan in the same amount of time, and tossed with a light thyme vinaigrette and artichoke hearts. This makes a quick, no-fuss, one-pot, one-bowl meal. If you can't find Wehani rice, you can substitute long-grain brown rice, or for non-gluten-free options, spelt berries, Kamut berries, or soft white wheat berries, all of which cook in about the same amount of time.

- ½ cup (100 g) raw Wehani rice
- ½ cup (95 g) green (French) lentils, rinsed and picked over
- 2 tablespoons freshly squeezed lemon juice
- Coarsely grated zest of ½ lemon
- 1 tablespoon Champagne or white wine vinegar
- ½ teaspoon grainy mustard
- ½ teaspoon salt
- ¼ teaspoon freshly ground black pepper
- 1 teaspoon fresh thyme leaves
- 2 tablespoons olive oil
- 1 (14-ounce / 400 g) can artichoke hearts (in water, not marinated), drained and rinsed, then chopped; or about 8 small frozen artichoke hearts, thawed and chopped

In a heavy 2-quart (2-L) saucepan, combine the rice, lentils, and 1½ cups (360 ml) water. Bring to a boil, then lower the heat and simmer until the rice and lentils are just tender, 25 to 30 minutes. Drain in a sieve and rinse in cold running water until cool; set aside to drain further in the sieve.

In a large bowl, whisk together the lemon juice and zest, vinegar, mustard, salt, pepper, and thyme. Gradually whisk in the oil. Add the artichoke hearts and rice and lentils and toss to coat well. Serve at room temperature.

ICY, SPICY SOBA NOODLE SALAD
Serves 2 | vegan

Just about any sentence in Charles Portis's classic novel *The Dog of the South* could be the one that sends you over the edge, the one that, remembering it later in the grocery-store parking lot, makes you fall to your knees weeping with laughter. For me it was this one: "No one seemed to be selling snow cones in this steaming land." (The humor's in the lead-up, I see now.) Here's the salad I made for lunch with some leftover soba noodles soon after reading about the dearth of snow cones in Central America. It was one of those Georgia-summer days when you can't bring yourself to leave any air-conditioned space, not even to hurry to the mailbox in hopes of a *Saveur*, or at least a *New Yorker*, when the thought of cooking a meal makes you want to lie supine on the floor, when putting crushed ice on a spicy and incredibly tangy salad seems like the most brilliant idea you've ever had.

- **6 tablespoons (90 ml) rice vinegar**
- **3 tablespoons tamari**
- **1 tablespoon mirin**
- **1 tablespoon chile paste (sambal oelek), or more to taste**
- **2 teaspoons grated fresh ginger**
- **2 scallions, thinly sliced**
- **2 bundles (about 6 ounces / 170 g) dried soba noodles, cooked and chilled (see Note)**
- **½ small head chilled iceberg lettuce, cored and thinly shredded**
- **½ cup finely crushed ice**

In a large bowl, whisk together the vinegar, tamari, mirin, chile paste, and ginger. Add the scallions, noodles, and lettuce and toss to coat with the dressing. Divide among serving plates and sprinkle with the ice. Serve immediately!

NOTE: To cook and chill soba noodles, bring a large pot of water to a boil. Add the noodles and stir. Return to a boil and cook until just al dente, about 4 minutes. Drain in a sieve or colander and rinse well under cold running water until cold; drain well, then put in a covered container and keep refrigerated until ready to use.

VARIATIONS

★ Instead of the crushed ice, top each serving with 1 tablespoon chopped roasted unsalted cashews or peanuts, or 1 teaspoon toasted sesame seeds.

★ To add some vegan protein: Press a couple slabs of firm or extra-firm tofu between paper towels to remove excess water, then dice and add to the salad. Or toss in some rinsed-off frozen shelled edamame beans (no need to thaw).

★ To add some nonvegan protein: Poach a few peeled and deveined shrimp in boiling water until opaque, drain, and plunge into ice water to cool, then coarsely chop and add to the salad. Or add shredded cooked chicken or pork.

★ If you can't bring yourself to consume iceberg lettuce, use ½ small head red or green cabbage, cored and very thinly sliced, or a few big handfuls of shredded Napa or Savoy cabbage.

COLD SOBA NOODLES
WITH TAHINI, LIME, CUCUMBER, AND SHREDDED CHICKEN
Serves 4

These spicy but surprisingly cooling noodles make an excellent quick lunch. Don't skimp on the lime juice or fresh chile, both of which are important elements that contrast with the creamy tahini–olive oil dressing.

- **2 bundles (about 6 ounces / 170 g) dried soba noodles**
- **3 tablespoons freshly squeezed lime juice**
- **3 tablespoons tahini (sesame seed paste)**
- **1 tablespoon olive oil**
- **1 tablespoon rice vinegar**
- **1 tablespoon honey or agave nectar**
- **1 teaspoon salt**
- **½ teaspoon grated fresh ginger**
- **1 tablespoon chopped fresh mint**
- **1 scallion, thinly sliced on the bias**
- **½ English cucumber**
- **1 cup (140 g) shredded cooked chicken (about 1 breast)**
- **1 small fresh hot red chile, thinly sliced into rounds**

Bring a large pot of water to a boil. Add the noodles and stir. Return to a boil and cook until just al dente, about 4 minutes. Drain in a sieve or colander and rinse well under cold running water until cold; drain well and set aside.

While the noodles are cooking, in a large bowl, whisk together the lime juice, tahini, oil, vinegar, honey, salt, ginger, and mint. Stir in the scallion, then add the cucumber and chicken and toss to coat with the dressing. Add the noodles and use tongs (or your hands) to combine them with the dressing and other ingredients. Transfer to serving plates, garnish with the chile, and serve.

BEET AND APPLE SALAD WITH SAVORY GRANOLA
Serves 4 | vegetarian, gluten free*

Here, sweet, tender beets meet tangy, crisp green apples in a bright red wine vinaigrette flecked with fresh herbs. The granola topping is intensely garlicky and pleasantly salty, the bits held together with grated Parmesan that melts and turns golden as the granola bakes. Use the leftover granola instead of croutons to add crunch to salads, or sprinkle it over a pureed soup or simply steamed vegetables.

FOR THE SAVORY GRANOLA
- 1 cup (160 g) raw rolled oats
- ¼ cup (25 g) freshly grated Parmesan cheese
- 2 tablespoons pine nuts
- 1½ tablespoons olive oil
- 2 teaspoons minced garlic
- 1 teaspoon fresh thyme leaves or chopped rosemary
- ¼ teaspoon salt
- ⅛ teaspoon freshly ground black pepper

FOR THE SALAD
- 1 pound (455 g) small beets, tops cut off
- 1 large green apple
- ¼ cup (60 ml) red wine vinegar
- Salt and freshly ground black pepper
- 2 tablespoons olive oil
- ¼ cup (20 g) torn fresh basil leaves
- 2 tablespoons torn fresh mint leaves

MAKE THE SAVORY GRANOLA
Preheat the oven to 300°F (150°C).

In a 9-inch (23-cm) square baking pan, preferably nonstick, combine all the ingredients, stirring to coat with the oil. Bake until golden brown, 25 to 30 minutes. Let cool to room temperature in the pan on a wire rack. The granola will keep in an airtight container in the refrigerator for up to 2 weeks.

MAKE THE SALAD
Put the beets in a small saucepan, cover with water, and bring to a boil. Lower the heat and simmer until the beets are tender, 20 to 30 minutes. Drain and cover with cold water; when cool enough to handle, rub the peels off the beets, dice them, and set aside to cool completely.

Core and dice the apples (no need to peel).

In a large bowl, whisk together the vinegar and salt and pepper to taste, then whisk in the oil until emulsified. Add the beets and apples to the dressing, along with the basil and mint, and toss to combine. (The salad will keep, covered, in the refrigerator for up to 4 hours; let sit at room temperature for 15 minutes before serving to allow the oil to reliquify.) Top each serving with a few tablespoons of the savory granola and serve.

* See page 25.

SPINACH AND OAT GROATS SALAD WITH BLUE CHEESE AND TOASTED WALNUTS

Serves 4 | vegetarian, gluten free*

QUINOA SALAD WITH PARSLEY, DRIED CRANBERRIES, BLACK WALNUTS, AND GOAT CHEESE

Serves 4 | vegetarian, gluten free

I'd never cooked whole oat groats before I started working on this book, but it was such a pleasant surprise to learn how easy they are to use in salads like this. I guess I just assumed they'd take forever to cook and wouldn't be worth the trouble, but I was wrong. In fact, the mild, slightly sweet flavor of the oats is a perfect match for the other naturally sweet ingredients in this dish—balsamic vinegar, honey, sweet onion, and grapes—and helps temper any bite from the spinach (other, spicier greens like arugula or young dandelion would work equally well here) and the saltiness of the blue cheese. That said, you could use farro or spelt berries instead.

- 2 tablespoons balsamic vinegar
- ½ teaspoon honey
- ¼ teaspoon salt, or more to taste
- ¼ teaspoon freshly ground black pepper
- 2 tablespoons olive oil
- ½ cup (80 g) very thinly sliced sweet onion
- ½ cup (75 g) red grapes, halved
- 2 cups (450 g) cooked oat groats (page 26), cooled
- 4 cups (120 g) torn fresh spinach leaves
- ½ cup (60 g) walnut halves, toasted
- 2 ounces (55 g) blue cheese

In a large bowl, whisk together the vinegar, honey, salt, and pepper. Gradually whisk in the oil. Add the onion, grapes, oat groats, spinach, and walnuts and toss to coat. Taste and add more salt if necessary, keeping in mind that the cheese will be salty. Pile on serving plates and crumble the cheese over the top. Serve.

---

* See page 25.

Black walnuts appear in grocery stores in the fall. Their flavor is hard to describe, as they're not much like regular English walnuts at all (though by all means use those if that's what you have!). They taste a bit the way an unripe walnut or pecan smells when it's knocked, still green, from the tree by a squirrel and you pick it up from the ground and tear the husk open with your fingernails, which turn deep mahogany with the effort: musky and winey and dark. Their bitterness pairs very nicely with the sweet dried cranberries and mild quinoa in this salad. (Use up the bag in the teff cookies on page 217.)

This surprisingly satisfying salad makes an excellent simple lunch, or a side dish next to a piece of lemony roast chicken (page 172) for a nonvegetarian meal. I love how the quinoa grains stick to the bits of creamy, tangy goat cheese, but feta broken into rough chunks would be a fine substitute. The salad can be made a day (or more) in advance; remove it from the refrigerator 15 minutes before serving and add the parsley at the last minute.

- ⅓ cup (80 ml) sherry vinegar or white wine vinegar
- ½ teaspoon salt, or more to taste
- Freshly ground black pepper to taste
- 1 teaspoon Dijon-style mustard
- ¼ cup (55 g) extra-virgin olive oil
- 3 cups (550 g) cooked quinoa (page 27), cooled
- ¼ cup (25 g) dried cranberries
- ¼ cup (30 g) chopped black walnuts
- ½ bunch fresh flat-leaf parsley, stemmed
- 2 ounces (55 g) goat cheese

In a large bowl, whisk the vinegar, salt, pepper, and mustard together until the salt is dissolved. Gradually whisk in the oil. Add the quinoa, cranberries, and walnuts and toss to combine with the vinaigrette. Let stand at room temperature for 30 minutes.

Add the parsley and more salt or pepper if needed. Transfer to a serving bowl, crumble the goat cheese over the top, and serve.

RED QUINOA AND CARROT SALAD
WITH YELLOW PEPPER, GRAPEFRUIT, AND CRISPED DULSE

Serves 4 | vegan, gluten free

My friend Regan pointed me toward a quinoa salad with sunflower seeds and seaweed in Peter Berley's tome-ish *Modern Vegetarian Kitchen*, and it inspired this one. I use mild, crowd-pleasing dulse seaweed here, quickly crisped in a little oil—it's a good choice if you're just beginning to use sea vegetables in your cooking, but you could substitute soaked and drained hijiki, arame, or a combination of several different seaweeds. Or instead, hold a square of nori with heatproof tongs and pass it over a gas or electric burner to toast it, then crumble it over the salad.

- ¹⁄₂ sweet onion, diced
- 1 yellow bell pepper, diced
- Ice water
- ¹⁄₂ cup (70 g) sunflower seeds
- ¹⁄₄ cup (55 ml) olive oil
- 8 g dulse seaweed (see Note), picked over and unfolded
- 1 grapefruit
- Juice of ¹⁄₂ lemon, or more if needed
- 1 to 2 serrano chiles, minced
- 1 carrot, peeled
- Salt
- 3 cups (550 g) cooked red quinoa (page 27), cooled

Put the onion and sweet pepper in a small bowl and cover with ice water; set aside.

In a small sauté pan over medium heat, toast the sunflower seeds, tossing frequently, until golden brown, about 3 minutes. Transfer to a plate to cool. Return the pan to medium-high heat and add the oil. Add the dulse and cook, pressing it down and turning with tongs or a spatula, until crisp and lightly browned, about 3 minutes. Remove from the oil and drain on a paper towel; set aside, reserving the oil in the pan.

With a sharp knife, cut the rind and white membrane off the grapefruit. Working over a large bowl, cut the segments from the inner membrane and let them fall into the bowl; squeeze juice from the empty membranes into the bowl. Add the lemon juice and chiles, then grate the carrot into the bowl. Stir in 1 teaspoon salt and the oil from cooking the dulse.

Dump the quinoa into the bowl with the grapefruit. Drain and add the onion and sweet pepper. Crumble in half of the crisped dulse. Taste and add more salt or lemon juice if necessary. Serve, sprinkled with the remaining dulse, or chill in the refrigerator for up to 1 day (keep the dulse at room temperature and add at the last moment) and serve cold.

NOTE: Dulse (rhymes with "pulse") is a beautiful red-purple algae that grows on wave-splashed rocks and on larger seaweeds in cold northern reaches of the Atlantic and Pacific oceans. It's dried and sold as whole leaves or ground into flakes or powder—use the larger leaves here rather than the finely ground. Dulse is a good source of iodine, which is important for those of us who prefer kosher salt to iodized. You can also use dulse for the rice balls on page 86.

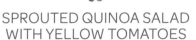

QUINOA WITH CORN, TOMATOES, AVOCADO, SWEET ONION, AND BALSAMIC REDUCTION

Serves 4 | vegan, gluten free

My friend Shari Miller's description of how her house smelled of balsamic vinegar as she was making a quinoa dish with creamy avocado and sweet vegetables was evocative enough that I had to make something like it immediately. (The aroma of vinegar simmering is oddly appealing to me, perhaps because it reminds me of pickle-canning days. And, you know, pickles.)

- 1 cup (160 g) diced sweet onion
- Ice water
- ½ cup (120 ml) balsamic vinegar
- 1 Hass avocado, peeled, pitted, and diced
- Juice of 1 lemon
- 1 cup (170 g) fresh or frozen (thawed) corn kernels
- 1 cup (180 g) diced tomato, drained in a colander
- 8 large fresh basil leaves
- 3 cups (550 g) cooked black or red quinoa (page 27), cooled
- Salt and freshly ground black pepper to taste

Put the onion in a small bowl of ice water. Set aside for 10 minutes.

Meanwhile, in a wide skillet or sauté pan, bring the vinegar to a boil; cook until reduced to about 3 tablespoons, about 3 minutes. Set aside.

Put the avocado in a large bowl and sprinkle with the lemon juice. Add the corn, tomato, basil, and quinoa. Drain the onion and add it to the bowl. Season with salt and pepper. Drizzle with the vinegar reduction and serve at room temperature.

SPROUTED QUINOA SALAD WITH YELLOW TOMATOES AND SCALLIONS

Serves 4 | vegan, gluten free

Tabbouleh is often made with different herbs, and here I use cilantro—beloved cilantro—and lots of mint (see page 110 for a more traditional version). It is not often made with grains other than bulgur, but it works very well with nutrient-dense, crunchy sprouted quinoa in this totally raw dish. If you'd like, grate a carrot into the salad for a little more sweetness.

- 2 cups (370 g) sprouted quinoa (page 28)
- 2 ripe yellow tomatoes, diced
- Juice of 1½ to 2 lemons
- Salt
- 1 cup (80 g) chopped fresh cilantro
- ½ cup (40 g) chopped fresh mint
- 2 scallions, thinly sliced on a bias
- 1 tablespoon extra-virgin olive oil

In a large bowl, combine the quinoa, tomatoes, the juice of 1½ lemons, and a pinch of salt. Let stand for 30 minutes, then add the cilantro, mint, and scallions. Taste and add more salt and lemon juice as needed. Serve at room temperature, drizzled with the oil, or cover and chill in the refrigerator for up to 4 hours and drizzle with the oil just before serving.

PEAR AND SPINACH SALAD WITH QUINOA, HAZELNUTS, AND LEMON-TAHINI DRESSING

Serves 4 | vegan, gluten free

Tahini is a great substitute for dairy: The smooth sesame-seed paste makes a creamy dressing that gently naps the crunchy quinoa and mingles with the sweet juice given off by the pears. Hazelnuts make this salad especially fancy, but you could use blanched toasted almonds or slivered almonds instead.

- 1/2 cup (55 g) hazelnuts
- 6 tablespoons (90 ml) freshly squeezed lemon juice
- 1/2 teaspoon salt
- 1/4 teaspoon freshly ground black pepper
- 2 tablespoons tahini
- 2 tablespoons olive oil
- 2 small pears
- 4 cups (120 g) baby spinach
- 3 cups (550 g) cooked quinoa (page 27), cooled

In a small sauté pan over medium-high heat, toast the hazelnuts until the skins crack and the loose bits start to smoke, 4 to 5 minutes. Remove to a plate and rub off the skins with your thumbs or a paper towel. Set aside.

In a very large bowl, whisk together the lemon juice, salt, pepper, and tahini, then drizzle in the oil, whisking until the dressing is emulsified.

Quarter the pears, cut out the cores, and dice the pears. Add the pears, spinach, quinoa, and hazelnuts to the dressing, toss to coat well, and serve.

MILLET AND SWEET CORN SALAD WITH POBLANO CHILES, GRAPE TOMATOES, AND CILANTRO

Serves 4 | vegan, gluten free

There are few things better, I think, than very good sweet corn, its milky kernels sliced off the cob in long rows that hold together a little even as you toss them in a salad. Here raw sweet corn is paired with toasty millet, mild but deep-flavored poblanos, and a lime-tart dressing flecked with mineral-tasting cilantro. To make this more of a main dish, add some protein in the form of blanched shelled edamame, or cooked, gently rinsed, and drained black beans (page 65).

- 3 tablespoons freshly squeezed lime juice
- 2 tablespoons cider vinegar
- 2 teaspoons agave nectar
- 3/4 teaspoon salt, or more to taste
- 1/4 teaspoon ground cayenne
- 1/4 cup (60 ml) olive oil
- 3 cups (525 g) cooked millet (page 24), cooled
- 1 pint (285 g) grape or cherry tomatoes, halved, or 2 medium tomatoes, diced
- 3 medium ears sweet corn, shucked, kernels cut off
- 1 poblano chile, seeded and diced
- 1/4 cup (20 g) chopped fresh cilantro
- 2 scallions, thinly sliced on the bias

In a large bowl, whisk together the lime juice, vinegar, agave nectar, salt, and cayenne, then whisk in the oil. Add the millet and toss to break it up a bit, then add the remaining ingredients and toss well. Taste and add more salt or cayenne if necessary. Serve at room temperature, or cover and keep in the refrigerator for up to 2 hours before serving cold.

WARM WHEAT BERRY AND BEET SALAD
WITH ANISE-SCENTED YOGURT CHEESE

Serves 4 | vegetarian

Tangy and sweet, with the comforting, mild nuttiness of warm wheat berries, this salad makes a swell light wintertime lunch. Serve it with hunks of dark bread for sopping up the dressing as it mingles with the fragrant anise yogurt. If you don't have time to drain the yogurt overnight, just use 1 cup (240 ml) Greek yogurt—its consistency won't be quite as cheeselike, but it'll taste the same.

- **Salt**
- **½ teaspoon ground anise seeds**
- **2 cups (480 ml) plain yogurt (not nonfat), drained overnight in a very-fine-mesh sieve (to yield 1 scant cup / 200 ml)**
- **1 bunch beets (about 1 pound), tops trimmed**
- **1 cup (180 g) raw wheat berries**
- **¼ cup (60 ml) cider vinegar or red wine vinegar**
- **2 tablespoons freshly squeezed lemon juice**
- **Freshly ground black pepper**
- **1 teaspoon honey or agave nectar**
- **¼ cup (60 ml) olive oil**
- **¼ cup (20 g) fresh parsley leaves**

Stir ½ teaspoon salt and the anise into the drained yogurt and set the yogurt cheese aside in the refrigerator for at least 1 hour for the flavors to develop.

Put the beets in a small saucepan, cover with water, and bring to a boil. Lower the heat and simmer until the beets are tender, 20 to 30 minutes. Drain and cover with cold water; when cool enough to handle, rub the peels off the beets, dice them, and set aside.

Put the wheat berries and 2½ cups (600 ml) water in a 2-quart (2-L) saucepan, cover, and bring to a boil. Lower the heat and simmer until the wheat berries are tender, about 50 minutes, adding ¼ teaspoon salt toward the end of the cooking. When the wheat berries are tender, pile the beets on top of them (no need to stir), cover, and cook until the beets are just heated through, about 4 minutes. Drain in a colander.

While the wheat berries are cooking, in a large bowl, whisk together the vinegar, lemon juice, ½ teaspoon salt, pepper to taste, and honey. Drizzle in the oil, whisking to emulsify the dressing. Add the warm wheat berries and beets and toss to combine. Serve warm, topped with dollops of cold yogurt cheese and sprinkled with parsley.

YOGURT CHEESE: When I'm feeling semi-organized (but not on the ball enough to have been making my own yogurt), I'll start draining a big container of yogurt as soon as I come home from the store with it. Then it's a simple matter of stirring in some salt and seasonings (minced fresh herbs; cracked black pepper; grated garlic; ground fennel, cumin, or nigella seeds) to make a dip for flatbreads or cracker shards (like those on pages 237 and 238), or for raw vegetables.

SPROUTED WHEAT BERRY SALAD WITH AVOCADO AND PICKLED RED ONION

Serves 2 | vegan

For such a simple collection of ingredients, this salad really packs a wallop of flavors, textures, and colors—the chewy, nutty wheat berries; crisp, cold, bright pink pickled onion; the green-yellow avocado that becomes creamy as you toss it with the wheat; and the heat of the little bits of fresh chile. It's nice spread on a big, thick piece of toasted or grilled rustic bread, or spooned into a pita.

- 2 cups (330 g) sprouted wheat berries (page 28)
- 1/2 cup (80 g) diced quick-pickled red onion (page 145)
- 1 hot green chile, seeded and minced
- 3 tablespoons chopped fresh cilantro
- 1 Hass avocado, halved, pitted, peeled, and diced
- Juice of 1 lime
- Salt to taste
- 1 tablespoon olive oil

Combine all the ingredients in a medium bowl and stir to combine. The avocado will break up a bit and make the salad creamy.

VARIATION

✱ Replace half or all of the wheat berries with sprouted quinoa, or use cooked wheat berries or quinoa.

SPICY BULGUR SALAD WITH PEACHES, JALAPEÑO, AND MINTED YOGURT

Serves 2 to 4 | vegetarian

This is a perfect midsummer salad, ideal for when you have perfectly ripe, sweet peaches, which are set against the heat of crisp fresh chiles and the crunch of pepitas. Abundant mint and thick Greek or other strained yogurt with at least a little fat content will help tame the chiles as well.

- 1 cup (240 ml) plain Greek yogurt
- Juice of 1 lime
- 1 teaspoon salt
- 1/8 teaspoon ground cumin
- 1 1/2 teaspoons minced fresh mint, plus whole sprigs for garnish
- 3 cups (570 g) cooked medium-grind bulgur (page 36), cooled
- 2 ripe peaches, diced
- 1 to 2 large jalapeño chiles, seeded and diced
- 2 tablespoons pepitas, toasted

In a medium bowl, whisk together the yogurt, lime juice, 3/4 teaspoon of the salt, the cumin, and minced mint.

In a separate large bowl, toss the bulgur with the peaches, chiles, half of the pepitas, and the remaining 1/4 teaspoon of salt. Transfer to serving plates, dollop the yogurt mixture over the top, scatter the remaining pepitas and the mint sprigs over the salad, and serve.

VARIATION

✱ Instead of the peaches, try this with honeydew or cantaloupe.

CLASSIC TABBOULEH
Serves 4 | vegan

I'm by no means opposed to shortcuts that involve food processors, but don't be tempted to use one to chop the herbs here: The whirling blades tend to rip the herbs into unpleasant shreds rather than cutting them into nice clean bits. Use a heavy, sharp knife and a large cutting board, and work out those forearms! And don't skimp on the parsley, which besides being the most important part of a true tabbouleh, is an underappreciated source of vitamins K, A, and C, as well as folate and iron.

- ½ cup (70 g) raw medium-grind bulgur
- 2 medium-size ripe tomatoes
- ½ small sweet onion
- ½ teaspoon salt
- Finely grated zest and juice of 1 large lemon
- 4 packed cups (320 g) stemmed fresh flat-leaf parsley (1 giant bunch), washed and spun dry
- A few sprigs of fresh mint, stems removed

In a heavy saucepan, bring 1 cup (240 ml) water to a boil. Stir in the bulgur, cover, and remove from the heat. Let stand until the bulgur is almost tender, about 10 minutes, then drain in a fine-mesh sieve. Rinse under cold running water to cool, then drain again, pressing out the excess water. Dump the bulgur into a large bowl.

Dice the tomatoes and add them, with their juices, to the bulgur. Dice and add the onion and stir in the salt and lemon zest and juice. Let stand until the bulgur is fully tender and has absorbed some of the tomato and lemon juices, about 30 minutes.

Meanwhile, on a large cutting board with a sharp chef's knife, finely chop the parsley and mint to make about 2 cups (160 g). Add to the bulgur mixture and toss to combine. Serve at room temperature, or cover and refrigerate for up to 2 days and serve cold.

VARIATIONS

★ Use baby arugula or half arugula and half spinach instead of the parsley.
★ Instead of parsley, use 1 cup (80 g) chopped fresh cilantro and 1 cup (80 g) chopped fresh Thai basil, and use the juice of 2 limes instead of the lemon zest and juice.
★ Add 1 seeded and diced cucumber to the salad.
★ Add 2 tablespoons toasted pine nuts.
★ Stir 1 tablespoon pomegranate molasses or 1 teaspoon tamarind concentrate (available in Middle Eastern and Indian stores) into the bulgur when you add the tomatoes.

BULGUR SALAD WITH BRISLING SARDINES, MEYER LEMON, AND ARUGULA

Serves 2 to 4 | vegetarian

By now most of us realize that overfishing and poorly executed aquaculture are significant problems that may very well lead to the permanent eradication of the large fish most loved in wealthier countries, and that it would behoove us to expand our appreciation of those smaller wild-caught fish—like sardines and anchovies—that mature quickly and are considered (aside from booms and busts mostly attributable to ocean water temperature fluctuations) generally not at risk. These fish are also exceptionally healthful, high in both essential omega-3 fatty acids (flax seeds, walnuts, and salmon are other good sources) and calcium (a can of sardines provides as much calcium as a tall glass of milk).

Small, delicate Nordic brisling sardines packed in olive oil (another good fat) are the ones to look for, especially if you're new to tinned fish; they're milder and cleaner-tasting than larger sardines that have been sectioned to fit in the cans. In this salad they're doused with plenty of floral-scented Meyer lemon juice, regular lemon juice, and white wine vinegar for a hit of acidity to offset the fish's richness.

- **Coarsely grated zest and juice of 1 Meyer lemon**
- **Juice of $\frac{1}{2}$ regular lemon**
- **2 tablespoons white wine vinegar or Champagne vinegar**
- **Salt**
- **$\frac{1}{2}$ teaspoon freshly ground black pepper**
- **2 tablespoons olive oil**
- **$3\frac{1}{2}$ cups (665 g) cooked medium-grind bulgur (page 36), cooled**
- **1 (3.75-ounce / 105–g) can brisling sardines in olive oil**
- **2 cups (85 g) fresh arugula**

In a large bowl, whisk together the Meyer lemon zest and juice, regular lemon juice, and vinegar. Whisk in a couple generous pinches of salt, the pepper, and oil. Add the bulgur and toss to combine.

Drain the sardines and add them, along with the arugula, to the bulgur; toss to combine. Taste and add more salt if necessary. Serve.

COUSCOUS, MELON, AND CUCUMBER SALAD

Serves 4 | vegan

I recently became enamored of the pretty taxicab-yellow-and-white-striped single-serving-size fruits sold in Asian shops as "Korean melons." They look a little like winter squash, but the flesh of ripe ones is honey-sweet and juicy, and they smell slightly of cucumber; specimens that are not perfectly ripe are even more similar to cucumber. Peel it with a vegetable peeler, or just halve it, scoop out the seeds (although many people eat the seeds too, as they're sweet and tender), and scrape the flesh from the skin. If you can't find these little melons, use chopped honeydew or cantaloupe. If you are able to find them, get a couple of extra—you can also halve them, fill the center, with or without seeds, with crushed ice sprinkled with a little sugar or drizzled with agave nectar, and eat it as a (very) light dessert.

- **1 tablespoon sesame seeds**
- **1 tablespoon pepitas**
- **2 tablespoons sliced almonds**
- **3 tablespoons Champagne or white wine vinegar**
- **Juice of 1 1/2 limes**
- **1/2 teaspoon salt, or to taste**
- **1/2 teaspoon crushed red pepper**
- **1/2 teaspoon ground cumin**
- **3 tablespoons olive oil**
- **3 cups (480 g) cooked whole wheat couscous (page 37), cooled**
- **1/2 small honeydew or canteloupe or 1 Korean melon, peeled, seeded, and diced (about 1 1/2 cups / 255 g)**
- **1/2 English cucumber, with peel, cut into 1/8-inch (3-mm) rounds or half-moons; or 3 Persian cucumbers, cut into rounds**
- **1 jalapeño chile, seeded and minced**
- **1/2 cup (40 g) fresh mint leaves**

In a small heavy sauté pan, toast the sesame seeds over medium-high heat until shiny and golden, about 1 minute, and transfer to a plate to cool. In the same pan, toast the pepitas and almonds until the pepitas are swelled and the almonds are golden, about 2 minutes; add to the sesame seeds and set aside.

In a large bowl, whisk together the vinegar, lime juice, salt, crushed red pepper, and cumin. Gradually whisk in the oil. Add the couscous, melon, cucumber, chile, and mint and toss to combine. Sprinkle with the toasted seeds and nuts and serve.

SQUID AND FARRO SALAD
WITH MANGO, LIME, AND BASIL
Serves 4

I've recently been looking for ways to bring more squid—a lean, inexpensive, abundant, and responsibly harvested protein—to my table. This Southeast Asian–style salad with mild, flavor-absorbing farro, sweet ripe mango, chiles, and plenty of lime juice may well make squid a staple at yours as well. You can find frozen squid, or calamari, in most good supermarkets and at any seafood market, and it's just as good as (or even better!) than fresh. To thaw it quickly, submerge the whole package in a container of cold water and set it in the sink under a barely dripping faucet for about 30 minutes.

- **1 pound (455 g) cleaned small squid**
- **1 tablespoon vegetable oil**
- **¼ cup (60 ml) freshly squeezed lime juice**
- **2 tablespoons fish sauce or 1 tablespoon soy sauce**
- **1 to 2 fresh hot red chiles, minced (seeded if desired)**
- **¼ teaspoon freshly ground black pepper**
- **4 cups (672 g) cooked farro (page 36), cooled**
- **1 ripe mango, peeled, pitted, and diced**
- **½ small red onion, diced**
- **3 sprigs fresh basil, torn**
- **2 sprigs fresh mint, torn**
- **Lime wedges**

Feel around inside the squid bodies (the tubes) and pull out anything that feels either softer or harder than the body flesh itself—any membranelike stuff or the clear hard blade-like pin bone. Depending on how well the squid have been cleaned, there may be more or less of this to do, but in any case, it's quick and easy. Pull off the fins on the outside of the body, and cut the tentacles off if they're still attached—discard the fins, which are tough, but save the tentacles. Rinse everything well and pat dry with paper towels. Cut each body in half lengthwise, then use a sharp knife to lightly score the inside surface of each one diagonally every ¼ inch (6 mm), then slice crosswise into ¼-inch (6-mm) strips. Alternatively, cut the bodies into ¼-inch (6-mm) rings.

In a large heavy sauté pan, heat the oil over high heat. Add the squid bodies and tentacles and cook, stirring frequently, until just opaque throughout, about 1 minute. Remove to a plate and set aside to cool.

In a large bowl, whisk together the lime juice, fish sauce, chiles, and black pepper. Add the farro, mango, onion, basil, mint, and calamari and toss to combine. Serve with lime wedges, either immediately or chilled for up to 4 hours.

WARM SPELT AND NEW-POTATO SALAD
WITH BACON AND DILL

Serves 6

Spelt berries—and the similar farro, which would be a good substitute here—absorb flavors readily, so they work well in a warm vinegary German potato salad, where they soak up the hot, bacon-enriched dressing just as the potatoes do. Crisp celery and onion, and plenty of celery leaves and dill, freshen up the dish. I could eat this as a meal in itself, but it would also be nice with simply steamed green beans and a piece of fish.

- 1 pound (455 g) new potatoes, cut in half if very small, quarters if larger
- Salt
- 4 ounces (115 g) bacon, diced
- 1 tablespoon olive oil
- ½ cup (120 ml) cider vinegar
- 2 teaspoons grainy mustard
- ½ sweet onion, diced
- 1 rib celery with leaves, diced
- 2 cups (390 g) cooked spelt berries (page 36)
- Freshly ground black pepper
- 2 teaspoons minced fresh dill

Put the potatoes and a generous pinch of salt in a large heavy saucepan and cover with cold water by 1 inch (2.5 cm). Bring to a boil and cook, uncovered, until just tender, 8 to 10 minutes. Drain in a colander.

While the potatoes are cooking, in a large, deep sauté pan, cook the bacon over medium heat until crisp, about 8 minutes. Remove with a slotted spoon and drain on a paper towel. Pour off most of the drippings in the pan and wipe out any burned bits. Return the pan to medium-high heat and add the oil, vinegar, mustard, onion, celery, spelt, and potatoes. Season with salt and lots of pepper to taste and cook, stirring frequently, until heated through and most of the vinegar is absorbed or evaporated, about 3 minutes. Fold in the dill and bacon and serve hot or warm.

FREEKEH AND FRISÉE
Serves 4

This is a heretical bastardization of salade niçoise and salade aux lardons, whole-grains style. I like the cracked green wheat called freekeh here because its faint grassy, oceanic aroma complements the tuna so well, but regular cracked wheat or, really, any other whole grain would work well too. Instead of bacon lardons (if I'm making a salad, it very often means I don't want to have to cook anything fresh), I use similar-size strips of sun-dried tomatoes, whose texture, when softened a bit in the dressing, at least vaguely *recalls* that of lardons.

- 6 ounces (170 g) French green beans, trimmed
- ¼ cup (60 ml) Champagne vinegar or white wine vinegar
- 1 teaspoon Dijon-style mustard
- ¾ teaspoon salt
- ¼ teaspoon freshly ground black pepper
- 6 tablespoons olive oil
- 6 sun-dried tomatoes
- 6 cups (240 g) pale yellow frisée or curly endive leaves, washed and spun dry
- ½ cup (40 g) fresh flat-leaf parsley leaves
- ½ cup (70 g) niçoise or Kalamata olives, pitted
- 2 cups (360 g) cooked freekeh (page 37), cooled
- 2 (4.5-ounce / 130-g) cans tuna in olive oil, drained
- 4 large eggs, hard-cooked, peeled, and quartered (see Note)

In a large saucepan of boiling water, blanch the green beans until just tender and bright green, about 2 minutes. Drain and transfer to a bowl of ice water to cool, then drain and set aside in the refrigerator.

In a medium bowl, whisk together the vinegar, mustard, salt, and pepper, then whisk in the oil until emulsified. Cut the sun-dried tomatoes into ⅛-inch-wide (3-mm-wide) strips and add to the dressing; if the tomatoes were not packed in oil, set them aside to soften in the dressing for at least 15 minutes.

Spread the frisée and parsley on a large serving platter. Make piles of the olives, freekeh, tuna, eggs, and beans; with a slotted spoon, transfer the tomatoes from the dressing to a pile in the frisée and drizzle everything with the dressing. Serve immediately.

NOTE: To hard-cook and peel eggs, put them in a small saucepan with just enough water to cover them. Place over high heat, cover the pan, and bring to a boil. Immediately remove from the heat and let stand, covered, for 8 minutes (for a creamy yolk) or 10 minutes (for a firm yolk). Drain, cover with cold water, and let stand until cool enough to handle. Tap the shell all over with the back of a spoon, then peel off the shell starting at the wider end. Dip back into the cool water to rinse them off, then use the eggs as desired.

4

Main Dishes

Whole grains are so incredibly versatile and easy to use that you could find yourself relying on them as the main ingredient in the main course at the supper table every everloving night. A risotto or farrotto, a soup or a pasta sauce, can be on the stove and simmering in minutes, and unless I overthink it, which I admit I often do, it can go something like this:

Turn on the burner under a pan or pot, whichever is already on the stovetop, and glug in some olive oil to start shimmering while you dice or slice an onion. Onion goes in the pan with a sprinkle of salt to help draw out the moisture and soften the onion a bit more quickly, and you smash a clove of garlic and add it, too. Then there's a brief moment of panic: What are you making, anyway? Here's where you can get creative. Add a spice or two to those now-browned onions (say, cumin and coriander to take it in an Indian direction; cumin, cayenne, and dried oregano for something Mexican), or just go right ahead and add some grains and liquid (farro or short-grain brown rice, a splash of wine, and stock for something Italian; millet, tomatoes, and water for that Indian thing; quinoa or amaranth and stock for Mexican).

For a soup, use more stock. Check the refrigerator drawers for vegetables; maybe you've stashed a bag of leftover diced zucchini or parsnips in there, or some cubes of butternut squash that didn't fit in the baking pan when you were roasting them the other night, or half a bag of greens that are no longer pretty enough for a salad. Add the hard vegetables and some leftover cooked chicken or turkey, or drain a can of beans and dump them in. Add the softer vegetables or greens toward the end. While it's all simmering, send the kid out to the yard for a handful of herbs. Clear the decks, get out the plates, and pour yourself another glass of wine. Soon the millet or what have you will be tender and supper will be ready. And of course it's all made even simpler if there are a few bags of different grains at the ready in your freezer—no need to think ahead of time, just break up the grains in a sieve or colander, run them under cold water for a minute, and they're good to go.

SMOKY AMARANTH CORN CHOWDER

Serves 4 | vegan, gluten free

As recently as a few years ago, I wouldn't have dreamed of making corn chowder without bacon, much less white potatoes, but I've actually come to prefer a lighter, cleaner-tasting corn soup (maybe it isn't even *chowder* anymore). Good milky sweet corn and a sweet potato make the soup a little creamy, and amaranth gives the broth body.

- **1 tablespoon olive oil**
- **1/2 onion, diced**
- **1/2 red bell pepper, diced**
- **1 rib celery, diced**
- **2 tablespoons chopped celery leaves**
- **1/2 teaspoon chipotle chile flakes or 1/4 teaspoon ground chipotle**
- **2 1/2 cups (600 ml) vegetable stock or water**
- **2/3 cup (130 g) raw amaranth**
- **2 cups (340 g) sweet corn kernels (from 2 or 3 large cobs, or frozen)**
- **1 sweet potato, peeled and diced**
- **Salt and cracked black peppercorns**
- **4 sprigs fresh basil**

In a 3-quart (2.8-L) saucepan, heat the oil over medium-high heat. Add the onion, bell pepper, and diced celery and cook, stirring frequently, for 5 minutes. Add the celery leaves, chipotle chile flakes, stock, amaranth, corn, and sweet potato. Bring to a boil, then lower the heat and simmer, stirring occasionally, until the amaranth grains are translucent and the sweet potato is very soft and falling apart, about 20 minutes. Season with salt and plenty of black pepper. Serve with a sprig of basil topping each bowlful.

CHICKEN AND TOMATILLO SOUP
WITH AMARANTH
Serves 4 | gluten free

AMARANTH-CRUSTED BAKED CATFISH
Serves 4 | gluten free

Here, roasted tomatillos, onion, chile, and garlic are pureed, then simmered with amaranth and leftover shredded chicken, and the resulting quick soup is showered with cilantro for a bright, tangy, light meal. Do add a little crème fraîche or sour cream if you have it. If you like, instead of using already cooked chicken, you can gently poach one or two uncooked chicken breast halves in the broth, then pull them out with tongs, let cool, and shred the meat before returning it to the soup.

Fried catfish is a fine treat every once in a while (it's the kind of down-home food the Krissoffs tend to eat only on road trips; heading out of Georgia in any direction, there's bound to be good catfish somewhere along the way). This baked fish, with a crisp-crunchy topping of tiny popped amaranth grains, is perfect as everyday—home-cooked—fare. Serve the fish fillets with a big pile of spinach or baby collard greens sautéed in olive oil with garlic on the side. Or tuck them into warmed flour tortillas with crisp shredded green cabbage, drizzled with crema or plain yogurt whisked with a little salt.

- **12 ounces (340 g) tomatillos, husked and rinsed**
- **1/2 onion, cut into 4 wedges**
- **1 hot green chile**
- **2 cloves garlic, peeled**
- **4 cups (960 ml) chicken or vegetable stock or water**
- **1 cup (200 g) raw amaranth**
- **2 cups (280 g) shredded cooked chicken**
- **Juice of 1 lime**
- **Salt and freshly ground black pepper**
- **1/2 cup (40 g) chopped fresh cilantro**
- **Crème fraîche or sour cream (optional; page 74)**

- **1/4 cup (1/2 stick / 55 g) unsalted butter, melted, plus more for the baking sheet**
- **1 1/2 cups (90 g) popped amaranth (page 20)**
- **8 (4- to 5-ounce / 115- to 140-g) catfish fillets**
- **Cajun spice blend or freshly ground black pepper**
- **Salt**
- **Lemon wedges**

Preheat the oven to 375°F (190°C) and set a rack in the lower third of the oven. Butter a baking sheet.

Preheat the broiler to high. Line a rimmed baking sheet with aluminum foil and put the tomatillos, onion, chile, and garlic on it. Broil, about 4 inches (10 cm) from the heat source, for 12 to 15 minutes, turning the vegetables over once halfway through, until nicely browned in spots. Using tongs, transfer the vegetables and any juices from the baking sheet to a blender or food processor and puree until smooth. Pour into a large heavy saucepan and add the stock and amaranth. Bring to a boil, then lower the heat and simmer until the amaranth is translucent and tender, about 20 minutes. Stir in the chicken and lime juice, and add salt and pepper to taste; bring to a simmer to heat through. Stir in the cilantro and ladle into soup bowls. Dollop with crème fraîche, if desired, and serve.

Put the amaranth in a shallow dish. Season the fillets with Cajun spice blend or pepper and salt to taste. Set each fillet in the amaranth and turn to coat well, pressing the amaranth gently onto the fish so it adheres. Arrange on the prepared baking sheet and drizzle with the butter. Bake in the lower third of the oven for about 10 minutes, until firm and lightly golden. Serve hot, with lemon wedges.

COLD CUCUMBER-YOGURT SOUP
WITH DILL AND BARLEY

Serves 2 to 4 | vegetarian

With a stash of cooked barley in the freezer, ready to be dumped into a sieve and rinsed under cold running water for a few seconds to just thaw it, could lunch be any easier?

- **1 medium cucumber, peeled, seeded, and roughly chopped**
- **1 hot green chile, seeded and chopped**
- **1 clove garlic, smashed**
- **1 tablespoon chopped fresh dill**
- **1 cup (240 ml) plain yogurt**
- **3/4 cup (180 ml) cold vegetable stock or water**
- **Salt and freshly ground black pepper**
- **1 1/2 cups (240 g) cooked hulled barley (page 20), cooled**

Put the cucumber, chile, garlic, dill, yogurt, stock, and salt and pepper to taste in a blender and puree until smooth. Stir in the barley and serve or, better, transfer to the refrigerator to chill for up to 1 day before serving cold. Taste and season with more salt if necessary before serving.

PORCINI AND BARLEY "RISOTTO"

Serves 3 or 4 | vegan

It's always been my belief that risotto, if made correctly, needs neither butter, nor cream, nor cheese—the special rice should release enough starch in the unique cooking-and-stirring process to make the broth creamy and thick. Barley, however, needs a little help releasing its starches, so I just hit it with an immersion blender for a few seconds to break up some of the grains. Though it wouldn't be vegan, you could also (or instead) go ahead and add a little heavy cream or crème fraîche, and sprinkle with freshly grated Parmesan.

- ½ cup (10 g) dried porcini mushrooms
- 1 cup (240 ml) boiling water
- 3 cups (720 ml) vegetable stock
- 2 tablespoons olive oil
- 6 ounces (170 g) cremini mushrooms, trimmed and sliced
- 1½ teaspoons fresh thyme leaves
- ½ onion, thinly sliced
- 1 clove garlic, minced
- 1½ cups (300 g) raw hulled barley
- Salt
- Juice of ½ lemon

Put the porcini mushrooms in a heatproof bowl and pour in the boiling water. Let soak for 30 minutes, then scoop out and chop the mushrooms; set aside. Pour the soaking liquid through a fine-mesh sieve into a small saucepan, add the stock, and heat over low heat; bring to a simmer, then cover and set aside.

In a heavy, deep sauté pan, heat 1 tablespoon of the oil over medium-high heat. Add the cremini mushrooms and cook, stirring occasionally, until they have released their liquid, the liquid has evaporated, and the mushrooms are nicely browned around the edges, about 8 minutes. Stir in the thyme, cook for 1 minute, then scrape into a bowl and set aside.

In the same sauté pan, heat the remaining 1 tablespoon of oil over medium-high heat. Add the onion and cook, stirring occasionally, until soft and nicely browned, about 10 minutes. Add the garlic and cook until tender, about 2 more minutes. Add the barley and stir to coat it with the oil. Cook, stirring constantly, until you can smell the barley, about 2 minutes. Stir in the chopped porcini mushrooms and the stock mixture. Bring to a boil, then lower the heat, cover, and simmer, stirring occasionally, until the barley is tender and most of the liquid is absorbed, 45 to 50 minutes.

Season with salt to taste. Using an immersion blender, blend for 5 to 10 seconds, just until the liquid remaining is thick and creamy. Stir well, then stir in the lemon juice and the cremini mushrooms. Cook to heat through, and serve hot.

VARIATIONS

★ For a nonvegan dish, remove the casing from one or two links of Italian-style sausage and add the meat to the pan with the cremini mushrooms; cook, breaking it up with the spoon, until the sausage and mushrooms are nicely browned, then add the thyme and continue with the recipe. Drain off any excess fat if necessary before returning the sausage and mushroom mixture to the pan.

★ Another nonvegan option is to stir some leftover cooked chicken into the risotto at the end of cooking and heat through.

SWEET-SPICED ROAST CHICKEN WITH BARLEY AND APRICOTS
Serves 4 to 6

This dish was inspired by a barley salad on the wonderful Simply Recipes website that featured ras al-hanout, a Moroccan spice mixture. With some bitter leaves like arugula or young dandelion greens dressed with a little salt, olive oil, and lemon juice on the side, this makes a lovely and special supper.

FOR THE DRESSING
- **2 small lemons**
- **1½ teaspoons salt**
- **1 teaspoon ground cinnamon**
- **1 teaspoon ground cardamom**
- **1 teaspoon ground ginger**
- **½ teaspoon ground cayenne**
- **¼ cup (60 ml) olive oil**

FOR THE CHICKEN
- **1 (3-pound / 1.4-kg) whole chicken, spatchcocked (see Note), or 4 pounds (1.8 kg) chicken leg quarters**

FOR THE BARLEY
- **1½ cups (300 g) raw hulled barley**
- **¼ teaspoon salt**
- **¼ cup (25 g) chopped dried apricots**
- **2 scallions, thinly sliced**
- **½ cup (40 g) chopped fresh cilantro**

MAKE THE DRESSING
Coarsely grate the zest from the lemons into a large bowl. Juice the lemons into the bowl, picking out the seeds. Add the remaining ingredients and whisk to combine.

MAKE THE CHICKEN
Preheat the oven to 425°F (220°C).

Put the chicken in a large baking dish or pan. Pour half of the dressing over the chicken (reserve the rest in the bowl), turning to coat it on all sides, and arrange skin side up. Roast for 45 minutes (for leg quarters) to 1 hour (for a spatchcocked whole chicken), or until a thermometer inserted in a thigh reads 160°F (70°C) and the skin is crisp and golden. Let rest for 10 minutes before serving.

MAKE THE BARLEY
While the chicken cooks, combine the barley, salt, and 4 cups (960 ml) of water in a heavy saucepan. Cover, bring to a boil, then lower the heat and simmer until the barley is tender and no trace of bright white is visible at the center when a grain is cut in half, about 40 minutes. Drain well. Add the barley, apricots, scallions, and cilantro to the reserved dressing and toss to combine. Serve the warm barley with the chicken.

VARIATION
★ To make this a vegan salad: Omit the chicken (duh). Reduce the dressing quantities by half and add 1 drained (15-ounce / 430-g) can chickpeas to the salad. Serve over bitter greens.

NOTE: To spatchcock a whole chicken, which helps it roast faster and more evenly than a whole specimen, use a heavy knife to cut down either side of the backbone and remove it. Turn the chicken breast-meat side up and press down on the center bone with your palm to flatten the bird. (Some people add a couple extra steps in here—cutting out part of the keel bone and doing some fancy wing tucking—that I find to be unnecessary.)

SOBA NOODLES
IN DASHI WITH TOFU AND KABOCHA SQUASH
Serves 2 or 3 | vegan

This healthful, refreshing soup couldn't be simpler: Soba noodles and tofu are piled in serving bowls while a broth simmers gently, flavored with kombu and dried mushrooms. Cubes of bright orange kabocha squash, still with the green peel on, are cooked quickly in the broth, and all is poured into the bowls to heat the noodles and tofu.

- **1 bundle (about 3 ounces / 85 g) dried soba noodles**
- **7 ounces (200 g) soft or firm tofu, diced**
- **1 scallion, thinly sliced**
- **1 (3-inch / 7.5-cm) square kombu seaweed, lightly rinsed, torn into thin strips**
- **4 large dried shiitake mushrooms, rinsed**
- **¼ small kabocha squash, seeded and cut into large chunks**
- **Tamari or soy sauce to taste**

Bring a large pot of water to a boil. Add the noodles and stir. Return to a boil and cook until just al dente, about 4 minutes. Drain in a sieve or colander and rinse well under cold running water until cold; drain well. Divide among 2 or 3 deep serving bowls and top with the tofu and scallion.

In a heavy 3-quart (2.8-L) saucepan, combine 6 cups (1.4 L) water, the seaweed, and mushrooms. Bring to a boil, then lower the heat and simmer for 15 minutes. With a slotted spoon, fish out the seaweed and mushrooms and remove and discard the mushroom stems; cut the mushroom caps into ¼-inch-wide (6-mm-wide) strips and divide the mushrooms and seaweed among the serving bowls.

Add the squash to the broth. Bring to a boil, then lower the heat and simmer until the squash is tender, 6 to 8 minutes. With the slotted spoon, transfer the squash to the serving bowls. Season the simmering broth with tamari, then ladle it over the noodles, tofu, and vegetables in the serving bowls. Serve hot.

VARIATIONS

★ In fall and winter, use peeled and chopped butternut or acorn squash—or any hard winter squash—in place of the kabocha and simmer until tender (these will take a bit longer to cook than kabocha). Or instead of hard squash, use carrots, parsnips, or sweet potatoes.

★ In summer, blanch strips of zucchini or yellow squash, or sugar-snap or snow peas, in the broth instead of the hard squash.

★ Stir ¼ cup (45 g) miso paste (any kind) into the simmering broth before seasoning with tamari.

★ Instead of the tofu, pile a small handful of shredded leftover roast chicken or pork (not vegan, obviously) on top of the noodles. Or poach a few thin slices of raw chicken breast or flank steak in the simmering broth until cooked through and divide them among the serving bowls.

SOBA NOODLES
WITH SHRIMP AND SUGAR-SNAP PEAS
Serves 4

I often forget about the bag of shrimp in the freezer, but maybe writing this recipe down will help me remember that a satisfying, family-pleasing meal can be easily put together at the last minute. Dump the shrimp into a bowl of cold water and put the bowl in the sink under a barely dripping faucet; they'll be thawed in about 15 minutes. If you don't have sugar-snap peas on hand (we do because of my recent hummus-dipped-pea obsession), use a couple handfuls of frozen peas from the freezer, or some diced sweet peppers and zucchini or yellow squash, instead.

- **3 bundles (about 9 ounces / 255 g) dried soba noodles**
- **1 tablespoon vegetable oil**
- **1 teaspoon sesame oil**
- **5 shallots or 1 small sweet onion, thinly sliced**
- **1 inch (2.5 cm) fresh ginger, peeled and julienned**
- **1 pound (455 g) large shrimp, peeled and deveined**
- **8 ounces (225 g) sugar-snap peas, strings removed**
- **¼ cup (20 g) fresh basil leaves**
- **¼ cup (20 g) fresh cilantro leaves**
- **1 cup (240 ml) vegetable stock or water**
- **2 tablespoons soy sauce, or to taste**
- **1 lime, cut into wedges**

Bring a large pot of water to a boil. Add the noodles and stir. Return to a boil and cook until just al dente, about 4 minutes. Drain in a sieve or colander and rinse well under cold running water until cold; drain well and set aside.

In a large heavy sauté pan, heat the vegetable and sesame oils over medium-high heat. Add the shallots and cook, stirring frequently, until soft and golden brown, about 6 minutes. Add the ginger and cook, stirring, for 2 minutes. Add the shrimp, peas, basil, cilantro, stock, and soy sauce and cook until the shrimp are opaque throughout and the peas are tender, about 4 minutes. Add the noodles and toss to combine and heat through. Serve with the lime wedges.

RUSTIC SHREDDED-BEEF TAMALE WITH FRESH CORN
Serves 6 to 8 | gluten free

This is a good dish to share with close friends, as it's basically one huge tamale baked in a dish lined with corn husks (which I believe add that special tamale flavor that might be missing in other "tamale pies"). I've even made this with two fillings in the same tamale, the shredded beef here and the greens filling described in the variation: Just spread each on one side of the tamale dough in the baking dish and try to remember which is which when you start scooping into it. The recipe is long, but this is a simple dish to put together if you braise the beef in advance or if you have some leftover pot roast or roast pork (shred about 2½ cups (375 g) meat, season it with cumin and ground cayenne or good hot paprika, and stir in a little stock to loosen the mixture to the consistency of the meat on a barbecue pork sandwich).

FOR THE FILLING
- **4 dried guajillo chiles (see Notes)**
- **1 tablespoon olive oil**
- **1 (2-pound / 910-g) boneless beef chuck roast, about 1½ inches (4 cm) thick**
- **Salt and freshly ground black pepper**
- **1 small onion, chopped**
- **1 clove garlic, peeled**
- **½ teaspoon ground cumin**

FOR THE DOUGH
- **2 cups (230 g) masa harina (preferably "for tamales")**
- **½ cup (50 g) lard or vegetable shortening**
- **1 teaspoon baking powder**
- **¾ teaspoon salt**
- **2 cups (340 g) corn kernels (from about 2 large ears), fresh or frozen (thawed)**

TO ASSEMBLE
- **12 to 14 large dried corn husks (see Notes)**

MAKE THE FILLING
Wipe the chiles clean with a paper towel, break in half, and remove the stems and seeds. In a 6-quart (5.7-L) Dutch oven, heat the oil over medium-high heat. Add the chiles and fry, stirring constantly, until crisp and fragrant, about 1 minute. Remove to a bowl and set aside. Return the pot to medium-high heat. Season the beef with salt and pepper and add to the hot oil. Cook without disturbing for 8 minutes, then turn the hunk of beef over and add the onion and garlic to the pot around it. Cook for 8 minutes longer, stirring the onion and garlic occasionally. Add 3 cups (720 ml) water and nestle the chiles in around the beef. Bring to a simmer, cover, and lower the heat to very low. Cook at a very slow simmer until the beef can be easily pulled apart, about 2 hours.

Remove the beef to a bowl and let cool. Let the cooking liquid cool, then pour it and the chiles, onion, and garlic into a blender and blend until smooth. Shred the meat with your hands or two forks, discarding any large pieces of fat. Hold a sieve over the meat and pour in just enough of the pureed cooking liquid to coat it well, about 1 cup (240 ml); it shouldn't be soupy (just about as moist as the pulled pork on a barbecue sandwich); reserve the remaining cooking liquid for another use. Stir the cumin into the meat. Taste and season with more salt and pepper. Set aside; or cover and refrigerate up to overnight, bringing to room temperature before using.

MAKE THE DOUGH
While the beef is cooking, combine the masa harina and 1½ cups (360 ml) water in a medium bowl. In a large bowl, using an electric mixer, beat the lard, baking powder, and salt together until light and fluffy, scraping the sides of the bowl once or twice, then beat in the masa harina mixture a spatula-full at a time until smooth. Beat in about ¼ cup (60 ml) water to make a very soft dough; it should be the consistency of very soft cookie dough. Beat in the corn. Cover the bowl and put in the refrigerator to chill for 1 hour or up to overnight.

ASSEMBLE THE TAMALE

Preheat the oven to 350°F (175°C).

Rinse the corn husks and put them in a heatproof container and cover with boiling water; let soak for 5 minutes. Remove the corn husks from the water one at a time, pat dry, and use them to line the bottom of a 9-by-13-inch (23-by-33-cm) baking dish, arranging them so they extend up all four sides of the dish and overlapping their long edges.

Spoon half of the dough mixture over the husks in the baking dish and spread it smooth. Spread the meat filling mixture over the dough in an even layer, then top with the remaining dough, gently spreading the dough with a spatula or dampened palms to cover the filling. Lay more husks over the dough to cover it, folding the ends of the husks from the bottom over them. Cover the dish with aluminum foil. Bake until the husks can be pulled away from the dough without it sticking to them, about 2 hours. To serve, remove and discard the husks from the top and scoop out portions of the tamale at the table.

VARIATION

✱ To make a vegan tamale: Use vegetable shortening instead of lard. Instead of the meat filling, use drained cooked black beans (page 65) and/or sautéed turnip, mustard, or collard greens: In a large saucepan, bring 2 inches (5 cm) water to a boil and add 1 pound (455 g) chopped greens, pushing them under the water as they wilt. Cook until just tender, 5 to 15 minutes depending on the type. Drain. In a large deep sauté pan, heat 1 tablespoon oil over medium-high heat. Add 1 sliced onion and cook, stirring, for 6 minutes. Add 1 minced clove garlic, ½ teaspoon ground cumin, and a generous pinch of crushed red pepper and stir for 1 minute. Add the greens, ½ cup (120 ml) water, and salt to taste. Cook until most of the water is evaporated, about 4 minutes. Let cool, then use to fill the tamale.

NOTES: Guajillo chiles are deep burgundy, with shiny skin, usually 4 to 6 inches (10 to 15 cm) long. They're available in most grocery stores in the Latino foods section or with the produce.

You'll find dried corn husks near the guajillos; you can also use banana leaves (available in the frozen foods section of some grocery stores and Asian or Latino markets): Dip them in a pan of boiling water for a few seconds to soften.

LONG-BRAISED PORK WITH GRITS AND CILANTRO-CHILE-LIME SAUCE

Serves 4 to 6 | gluten free

I've made two braised pork recipes—a picadillo with cinnamon and raisins by Rick Bayless, and Lynne Rossetto Kasper's Emilia-Romagna stew with black olives and basil served over polenta—so many times that over the years they've gradually melded together into one. This is a fantastic dinner-party dish to serve with a simple green salad and maybe a loaf of good bread for tearing off pieces at the table. The pork can be made a day in advance and reheated just before serving—in fact, it may be better the second day.

Grits and coarse cornmeal have widely varying cooking times among brands and different grinds; yours could take just 15 minutes to cook or more like half an hour, so if you haven't cooked the particular type before, leave plenty of time before supper: If they finish early, they can be easily reheated, with a little more water if necessary, over low heat.

FOR THE PORK

- 1 tablespoon olive oil
- 2½ to 3 pounds (1.2 to 1.4 kg) country-style pork ribs (with or without bones) or boneless shoulder meat, cut into 2-inch (5-cm) pieces
- Salt and freshly ground black pepper
- 1 large onion, diced
- 1 clove garlic, minced
- 1 bay leaf
- 1 teaspoon ground cumin
- ½ teaspoon ground cinnamon
- ¼ teaspoon ground cayenne
- ½ cup (120 ml) wine (white or red)
- 1 (28-ounce / 800-g) can whole tomatoes with juice, roughly chopped
- ¼ cup (40 g) raisins

FOR THE CILANTRO SAUCE

- 1 cup (80 g) roughly chopped fresh cilantro (including stems)
- 1 hot green chile, roughly chopped
- Juice of 1 lime
- ½ teaspoon salt
- ¼ cup (60 ml) olive or vegetable oil

FOR THE GRITS

- 4 cups (960 ml) chicken or vegetable stock
- ½ teaspoon salt (or less if the stock is already salty)
- 1 cup (160 g) raw speckled or other stone-ground coarse grits or cornmeal

MAKE THE PORK

In a 6-quart (5.7-L) Dutch oven or a large deep sauté pan, heat the oil over medium-high heat. Season the pork with salt and pepper and add it to the pot in one layer (do this in batches if necessary). Cook without disturbing for about 6 minutes, until nicely browned on the bottom, then turn the pieces over with a metal spatula and brown the other sides, turning occasionally; it should take about 15 minutes to brown the pork. Remove the pork to a plate and set aside.

Return the pot to medium heat and add the onion. Cook, stirring frequently, until nicely browned, about 8 minutes, then add the garlic, bay leaf, cumin, cinnamon, and cayenne and cook for 1 minute. Add the wine and stir to release the browned bits from the bottom of the pot; simmer for 1 minute. Add the tomatoes, raisins, and pork with its juices. Bring to a simmer, then cook, partially covered, until the pork is very tender, about 1½ hours. Season the broth with salt and pepper to taste.

MAKE THE CILANTRO SAUCE

While the pork is cooking, put all the ingredients in a mini food processor or blender and pulse until smooth. Set aside at room temperature for up to 2 hours.

MAKE THE GRITS

In a heavy 2-quart (2-L) saucepan, bring the stock and salt to a boil. Gradually whisk in the grits. Bring to a boil, then lower the heat and simmer until the grits are thick but still pourable and the grains are tender, 15 to 35 minutes, depending on the brand and type.

Spoon some of the grits onto each plate and top with the pork and its sauce, and a drizzle of the cilantro sauce.

RED POSOLE
WITH PORK AND MUSTARD GREENS
Serves 6 to 8 | gluten free

I've been making my husband, Derek's, favorite food in the world, posole rojo—a New Mexican red chile stew with hominy and, usually, pork—for years, and why I never thought to add peppery mustard greens until very recently I do not know. They really fill out the dish and make it a complete meal.

- **2 ounces (55 g) dried guajillo chiles (about 10 medium; see Note on page 129)**
- **1 tablespoon olive or vegetable oil**
- **2 pounds (910 g) boneless pork shoulder, well trimmed and cut into 1½-inch (4-cm) cubes**
- **Salt and freshly ground black pepper**
- **1 small onion, chopped**
- **1 clove garlic, chopped**
- **3 cups (720 g) cooked hominy (page 23) or 2 (15.5-ounce / 445-g) cans, drained and rinsed**
- **4 packed cups (170 g) chopped mustard greens**
- **Corn tortillas, warmed in a skillet**
- **Lime wedges, sliced radishes, sliced scallions, and/or fresh cilantro sprigs, to taste**

Preheat the oven to 300°F (150°C).

Wipe the chiles clean with a paper towel, then pull off their stems and shake out as many seeds as you can. Tear the chiles roughly into thirds and toast in a dry sauté pan over high heat, pressing down on them with a metal spatula or a smaller skillet and turning frequently, until blackened in spots. Place in a heatproof bowl and cover with boiling water. Set a plate on top of the chiles to keep them submerged. Let soak for about 15 minutes, then use a slotted spoon to transfer the chiles to a blender or food processor and puree until very smooth, adding up to 1 cup (240 ml) of the soaking liquid if necessary. If you want to be fancy, push the puree through a medium-mesh sieve with a rubber spatula and discard any bits of peel or seeds. Set the puree aside.

In a heatproof Dutch oven, heat the oil over medium-high heat. Season the pork with salt and pepper and add it to the Dutch oven in one layer (work in batches if necessary so you don't crowd the pot). Cook without disturbing the pork until it is nicely browned on the bottom and releases easily from the pan when you turn it with a metal spatula. Turn and cook until most of the sides are well browned, about 8 minutes. Add the onion and garlic and cook, stirring frequently, for 3 minutes. Add 3 cups (720 ml) water, the chile puree, and several pinches of salt, stir to scrape up the browned bits, and bring to a boil. Cover and transfer to the oven. Bake until the pork is very tender and can be easily pulled apart with a fork, about 2 hours.

Add the hominy and mustard greens and simmer on the stovetop until the stems of the greens are tender, about 15 minutes. Taste and add more salt if necessary. Serve with corn tortillas and whatever accompaniments sound good to you.

VARIATIONS
★ To make a green posole with chicken: Roast about 6 large poblano chiles under the broiler, turning to blacken all sides; remove the peels, stems, and seeds and dice the chiles. Substitute trimmed boneless, skinless chicken thighs for the pork; brown the onion and garlic in the pot first, then add the chicken, water, chiles, and ¼ to ½ teaspoon ground cayenne. Reduce the cooking time in the oven to 1 hour. Instead of mustard greens, use a milder green like spinach, kale, or young collards.

★ To make a tomatillo posole: Use the chicken variation above, but instead of the poblano chiles, broil 6 large husked and rinsed tomatillos, then puree them in a food processor or blender and add them to the pot with the chicken.

MILLET AND WHEAT BERRY DAL
WITH CAULIFLOWER AND YELLOW SPLIT PEAS

Serves 6 | vegetarian

- 1½ tablespoons ghee
- 1 onion, diced
- 2 teaspoons ginger–garlic paste (page 62) or 1 teaspoon each minced fresh ginger and garlic
- 1 teaspoon ground cumin
- 1 teaspoon ground coriander
- ¼ teaspoon ground cayenne, or more to taste
- ½ cup (100 g) raw millet, rinsed
- 1 cup (200 g) yellow split peas, rinsed
- ½ cup (90 g) raw wheat berries, rinsed
- ½ head cauliflower, cut into small florets
- 1½ teaspoons salt, or to taste
- ¼ cup (20 g) chopped fresh cilantro
- Juice of 1 lemon
- 1 teaspoon cumin seeds
- 1 teaspoon yellow mustard seeds

I've been tinkering with cauliflower dal for years, and this is my current favorite combination of grains and split peas. That said, feel free to use whatever grains you have on hand: You'll want at least one firm, chewy grain, like rye berries, spelt berries, or oat groats, and one filler grain like quinoa or amaranth to thicken the mixture. You can also omit the cauliflower and use diced parsnips or another hard vegetable instead.

This recipe features a technique common in Indian vegetarian cooking called tempering: Just before serving the dal, oil or ghee is heated in a separate small pan (traditionally a tiny cup-shaped pan with a long handle, but a small sauté pan does just as well), and spices are added and cooked until they sizzle and become fragrant. Then the hot spiced oil or ghee is drizzled into the dal, and the pot is quickly covered and left to stand for a moment so the aromas of the spices fully infuse the dal. If you don't have ghee, you could use Niter Qibe (spiced butter, page 66), plain clarified butter, or olive or vegetable oil.

In a Dutch oven over medium-high heat, melt ½ tablespoon of the ghee. Add the onion and cook, stirring frequently, until just softened, about 4 minutes. Add the ginger-garlic paste and cook for 2 minutes. Add the cumin, coriander, cayenne, and millet and cook, stirring frequently, until very fragrant, about 3 minutes. Add 6 cups (1.4 L) water, the split peas, wheat berries, and cauliflower. Increase the heat to high and bring to a boil, then lower the heat and simmer, stirring occasionally, until the split peas and wheat berries are tender and the cauliflower and millet are soft and falling apart, about 1 hour, adding the salt after 45 minutes. Stir in the cilantro and lemon juice.

In a small sauté pan over high heat, melt the remaining 1 tablespoon ghee. Add the cumin seeds and mustard seeds and cook, stirring, for 30 seconds. Scrape the mixture into the stew and immediately cover the pot. Let stand for 5 minutes, then stir, taste and season with more salt if necessary, and serve.

GINGERY SWEET POTATO AND MILLET STEW
WITH EDAMAME

Serves 6 | vegetarian

This certainly sounds like hippie food, but the curry spices and the heat of fresh ginger make it much more interesting and brighter than you might expect. The millet is tinted an appealing deep yellow by the turmeric, and the sweet potatoes and chartreuse edamame add hits of color and texture.

- **1 tablespoon olive oil**
- **1 sweet onion, diced**
- **Salt**
- **2 teaspoons minced fresh ginger**
- **1/2 teaspoon cumin seeds**
- **1/2 teaspoon turmeric**
- **1 cup (200 g) raw millet**
- **2 small sweet potatoes (about 1 pound / 455 g), peeled and diced**
- **Generous pinch of crushed red pepper**
- **1 cup (155 g) shelled edamame beans (frozen is fine)**
- **Juice of 1/2 lemon**

In a Dutch oven or large heavy saucepan, heat the oil over medium-high heat. Add the onion and a pinch of salt and cook, stirring occasionally, until soft and translucent, about 8 minutes. Add the ginger, cumin, turmeric, and millet and cook, stirring frequently, until the millet is fragrant, about 3 minutes. Add the sweet potatoes, crushed red pepper, 1 teaspoon salt, and 4 cups (960 ml) water. Bring to a boil, then lower the heat and simmer until the millet and sweet potatoes are tender, about 20 minutes. Smash a few of the sweet potato pieces against the side of the pan to thicken the broth. Add the edamame and lemon juice and cook to heat through. Season with more salt if necessary, then serve.

VARIATION

✱ Instead of the edamame, use 1 (14-ounce / 400-g) can chickpeas, drained and rinsed.

MILLET MAKI ROLLS WITH AVOCADO PUREE
Serves 4 | vegan, gluten free

Millet, toasted and then steamed until fluffy and a bit sticky, makes an excellent substitute for white sushi rice in these simple rolls. The millet's fresh tortilla–like fragrance is a nice match for the jicama and the avocado puree, especially if you spike the puree with smoky ground dried chipotles.

Fish-free maki rolls like these are perfect for packing into lunchboxes or taking on a picnic; remember to bring a little container of tamari for dipping. They'd be good with a vinegary jicama and cabbage slaw on the side.

- **1 cup (200 g) raw millet**
- **Pinch of salt**
- **1 teaspoon rice vinegar**
- **¹⁄₂ teaspoon sugar**
- **4 sheets nori**
- **¹⁄₂ cucumber, peeled, seeded, and julienned**
- **¹⁄₄ small jicama or 1 carrot, peeled and julienned**
- **¹⁄₄ cup (60 ml) avocado puree (below)**
- **Tamari**

Toast the millet in a dry heavy 1¹⁄₂- to 2-quart (1.4- to 2-L) saucepan over medium-high heat, stirring frequently, until fragrant, about 3 minutes. Add 2 cups (480 ml) water and the salt, bring to a boil, then cover and simmer until the liquid is absorbed, about 25 minutes. Let cool for a few minutes, then turn out into a large bowl. Add the vinegar and sugar and toss gently to combine.

Lay a sheet of nori on a work surface, shiny side down and with a long side closest to you. Spread one-quarter of the warm millet mixture over the nori in a layer about ¹⁄₄ inch (6 mm) thick, leaving 1 inch (2.5 cm) uncovered at the long side farthest from you. Arrange cucumber and jicama strips in a row near the end closest to you and dab them evenly with avocado puree. Lightly brush the uncovered 1 inch (2.5 cm) of nori with water. Beginning at the side closest to you, roll up the nori tightly and gently press the dampened nori to the outside of the roll to seal. Repeat with the remaining nori, millet, and filling to make three more rolls. Cut each roll crosswise into 6 pieces and serve with small bowls of tamari for dipping.

AVOCADO PUREE
Makes about 1 cup (240 ml) | vegan, gluten free

If you don't have a mini food processor, just mash all the ingredients together as well as you can with a pestle or fork. Use leftover avocado puree in place of mayonnaise on sandwiches or dollop it onto salads, or serve as a dip for raw vegetables.

- **2 ripe Hass avocados**
- **Juice of 1 lemon**
- **¹⁄₂ teaspoon agave nectar**
- **Salt**
- **¹⁄₄ teaspoon ground chipotle (optional)**
- **2 tablespoons extra-virgin olive oil**

Halve the avocados and remove the pits. Scrape the flesh into a mini food processor and add the lemon juice, agave nectar, ¹⁄₂ teaspoon salt, and the chipotle powder (if using). Process until very smooth, scraping down the side of the bowl occasionally. Through the hole in the lid, add the oil in a thin stream, continuing to process. Drizzle in a little water if necessary to yield a mayonnaise-like consistency. Taste and add more salt if necessary. The avocado puree will keep, covered with plastic wrap pressed onto the surface, in the refrigerator for several days.

PINHEAD OAT–CRUSTED CATFISH,
ROASTED CAULIFLOWER AND MUSTARD GREENS, AND LEMON CREAM

Serves 4 | gluten free*

Pinhead oats, which are similar to steel-cut oats but contain some oats that are ground finer, like flour, make a foolproof crunchy-crisp gluten-free crust for pan-fried fish. You can exchange the catfish for just about any common white fish here—use a lower heat level under the pan and a longer cooking times for thicker fillets. Some good options include U.S. farmed tilapia, ocean perch, Pacific halibut, and line-caught Atlantic cod. Wild salmon would also be delicious—just be sure to avoid overcooking it.

- **2 packed cups (85 g) chopped mustard greens**
- **3 tablespoons plus 1 teaspoon olive oil**
- **Salt and freshly ground black pepper**
- **1/2 head cauliflower**
- **4 cloves garlic, peeled**
- **2 tablespoons unsalted butter**
- **1 large shallot, minced**
- **1/2 cup (120 ml) white wine**
- **1 cup (240 ml) heavy cream**
- **Finely grated zest of 1/2 lemon**
- **1 tablespoon freshly squeezed lemon juice**
- **1/2 cup (90 g) raw pinhead (Scottish) oats**
- **4 (6-ounce / 170-g) pieces catfish fillet**

Preheat the oven to 400°F (205°C).

In a large bowl, toss the mustard greens with 1 teaspoon of the oil and season with salt and pepper. Set aside.

Trim the cauliflower and break it into florets. Put the cauliflower and garlic in a 9-by-13-inch (23-by-33-cm) baking dish, drizzle with 1 tablespoon of the oil, and sprinkle with salt and pepper to taste. Toss to coat with the oil. Roast until the cauliflower is very tender and golden brown, about 40 minutes.

Meanwhile, in a small saucepan, heat 1 tablespoon of the butter over medium-high heat. Add the shallot and a pinch of salt and cook, stirring occasionally, until just starting to brown, about 5 minutes. Add the wine and cook until reduced by about half, then add the cream and lemon zest. Simmer over medium heat until reduced and thickened, about 6 minutes, then whisk in the lemon juice. Remove from the heat. Season with salt to taste and set aside, covered to keep warm.

Add the greens to the cauliflower and toss with a metal spatula. Sprinkle with a little water and roast until the greens are wilted and tender and beginning to crisp, 5 to 7 minutes.

In an extra-large sauté pan (or two large ones), heat the remaining 1 tablespoon butter and 2 tablespoons oil over medium-high heat. Spread the oats on a plate. Season the fish with salt and pepper and lay each fillet on the oats, pressing gently so the oats adhere to one side. Put the fish in the pan (or pans), oat side down, and cook without disturbing until the oats are nicely browned and the opaqueness has moved about a third of the way through the thickest part of the fish, about 4 minutes depending on the thickness of the fillets. Use a metal spatula to carefully turn the fish over and cook until just opaque throughout, about 4 minutes. Pile the cauliflower, garlic, and greens on 4 serving plates, top with the fish, and spoon some of the sauce over everything. Serve immediately.

---

* See page 25.

SPICED PAN-SEARED WILD SALMON
WITH QUINOA AND ORANGE REDUCTION
Serves 4 | gluten free

Look for wild king salmon in the summer months, when it's in season; sometimes you can find it at a better price than farmed salmon—which is much less flavorful and environmentally unsound—though even then, I still consider the wild salmon a luxury. Its preparation is best kept simple. While my husband and daughter would happily eat a side of salmon (each) with nothing more than salt and a drizzle of olive oil, I like it with a light coating of spices, which crisp up beautifully in a heavy stainless-steel pan and keep the fish from sticking. The quinoa (also simply done with just a little butter and cilantro) and salmon would be excellent with a little pile of steamed and minted sugar-snap peas alongside, or some garlicky sautéed green beans or flash-cooked spinach.

- **1 teaspoon ground coriander**
- **1 teaspoon ground cumin**
- **1/2 teaspoon ground cinnamon**
- **1/2 teaspoon freshly ground black pepper**
- **Finely grated zest of 1 orange**
- **4 (4- to 6-ounce / 115- to 170-g) pieces wild king salmon fillet (3/4 to 1 inch / 2 to 2.5 cm thick in the center)**
- **Salt**
- **2 tablespoons cold unsalted butter**
- **1 small shallot, minced**
- **3/4 cup (180 ml) freshly squeezed orange juice (from about 2 1/2 Valencia oranges)**
- **1 teaspoon balsamic vinegar**
- **3/4 teaspoon sugar**
- **1 cup (170 g) raw ivory quinoa, well rinsed**
- **2 tablespoons olive oil**
- **1/4 cup (20 g) torn fresh cilantro leaves**

In a cup, combine the coriander, cumin, cinnamon, pepper, and orange zest. Remove any pin bones from the fish, then sprinkle with salt and rub about 1 teaspoon of the spice mixture all over the flesh side. Cover and set aside at room temperature while you make the sauce and quinoa.

In a small heavy saucepan, melt 1/2 tablespoon of the butter over medium heat. Add the shallot and a pinch of salt and cook, stirring frequently, until the shallot is soft and nicely browned, about 4 minutes. Add the orange juice, vinegar, sugar, and 1/2 teaspoon of the spice mixture. Simmer briskly until the sauce is reduced and slightly thickened, about 8 minutes, then stir in 1/2 tablespoon of the butter. Season with salt and pepper to taste and set aside.

In a heavy 2-quart (2-L) saucepan, combine the quinoa, 1 1/2 cups (360 ml) water, 1/4 teaspoon salt, and the remaining 1 tablespoon of butter and bring to a boil, then lower the heat, cover, and cook until the quinoa is tender and the water is absorbed, about 15 minutes. Fluff with a rubber spatula, cover, and set aside while you cook the fish.

In a large heavy sauté pan, heat the oil over medium-high heat. Add the fish, flesh side down, and cook without disturbing for 2 to 3 minutes, until the bottom is crusty. Use a thin metal spatula to turn the fish over and cook on the skin side until the fish is cooked to your liking—ideally it should be still a little translucent in the center—2 to 3 more minutes, depending on the thickness of the fillets. Meanwhile, gently reheat the sauce. Pile the quinoa on serving plates and scatter the cilantro over it. Put a piece of fish on each plate and drizzle the sauce over everything. Serve immediately.

VARIATION

★ If you like, begin the sauce by searing a few thin slices of spice- and salt-dusted orange in a little butter in a hot pan until caramelized on both sides, then add more butter and the shallot and proceed as above, simmering until the orange slices are tender; serve the slices with the fish and quinoa.

PAN-FRIED TOFU
WITH QUINOA, ALMONDS, AND RED CHILES

Serves 2 | vegan, gluten free

A simple, quick way to use leftover quinoa, this can be made in the morning, cooled, and packed into a bento box for lunch—it would be especially appealing with some sliced oranges nestled alongside.

- **7 ounces (200 g) extra-firm tofu**
- **2 tablespoons vegetable oil**
- **2 teaspoons minced fresh ginger**
- **1 clove garlic, minced**
- **2 large scallions, thinly sliced, green and white kept separate**
- **¼ cup (30 g) sliced almonds**
- **3 dried red chiles, stemmed, broken in half, seeds shaken out**
- **1½ cups (275 g) cooked black or red quinoa (page 27)**
- **1 tablespoon tamari**
- **Chile paste (sambal oelek) for serving (optional)**

Drain the tofu, cut it into ¼-inch-thick (6-mm-thick) slabs, and arrange in one layer on a double layer of paper towels. Put another paper towel over the top and press with your palms until the paper towels are soaked. Uncover the tofu and cut the slabs into ½-inch (12-mm) squares. Set aside.

In a large sauté pan, heat the oil over medium-high heat until it shimmers. Add the tofu in a single layer and cook, turning occasionally with a metal spatula, until both flat sides are well browned, about 8 minutes total. Add the ginger, garlic, scallion whites, almonds, and chiles and cook, turning with the spatula, until the ginger and garlic are tender, about 3 minutes. Add the scallion greens, quinoa, and tamari and cook, turning with the spatula, until heated through, about 1 minute. Serve with chile paste on the side, if desired.

ROASTED BUTTERNUT SQUASH
WITH QUINOA AND SAUSAGE

Serves 4 | gluten free*

This simple dish is the one that made me fall hard in love with quinoa, and if you've never cooked with the supergrain before, I'd suggest starting here. The way the quinoa absorbs the rich flavor of the sausage (and you don't have to use much of the latter) and sticks to the tender chunks of sweet butternut squash is just irresistible.

- **1 small butternut squash (about 1½ pounds / 680 g)**
- **2 shallots**
- **2 tablespoons olive oil**
- **Salt and freshly ground black pepper**
- **8 ounces (225 g) mild Italian sausage (3 small links), casings removed (see Note)**
- **2 sprigs fresh sage, chopped**
- **1 cup (170 g) raw ivory quinoa, rinsed well**

Preheat the oven to 400°F (205°C).

Peel the squash and cut it into 1- to 1½-inch (2.5- to 4-cm) chunks, scraping out the seeds. Put in a baking pan or dish in one layer. Peel and quarter the shallots, leaving the root ends intact, and add them to the squash. Drizzle the vegetables with 1 tablespoon of the oil and season with salt and pepper; toss to coat. Roast until tender and lightly browned, turning the vegetables over once during roasting if you have a chance, 30 to 40 minutes.

Meanwhile, in a heavy 2-quart (2-L) saucepan over medium-high heat, heat the remaining 1 tablespoon of oil and add the sausage. Cook, breaking the sausage up into small pieces with a spatula, until the sausage is cooked through and nicely browned, about 15 minutes. Drain off any excess fat, if necessary. Return to high heat and add the sage, ½ teaspoon salt, and 1½ cups (360 ml) water, stirring to scrape up any browned bits. Add the quinoa. Cover, bring to a boil, then lower the heat and simmer until the quinoa is tender and the water is absorbed, about 15 minutes.

Transfer the quinoa mixture to the baking pan with the roasted squash and shallots and gently fold to combine. Taste and add more salt and pepper if necessary. Serve hot.

* If gluten is an issue, be sure to check the ingredients of the sausage, or make your own (page 60; omit the sage and maple syrup, and add a good pinch of fennel seeds).

MOM'S QUINOA MEAT PIE
WITH OLIVE OIL CRUST
Serves 6 to 8

My mom is the queen of meat pies. When we lived in Montana, she learned to make perfect Butte-style pasties (which is Butte's only culinary claim to fame, unless you count the pork chop sandwich). When we lived in Virginia, she made hand-held meat turnovers and full-size pies filled with shredded venison shoulder and whatever random vegetables she happened to have (my dad always wanted a boat of gravy to pour over his). This is her latest addition to the genre, with quinoa—dark or ivory will work equally well—instead of the more typical white potatoes and enriched with soft sweet potatoes and lots of still-slightly-crisp celery.

FOR THE CRUST
- 2¾ cups (385 g) white whole wheat flour
- ¾ teaspoon salt
- ⅔ cup (160 ml) olive oil, frozen until soft-solid and opaque
- 1 tablespoon cider vinegar
- 4 to 6 tablespoons (60 to 90 ml) ice water

FOR THE FILLING
- 1 tablespoon olive oil
- 1 onion, diced
- 1 medium sweet potato, peeled and finely diced
- Salt
- 2 ribs celery, diced
- 1 teaspoon minced fresh rosemary, winter savory, or marjoram
- ½ teaspoon celery seeds
- ½ teaspoon freshly ground black pepper
- 1 pound (455 g) lean ground beef
- ½ cup (120 ml) beer or water
- 1½ cups (275 g) cooked quinoa (page 27)
- 4 ounces (115 g) fresh mozzarella cheese, shredded (about ¾ cup)

TO ASSEMBLE
- 1 large egg, beaten

MAKE THE CRUST
In a large bowl, combine the flour and salt. Dump in the oil and mix quickly with your fingertips or a pastry cutter until the largest bits of oil are about the size of small peas. Make a well in the center and add the vinegar and 4 tablespoons ice water. Using a rubber spatula, quickly toss together, adding more water if necessary, until the dough holds together when squeezed gently. Briefly knead in the bowl, then divide the dough in half and wrap each in plastic wrap, shaping each piece of dough into a smooth disk. Put in the refrigerator while you make the filling.

MAKE THE FILLING
In a large deep sauté pan, heat the oil over medium-high heat. Add the onion and sweet potato and a pinch of salt and cook, stirring frequently, until the onion is translucent, about 5 minutes. Add the celery, rosemary, celery seeds, and pepper and cook, stirring occasionally, until the sweet potato is just tender, about 5 minutes. Scoot the vegetables to the outside of the pan and add the beef to the center. Cook, stirring frequently, until the beef is no longer pink and is starting to brown. Stir in the beer and bring to a boil. Fold in the quinoa and cook to just heat through. Season with salt to taste. Transfer to a large bowl and let cool for a few minutes, then fold in the cheese. Set aside.

ASSEMBLE THE PIE
Preheat the oven to 400°F (205°C).

Between two sheets of freezer paper, waxed paper, or plastic wrap, roll out one disk of dough to ⅛ inch (3 mm) thick and about 12 inches (30.5 cm) round; fit it into the bottom and up the sides of a 9- to 10-inch (23- to 25-cm) glass pie plate, repairing any tears as necessary. Pile in the filling and spread it evenly in the crust. Roll out the second disk of dough and lay it over the filling; seal the edges of the bottom and top crusts (it's okay if there are a few small gaps—the filling isn't too juicy and won't leak out). Make a few slits in the top to allow steam to escape, then brush the top and sealed rim with the egg. Bake in the center of the oven until nicely browned on top and bottom, 50 to 60 minutes. Cut into wedges and serve hot.

BLACK QUINOA
WITH CHICKEN CONFIT, MUSHROOMS, AND QUICK-PICKLED ONION
Serves 4 | gluten free

This dish has several elements, but all of it can be prepared well in advance and kept in the refrigerator; putting it all together to serve at a dinner party is a simple matter. The confit, covered in its own fat, can be refrigerated for at least a couple weeks; you won't use all of it here, but it's great to have the leftovers on hand—crisp some up in a skillet and toss with pasta or put it on a sandwich with a grind of black pepper and a slather of good mayonnaise and a few left-over pickled onions. If you'd prefer not to make the confit yourself, you can purchase prepared duck confit at specialty grocery stores. You can cook the quinoa up to three days in advance, and the pickled onion, of course, can be kept in the fridge for weeks.

FOR THE CONFIT
- **4 chicken leg quarters (about 4 pounds / 2 kg)**
- **1 teaspoon salt**
- **1/2 teaspoon freshly ground black pepper**
- **4 sprigs fresh thyme**
- **4 sprigs fresh parsley**
- **1 1/2 cups (360 ml) olive or vegetable oil, or a combination**

FOR THE PICKLED ONION
- **3/4 cup (180 ml) cider vinegar**
- **1/2 teaspoon salt**
- **Pinch of sugar**
- **A few black peppercorns, coarsely crushed**
- **A few allspice berries, coarsely crushed**
- **1 bay leaf**
- **1 medium red onion, sliced 1/4 inch (6 mm) thick**

TO SERVE
- **1 navel orange**
- **8 ounces (225 g) mushrooms, sliced**
- **1 teaspoon fresh thyme leaves**
- **Salt**
- **1 1/2 cups (275 g) cooked black quinoa (page 27)**
- **Freshly ground black pepper**

MAKE THE CONFIT
Preheat the oven to 250°F (120°C). Or, better, ready a 6- to 8-quart (5.7- to 7.5-L) slow cooker.

Season the chicken all over with the salt and pepper. Nestle the chicken in a 9-by-13-inch (23-by-33-cm) baking dish or in the slow cooker (you'll have to stack them, if using a cooker, which is fine) and tuck the herb sprigs around the chicken pieces. Pour the oil over the chicken; if you have any chicken fat saved in the freezer, rendered or unrendered, go ahead and add it to the baking dish; the fat should almost cover the chicken. Cover with foil and bake for at least 10 hours, or, if using a slow cooker, cover and cook on the low setting for 8 to 10 hours. The chicken should be nearly covered with oil and fat and is extremely tender; you should be able to pull a leg bone out cleanly with no effort. Uncover and set aside until the chicken is cool enough to handle, then pick all of the meat off the bones, discarding the bones, skin, and cartilage but reserving all of the liquid fat. If not using right away, pack the meat in one or two containers and strain in the oil and fat to cover the meat completely. Let cool, then cover and refrigerate until ready to use, up to 2 weeks.

MAKE THE PICKLED ONION

In a glass measuring cup, combine the vinegar, ½ cup (120 ml) water, and the salt, sugar, pepper, allspice, and bay leaf. Bring a saucepan of water to a boil, add the onion, and blanch for 30 seconds. Drain and put in a clean glass jar or other non-reactive container. Pour the vinegar mixture over the onion to cover. Cover the container and refrigerate until very cold and brilliant pink, at least 1 hour and up to several weeks.

ASSEMBLE THE DISH

Finely grate ½ teaspoon of zest from the orange and set aside. Cut the peel off the orange and cut the segments from the membranes, working over a bowl to catch the segments and juice; squeeze the juice from the empty membranes into the bowl with the orange segments. Set the juice and segments aside.

In a large sauté pan, heat 1 tablespoon of the oil from the confit over medium-high heat. Add the mushrooms, thyme, and a pinch of salt and cook, stirring occasionally, until the mushrooms have released their liquid, the liquid has evaporated, and the mushrooms are nicely browned, 8 to

10 minutes. Meanwhile, fish about 2 cups of the chicken confit from the surrounding fat, scraping off as much excess fat as you can (alternatively, gently warm the confit and use a slotted spoon to remove the meat from the fat). Add the confit to the mushrooms, then add the quinoa and orange zest; cook, stirring and turning with a metal spatula, until heated through, about 3 minutes. Drizzle in 3 tablespoons of the orange juice and season with salt and pepper to taste.

Mound the quinoa mixture on a serving plate. Top each serving with some of the cold pickled onion and scatter pieces of the orange segments and drops of the remaining orange juice around the quinoa. Serve.

BROWN RICE KAYU
(JAPANESE PORRIDGE) WITH GREENS

Serves 4 | vegan, gluten free

In Japan, kayu—nothing more than a porridge of overcooked rice with simple garnishes—is commonly served to the sick, the old, and the very young, much as chicken soup is in this country. Like chicken soup, kayu is a comforting, warming bowl of goodness anytime you crave a meal that doesn't make you think too hard. Usually made with white rice, like Chinese congee, it's just as good (no, better) with heartier brown rice, and I've seen several recipes that supplement the rice with a handful of adzuki beans for a more substantial dish.

A wild-herb-specked version of kayu, the inspiration for this recipe, is served for the Japanese Festival of Seven Herbs, or Nanakusa-no-sekku, celebrated on January 7. The first herbs of the year were traditionally believed to be the most nutritious—and indeed, in midwinter any greens would certainly have been welcome in the diet—but now the austere dish is eaten less as a tribute to the herbs and more as a culinary respite from the indulgences of New Year celebrations. Included among the seven wild herbs are turnip and daikon tops—try those with some wild dandelion greens if you can find them, or arugula, watercress, water spinach, winter parsley, or whatever you have on hand. Gomashio—salted sesame seeds, sometimes with seaweed for an extra nutritive boost—is the main seasoning here. Salty, tangy preserved umeboshi plums, which are available in jars at Asian grocery stores, are another common garnish.

- **1 cup (190 g) raw short-grain brown rice, rinsed**
- **2 cups (85 g) roughly chopped tender greens**
- **4 umeboshi plums (optional)**
- **About 4 teaspoons Gomashio (page 248)**

Put the rice and 4 cups (960 ml) water in a heavy 3- to 4-quart (2.8- to 3.8-L) saucepan. Bring to a boil, then put the lid on slightly askew, lower the heat, and simmer, stirring occasionally, until the rice is very soft and falling apart, about 1 hour. The mixture should have a loose porridgelike consistency. Stir in the greens and cook until just wilted and heated through. Spoon into small bowls, top each with an umeboshi plum, if using, sprinkle with gomashio, and serve.

FRIED BROWN RICE
WITH GREEN BEANS AND BALSAMIC VINEGAR
Serves 2 or 3 | vegetarian

I've read so many otherwise reasonable food writers on the unsuitability of brown rice for fried rice that I had to include a recipe for some here. It works perfectly, especially if you used the steaming method to cook the rice to prevent mushiness, and it has so much more character than fried white rice that I can't understand what these people are expecting. (Perhaps *less* character?) Feel free to use whatever vegetables you happen to have available (or cooked meat, if you like). Fried rice is best made with leftovers, of course, and is endlessly adaptable.

- 2 tablespoons soy sauce, preferably light (not "lite") Chinese
- 1 tablespoon balsamic vinegar
- 2 teaspoons chile paste (sambal oelek), plus more for serving
- 2 large eggs
- 3 tablespoons vegetable oil
- 1½ cups (150 g) diced green beans
- 1 large carrot, diced
- ½ cup (50 g) chopped scallions (about 3)
- 1 clove garlic, minced
- 1 inch (2.5 cm) fresh ginger, peeled and minced
- Pinch of salt
- 3 cups (585 g) cooked long-grain brown rice (pages 29–30), cooled and refrigerated for at least 4 hours or overnight
- 1 tablespoon chopped fresh cilantro

In a small cup, stir together the soy sauce, vinegar, and chile paste; set aside. In a small bowl, beat the eggs together with 1 teaspoon water.

In a large deep sauté pan or wok, heat 2 tablespoons of the oil over high heat. When it shimmers, add the egg mixture; it should start to cook immediately. After about 10 seconds, begin to stir it gently, cooking just until it's barely firm, about 30 seconds total. Remove to a plate and set aside. Return the pan to high heat and add about ½ tablespoon of the oil. Add the green beans, carrot, scallions, garlic, ginger, and salt. Cook, stirring constantly, until the vegetables are just tender, about 4 minutes. Drizzle in the remaining ½ tablespoon of oil, then add the rice and cook, turning with a metal spatula, to heat through, about 1 minute. Drizzle in the soy sauce mixture, turn to coat the rice, then add the cooked egg and the cilantro and turn with the spatula until heated through, about 1 minute. Serve with more chile paste on the side.

1,001 LENTILS AND BROWN BASMATI RICE
WITH CUCUMBER-TOMATO SALAD

Serves 6 | vegetarian, gluten free

Years ago, before Derek and I were even a couple, we impulsively left New York and moved to an apartment in a powder-blue mansion in Old Louisville, Kentucky, in the middle of the largest concentration of Victorian houses in the country. My parents, my brother, and my grandmother came to visit that summer (probably in no small part to get the measure of this fellow I'd gone off to Kentucky with all of a sudden), and we had lunch at a '90s-funky semi-vegetarian café on Bardstown Road. I remember nothing of that meal except the dish evocatively titled "A Thousand and One Lentils," a classic Middle Eastern dish also known as mujaddara: lentils and basmati rice spiced simply with cinnamon and cumin and topped with sweet caramelized onions. I'm thankful that my mom had the foresight to take notes. What follows is her rendition, made many times since the Kentucky days, and it may well be the most comforting, satisfying meal in this book. If you don't want to serve the dish with yogurt, serve a tongue-tying meal of mujaddara with muhamarra (page 254) thinned a bit with water or vegetable stock.

Be sure to let the onions soften and caramelize very slowly—don't rush it. They become sweet and silky, and that's important to this dish. You can make the salad up to four hours in advance (cover and refrigerate), and you can use precooked rice and lentils if you wish: Just add a splash of water to the pan when you add the rice and lentils to the celery, then stir, cover, and let everything steam and heat through for a couple minutes.

FOR THE SALAD

- **3 medium tomatoes, cut into chunks**
- **1 regular cucumber, seeded and chopped, or ½ English cucumber, chopped**
- **¼ cup (20 g) chopped fresh cilantro**
- **1 tablespoon olive oil**
- **3 tablespoons freshly squeezed lime juice**
- **½ teaspoon salt**
- **Freshly ground black pepper to taste**

FOR THE RICE AND LENTILS

- **1 cup (190 g) raw brown basmati rice**
- **Salt**
- **1 cup (190 g) brown or green lentils, rinsed and picked over**
- **2 teaspoons cumin seeds**
- **1 tablespoon unsalted butter**
- **2 medium onions, sliced (about 1 pound / 455 g)**
- **3 tablespoons olive oil**
- **1 cup (100 g) thinly sliced celery**
- **1½ teaspoons ground cinnamon**
- **2 cups (480 ml) plain yogurt**

MAKE THE SALAD

In a large bowl, toss all the ingredients together. Set aside.

MAKE THE RICE AND LENTILS

Rinse the rice in at least three changes of water, until the water is clear; drain well and put in a heavy 2-quart (2-L) saucepan with 1½ cups (360 ml) water. Let soak for 30 minutes. Bring to a boil over high heat. Add ½ teaspoon salt, stir once, then cover and lower the heat to very low; cook until all the water is absorbed and the rice is tender, without stirring, about 15 minutes. Remove from the heat and let rest, covered, for 5 minutes. Fluff gently with a heatproof spatula and set aside.

Put the lentils in a heavy 2-quart (2-L) saucepan and add water to cover by 2 inches (5 cm). Bring to a boil, then lower the heat and simmer until tender, 25 to 30 minutes. Drain in a sieve and set aside.

Heat a small sauté pan over medium-high heat and add the cumin. Toast, stirring, until fragrant and a shade darker, about 3 minutes. Transfer to a mortar and lightly crush with a pestle.

In a large heavy sauté pan, melt the butter over medium heat. Add the onions and a pinch of salt and cook, stirring occasionally, until very soft and golden, lowering the heat and adding a splash of water if necessary to keep them from browning too quickly, about 30 minutes. Scrape into a bowl and set aside.

In the same sauté pan, heat 1 tablespoon of the oil over medium-high heat, then add the celery and cook until just starting to become tender, about 3 minutes. Add the remaining 2 tablespoons of oil, the rice, lentils, cumin, cinnamon, and salt to taste. Turn with a metal spatula to combine and just heat through, about 2 minutes. Transfer to a serving platter and pile the onions on top. Serve with the salad and lots of yogurt for generous dolloping.

BROWN RICE RISOTTO WITH SHRIMP, FENNEL, AND AMARO

Serves 3 or 4 | gluten free

Amaro is a not-too-sweet liqueur in the bitters category. Its character varies significantly from producer to producer, but it's always deeply herbal, almost medicinal (in a good way!), making it a natural with fennel: It brings out the licorice scent and flavor of the bulb. If you don't happen to have a bottle of amaro hanging around, a dash of bitters (such as Angostura), Campari, or dry or sweet vermouth would work well as a substitute.

- 12 ounces (340 g) large shrimp with peels
- 5 to 6 cups (1.2 to 1.4 L) vegetable stock or water
- 1/2 teaspoon whole black peppercorns
- 1 fennel bulb
- 1 tablespoon olive oil
- 1 sweet onion
- Salt
- 1 cup (190 g) raw short-grain brown rice
- 1/2 cup (120 ml) white wine
- Freshly ground black pepper
- 1 tablespoon unsalted butter
- 1 tablespoon amaro

Peel and devein the shrimp and put the shells in a large saucepan with the stock and peppercorns; set the shrimp aside in the refrigerator. Bring the stock to a boil, then lower the heat and simmer gently.

Cut the stalks off the fennel bulb. Wash and roughly chop a handful of the stalks and fronds and add them to the simmering stock; reserve a few fronds and chop about 1 tablespoon for garnish. Cut the bulb into quarters lengthwise, cut out and thinly slice the core, then cut the bulb into 1/4-inch-thick (6-mm-thick) slices lengthwise.

In a large deep sauté pan, heat the oil over medium heat. Add the sliced fennel, onion, and a pinch of salt and cook, stirring occasionally, until soft and golden brown, about 10 minutes. Add the rice and stir to coat with the oil. Add the wine and cook, stirring frequently, until it is almost all evaporated and absorbed, about 3 minutes. Hold a fine-mesh sieve over

the pan and ladle in about half of the simmering stock, to just cover the rice and vegetables (return any solids to the saucepan of stock). Add salt and pepper to taste, cover the sauté pan, and simmer, stirring occasionally and adding more simmering stock if needed to keep the rice just covered, for 30 minutes.

Uncover the pan and add stock to cover if necessary. Cook uncovered, stirring more frequently now, until the rice is tender and most of the liquid has evaporated and what remains is more opaque and slightly thickened, 10 to 15 minutes. Stir in the butter until it melts. Gently fold in the shrimp and cook, stirring, until the shrimp are pink and opaque throughout, about 5 minutes, adding a little more stock if necessary. Sprinkle in the amaro and reserved chopped fennel fronds and serve hot.

SHRIMP AND CHORIZO WITH BLACK RICE
Serves 4 | gluten free

Seafood with crumbles of bright orange fresh chorizo clinging to it is a classic combination all over Latin America. Here the simple sauce is made with grated fresh tomatoes (you can also use canned) and plenty of garlic and parsley, and kept thin enough that it will seep down into the bed of risotto-like black rice beneath. Black rice needs to be soaked for at least 4 hours before cooking, so plan ahead.

- **1 cup (190 g) raw black rice**
- **1½ cups (360 ml) chicken stock or water**
- **Salt (if needed)**
- **4 ounces (115 g) fresh chorizo (Mexican style; see Note), plastic casing removed**
- **1 onion, diced**
- **2 cloves garlic, minced**
- **1 pound (455 g) large shrimp, peeled and deveined**
- **2 juicy ripe tomatoes, grated (about 1 pound / 455 g) or 1¼ cups (225 g) crushed tomatoes plus ¼ cup (60 ml) water**
- **¼ cup (20 g) chopped fresh parsley**
- **Juice of ½ lemon**

Put the rice in a sieve and rinse it well under cold running water. Put in a heavy 2-quart (2-L) saucepan and add cold water to cover by at least 1 inch (2.5 cm). Let soak for 4 hours. If using "Forbidden rice," there's no need to soak.

Drain and return the rice to the saucepan. Add the stock (or use the water and about ¼ teaspoon salt). Bring to a boil, then lower the heat, cover, and simmer until tender and most of the liquid has been absorbed, about 40 minutes. Turn a few times with a spatula (it will not really be fluffy, but rather a bit risotto-like); cover and set aside off the heat for 5 minutes.

In a large heavy sauté pan over medium heat, cook the chorizo, breaking up the meat with a heatproof spatula, until beginning to brown, about 4 minutes. Add the onion and garlic and cook, stirring frequently, until the onion is translucent, about 5 minutes. Add the shrimp, tomatoes, and half of the parsley. Bring to a simmer and cook until the shrimp are pink and opaque throughout, 6 to 8 minutes. Stir in the

lemon juice. Taste and add salt if necessary (you probably won't need any).

Scoop the rice into shallow serving dishes and spoon the shrimp and sauce over it. Sprinkle with the remaining parsley and serve.

VARIATIONS
★ Instead of shrimp, use 1 pound (455 g) cleaned squid (bodies sliced into rings, tentacles cut into manageable pieces), 1 pound white fish fillets (cut into 1-inch / 2.5-cm chunks), 2 pounds (910 g) scrubbed mussels or littleneck clams, or a combination of seafood.
★ Instead of the shrimp, use 6 well-trimmed boneless, skinless chicken thighs. Cut them each into 3 or 4 chunks and add them with the onion.

NOTE: Fresh chorizo can be found in most regular supermarkets. If your grocery store has a refrigerated section in the "international" foods aisle, it'll be there; otherwise check the meat cases, where chorizo is usually next to the Mexican cheeses. (Why they put Mexican cheeses in the meat case instead of with the other cheeses I do not profess to know.)

SOFRITO-BAKED BROWN RICE WITH CLAMS, MUSSELS, AND SHRIMP

Serves 4 | gluten free

Sofrito is a thick, intense mixture of aromatics and, usually, tomato that serves as the flavor base for countless rice and bean dishes throughout the Mediterranean and Latin America. For this one-dish, one-skillet meal, you cook and stir the onion, garlic, tomato, and paprika until it becomes pasty and a shade darker, then stir in stock and brown rice. You can cook it all the way on the stovetop, or stick the skillet in the oven to bake while you wipe down your cutting board and knife, open a bottle of wine, maybe read a magazine article or corral the kids. To finish the dish, put the skillet back on the stovetop, top the rice with the seafood—in a few minutes the shellfish will steam open and the rice at the bottom of the skillet will crisp up, and dinner will be ready to eat.

- 1 cup (190 g) raw short-grain brown rice
- 2 cups (480 ml) chicken stock or water
- Pinch of saffron threads (optional)
- 1 tablespoon olive oil
- 1 large onion, diced
- 2 cloves garlic, minced
- Salt
- 1 large tomato
- 1 teaspoon Hungarian or smoked Spanish paprika
- 1 pound (455 g) small clams, such as littlenecks, scrubbed
- 1 pound (455 g) mussels, scrubbed
- 8 ounces (225 g) large shrimp (if the tracts are clean you can leave the shells on; peel and devein if not)
- Chopped fresh flat-leaf parsley
- Lemon wedges

Preheat the oven to 375°F (190°C).

Put the rice in a bowl and rinse well with water; drain. In a glass measuring cup, combine the stock and saffron, if using.

In a deep 10-inch (25-cm) ovenproof skillet or flameproof casserole or Dutch oven with a lid, heat the oil over medium heat. Add the onion and garlic and a pinch of salt. Cook, stirring occasionally, until the onion is translucent, about 10 minutes. Cut the tomato in half horizontally and grate the flesh into the skillet, discarding the skins left behind. Add the paprika, season generously with salt, increase the heat to medium-high, and cook, stirring frequently, until the mixture is thick and jamlike, 8 to 10 minutes. Stir in the stock mixture and rice. Bring to a boil, then cover and transfer to the oven. Bake until most of the liquid is absorbed and the rice is tender, 40 to 50 minutes; do not stir.

Arrange the clams, mussels, and shrimp over the rice mixture. Cover the skillet and return to the stovetop over medium-high heat until the clams and mussels have steamed open and the shrimp are pink and opaque throughout and you can hear the rice toasting on the bottom of the skillet, 5 to 8 minutes. Discard any clams or mussels that do not open after the others have. Sprinkle with plenty of parsley and scatter lemon wedges over the top. Serve straight from the skillet, but remember to cover the handle with a potholder because it'll be *hot*. Set out a large bowl for shells.

VARIATION

★ Make this with chicken: Omit the shellfish. Reduce the stock to 1 cup (240 ml). Just before you put the rice in the oven, season 6 to 8 well-trimmed boneless, skinless chicken thighs with salt and pepper and nestle them in the liquid.

BROWN RICE STUFFED CABBAGE
Serves 6 to 8 | gluten free

This is based on one of my mom's old recipes. She is even more of a tinkerer than I am, and doesn't stop changing how she cooks a dish even after she's hit on the very best way to do it. One thing she doesn't leave out of this no matter what other adjustments she makes according to whim or availability, is the chopped lemon, which becomes tender little bits of intense flavor in the slightly sweet, tart tomato sauce. That said, I sometimes make it with just lemon juice and sweet spices to make an especially deep, cold-weather sauce (see the variation below).

I like to bake the stuffed cabbage, but that's mostly because this is the kind of dish that's meant for cool, dark winter evenings and turning on the oven cozies up the house and stowing a Dutch oven full of supper lets you get right back under the afghan on the couch for a while; that said, it's just as good simmered on the stovetop if your oven's occupied in some way.

- **1 medium head green cabbage**
- **1 tablespoon olive oil**
- **1 onion, diced**
- **Salt**
- **1 (28-ounce / 800-g) can crushed tomatoes**
- **1/2 lemon, seeded and chopped**
- **2 tablespoons brown sugar or 1 tablespoon honey or agave nectar**
- **1/2 teaspoon freshly ground black pepper**
- **1/2 cup (80 g) raisins**
- **3 cups (585 g) cooked brown rice (pages 29–30), cooled**
- **1 large egg**
- **1 pound (455 g) ground turkey**

Cut the core from the bottom of the head of cabbage. Put the cabbage, cored side down, in a deep pot and pour in 1 inch (2.5 cm) water. Cover, bring to a boil, and cook for 5 minutes. Drain, then fill the pot with cold water to cool the cabbage. Carefully pull off 8 whole large leaves, cut out and discard the thick bottom portion of the center rib (in a small triangle), and set the leaves aside. Chop enough of the remaining cabbage to make 3 cups (270 g).

Preheat the oven to 350°F (175°C).

In a nonreactive Dutch oven or large saucepan, heat the oil over medium-high heat. Add the onion, chopped cabbage, and a pinch of salt and cook, stirring frequently, until the onion and cabbage are tender and lightly browned, about 8 minutes. Scrape about half of the mixture into a large bowl and set aside to cool.

Return the Dutch oven with the remaining cabbage mixture to medium-high heat and stir in 2 cups (480 ml) water, the tomatoes, lemon, brown sugar, 1/2 teaspoon salt, 1/4 teaspoon of the pepper, and the raisins. Bring to a boil, then lower the heat and simmer for 10 minutes; taste and season with more salt if necessary. Spread about 1/2 cup (120 ml) of the sauce in the bottom of a 9-by-13-inch (23-by-33-cm) baking dish or shallow casserole and set aside.

To the cabbage mixture in the bowl, add the rice, egg, and turkey, along with 1 teaspoon salt and the remaining pepper. Mix until thoroughly combined; in the bowl, divide the filling into 8 portions. Lay out 1 whole cabbage leaf with the stem end facing you and the inside facing up. Spoon 1 portion of the filling onto the cabbage leaf, gently fold in the edges, roll it up away from you to enclose, then set it seam side down in the baking dish. Repeat with the remaining leaves and filling. Pour the remaining tomato sauce over the rolls. Cover the baking dish with aluminum foil and bake for 45 to 55 minutes, until very bubbly and cooked through (the internal temperature of a roll should be at least 160°F / 70°C). Serve hot.

VARIATIONS

★ To cook the stuffed cabbage on the stovetop instead of in the oven: Bring the sauce to a boil in the Dutch oven, then carefully nestle the cabbage rolls in the sauce, gently nudging them so they're mostly covered. Cover the pot and simmer, without stirring, for 45 to 55 minutes.

★ Instead of turkey and brown rice, try beef and barley or spelt berries (not gluten free).

★ To make vegetarian stuffed cabbage: Increase the rice to 4 cups (780 g). Chop enough cabbage to make 5 cups (450 g)—a medium head of cabbage will yield plenty—and scrape about two-thirds of it into the bowl for the filling.

Use 2 eggs in the filling. (Omitting the eggs will yield a very tasty vegan dish, though the filling will be looser.) Cover ½ cup (10 g) dried porcini mushrooms with hot water and let soak until soft, then fish them out of the water and dice them; add the mushrooms to the filling instead of the turkey, and strain the soaking liquid into the sauce instead of using plain water.

★ Winter-spiced sauce: Use the juice of ½ lemon instead of the chopped lemon, and add ¾ teaspoon ground cinnamon, ½ teaspoon ground ginger, ¼ teaspoon ground cloves, and ¼ teaspoon ground allspice to the sauce.

PERSIAN-STYLE LAMB, BUTTERNUT SQUASH, AND BROWN BASMATI RICE PILAF

Serves 6 | gluten free

The golden crust of buttery rice at the bottom of the pot—the tahdig—is the best part of any fancy Persian rice dish, this one included, and well worth the effort of lining the bottom of your pot with buttered parchment and mixing part of the parboiled rice with yogurt to help bind it before piling in the remaining ingredients. Sweet winter squash and prunes are the other highlights here; the lamb can be omitted or replaced with stew beef or boneless, skinless chicken thighs (in the latter case, reduce the browning time a bit).

- 1 teaspoon ground cardamom
- 1 teaspoon ground cinnamon
- ½ teaspoon ground cumin
- 1 tablespoon olive or vegetable oil
- 1 pound (455 g) lamb stew meat (from shoulder or leg)
- Salt and freshly ground black pepper
- 1 onion, diced
- 1 small butternut squash (about 1 pound / 455 g), peeled, seeded, and cut into 1-inch (2.5-cm) pieces
- ½ cup (90 g) pitted prunes
- 3 cups (570 g) raw brown basmati rice
- 1 tablespoon softened unsalted butter plus ½ cup (1 stick / 110 g) butter, melted
- 2 tablespoons plain yogurt
- Pinch of crushed saffron threads or turmeric
- Fresh flat-leaf parsley sprigs

In a small cup, combine the cardamom, cinnamon, and cumin and set aside. In a large deep sauté pan, heat the oil over medium-high heat. Add the lamb and sprinkle with salt and pepper; cook, turning occasionally, until deeply browned, about 10 minutes. Add the onion and cook, stirring occasionally, until just tender, about 5 minutes. Add 1 teaspoon of the spice mixture, 1 cup (240 ml) water, 1 teaspoon salt, and the squash and simmer gently, uncovered, until the squash is just tender, about 25 minutes. Stir in the prunes.

While the lamb and squash are cooking, in a large heavy saucepan, rinse the rice in at least three changes of cold water, until the water is clear when you pour it off. Drain well,

return the rice to the pan, and add 6 cups (1.4 L) water. Bring to a boil, then boil until the rice has swelled a bit but is still hard on the inside, about 12 minutes. Drain, rinse briefly in cold water, and drain well.

Preheat the oven to 375°F (190°C). Cut a piece of parchment paper to fit in the bottom of a Dutch oven. Lightly oil the Dutch oven, put in the parchment, and generously grease with the 1 tablespoon of softened butter.

Put 2 cups (330 g) of the parboiled rice in a small bowl and stir in ¼ cup (60 ml) water, the yogurt, ¼ cup (60 ml) of the melted butter, and ¼ teaspoon salt. Spread the rice mixture in the prepared Dutch oven to cover the bottom evenly. Top with one-third of the remaining rice and sprinkle with some of the remaining spice mixture and ¼ teaspoon salt. Spoon half of the lamb mixture over the rice, piling it in the center of the rice layer. Top with another third of the rice, mounding it in the center, and sprinkle with some of the spice mixture and ¼ teaspoon salt. Spoon the remaining lamb mixture over the rice, again mounding it into a rough cone shape (the idea is to create space all around the cone for the rice to expand as it steam-cooks), then top with the remaining rice; sprinkle with spice mixture and ¼ teaspoon salt.

In a small bowl, stir together the remaining ¼ cup (60 ml) melted butter, the saffron, and ½ cup (120 ml) water. Drizzle the mixture over the top layer of rice. Put a double layer of paper towels over the top of the Dutch oven and put the lid on tightly (the paper towels can stick out a bit). Put in the oven and bake for 1½ hours, or until the rice is tender and the liquid is absorbed.

Peek at the bottom layer of rice to see if a tahdig—a crusty browned bottom—has formed. If not, remove the paper towels and put the Dutch oven, covered, over medium-high heat and cook until the bottom is crusty (you will hear it sizzling), no longer than 7 minutes (you don't want to risk burning the parchment). Spoon the pilaf onto a large serving platter. Scoop up the crusty browned rice from the bottom (leaving the parchment behind) and arrange pieces of it over the pilaf. Garnish with the parsley and serve.

PORK AND RYE BERRY STEW WITH CARAWAY AND SAUERKRAUT
Serves 6

I can't imagine many things more comforting on a bitterly cold winter afternoon than to have this hearty, deep-dark pork stew simmering away on the stove. You could try to cook the rye berries right in the stew, but I find that sometimes the salt in a stock can prevent firmer grains from softening, so I hedge my bets and cook the grain separately (I usually just pull a hunk of cooked rye out of the freezer and submerge it in the stew until it breaks apart and thaws).

- 1 to 2 tablespoons olive oil
- 2 pounds (910 g) boneless pork shoulder, well trimmed, cut into 1-inch (2.5-cm) chunks
- Salt and freshly ground black pepper
- 2 carrots, peeled and chopped
- 2 ribs celery, chopped
- 1 onion, chopped
- 2 bay leaves
- 1 teaspoon caraway seeds, coarsely crushed
- 1 tablespoon tomato paste
- 1 cup (240 ml) red wine
- 2 cups (480 ml) beef, chicken, or vegetable stock or water
- 2½ cups (440 g) cooked rye berries (page 31)
- 2 cups (280 g) drained sauerkraut

In a heavy Dutch oven, heat 1 tablespoon of the oil over medium heat. Add half of the pork, season with salt and pepper, and cook, turning occasionally, until well browned on all sides; remove the pork to a plate and repeat with the remaining pork, removing it to the plate as it browns; it should take about 15 minutes to brown all the pork. Add more oil if needed.

To the Dutch oven, add the carrots, celery, onion, bay leaves, and caraway and cook until the caraway is very fragrant, about 2 minutes. Stir in the tomato paste, then stir in the wine, scraping up the browned bits from the bottom of the pot. Bring to a boil, then add the stock. Return the pork and any accumulated juices to the pot, bring to a boil, then lower the heat, cover, and simmer gently until the pork and vegetables are very tender, about 1 hour and 15 minutes.

Stir in the rye berries and sauerkraut and cook just to warm through. Taste and add more salt and pepper if necessary. Serve.

VARIATION

★ To make a vegan rye berry and sauerkraut stew, omit the pork. Double the carrots and celery and cook the vegetables in the oil over medium-high heat until some are lightly browned. Use vegetable stock or water, and add a peeled and chopped turnip, rutabaga, or potato when you add the stock. Simmer for about 20 minutes, until the vegetables are just tender, then stir in the rye and sauerkraut.

CURRIED CAULIFLOWER AND SORGHUM

Serves 4 | vegan, gluten free

You could use any of the firmer grains in this quick, everyday curry, but I do like sorghum because it readily absorbs the flavorful sauce and the little spherical grains sort of resemble broken-up cauliflower florets. With just two green chiles, this is fairly mild—I am most often cooking for a kid these days, so I leave them whole, which makes it easy for me to scoot them onto my own plate—but feel free to add more chiles, or a good dose of ground cayenne.

- **1 tablespoon olive or vegetable oil**
- **½ onion, thinly sliced**
- **1 large clove garlic, chopped**
- **1 inch (2.5 cm) fresh ginger, peeled and julienned**
- **1½ teaspoons mustard seeds**
- **1 teaspoon cumin seeds**
- **½ teaspoon turmeric**
- **2 hot green chiles, slit but left whole**
- **½ head cauliflower, separated into florets (about 14 ounces / 400 g)**
- **1 (14-ounce / 400-g) can diced tomatoes with juice**
- **Salt**
- **3 cups (480 g) cooked sorghum (page 32)**
- **Juice of 1 lemon**
- **Chopped fresh cilantro**

In a large, deep sauté pan, heat the oil over medium-high heat. Add the onion and cook, stirring occasionally, until softened and nicely browned, about 8 minutes. Add the garlic and ginger and cook for 10 seconds, then add the mustard seeds, cumin seeds, turmeric, and chiles and cook for 30 seconds. Add the cauliflower and ½ cup (120 ml) water and stir to coat the cauliflower as well as you can with the spices, then add the tomatoes and ½ teaspoon salt. Cover and bring to a boil, then lower the heat and simmer until the cauliflower is quite tender, 10 to 15 minutes.

Stir in the sorghum and bring to a simmer, then add in the lemon juice and cook to heat through. Sprinkle with the cilantro and serve.

WHEAT BERRIES AND BLACK-EYED PEAS
WITH TURNIP GREENS
Serves 4 as a main course or 8 as a side dish

I used to put two pots on the stove on New Year's Day: one containing a big mess of collard greens and one full of hoppin' John—black-eyed peas cooked with whatever form of smoked pork I had in the freezer, lots of onion, and white rice (the rice always cooked *together* with the black-eyed peas, not separately, so the flavors and textures of everything meld together into a coherent dish). The idea, at least where my mom grew up, in western Pennsylvania, was to eat poor on New Year's so you'll eat rich the rest of the year, though in the South the various parts of the traditional meal are more specifically totemic—collards representing paper money, peas representing coins, pork representing . . . pork. But after making it this way, with pop-in-your-mouth wheat berries instead of white rice, and tender turnip greens cooked right in the same pot, I've decided that new traditions have to start somewhere. And also that this hoppin' John—a meal in itself—should most definitely not be confined to January 1.

- 1 cup (225 g) dried black-eyed peas
- 6 slices bacon, diced
- 1 large onion, diced
- 1 bay leaf
- 1 cup (180 g) raw wheat berries
- Salt and freshly ground black pepper
- 1 bunch turnip greens (1 pound / 455 g), tough stems discarded, coarsely chopped

Rinse and drain the black-eyed peas. Put them in a heavy 4-quart (3.8 L) pot with water to cover by 1 inch (2.5 cm) and bring to a boil. Cover the pot and remove from the heat; let stand for 1 hour, then drain in a colander and set aside.

Put the bacon in the pot and cook, stirring frequently, over medium-high heat until nicely browned, 8 to 10 minutes. Remove the bacon with a slotted spoon and drain on paper towels; set the bacon aside.

Pour off all but 1 tablespoon of the bacon fat in the pot. Return the pot to medium heat and add the onion. Cook, stirring frequently, until translucent, about 10 minutes. Add 5 cups (1.2 L) water, the bay leaf, and wheat berries. Bring to a boil, skim off any foam from the surface, then cover the pot, lower the heat, and simmer until the wheat berries are just barely tender but still very chewy, about 25 minutes. Add the black-eyed peas, 1 teaspoon salt, and pepper to taste. Bring to a boil, then lower the heat and simmer for 25 minutes.

To finish, fold in the turnip greens and bacon and cook over high heat until the greens and black-eyed peas are tender, about 10 minutes. If the mixture is too soupy (some of the water will continue to be absorbed by the beans as the dish sits), carefully pour off some of the excess liquid. Taste and season with more salt and pepper if necessary. Remove the bay leaf and serve.

VARIATIONS
★ To make this vegan: Omit the bacon and use 1 tablespoon olive oil to sauté the onion; sprinkle the onion with about ½ teaspoon smoked Spanish paprika and stir for a few seconds before adding the water.
★ Use brown rice instead of wheat berries. After the peas are parboiled, add the rice and black-eyed peas back to the pot at the same time and simmer until everything is tender, about 40 minutes.

WHOLE ROASTED RAINBOW TROUT
STUFFED WITH ZUCCHINI COUSCOUS
Serves 4

Rainbow trout is a beautiful, delicately flavored, responsibly farmed fish that's easy to cook and serve whole—one trout makes a decent-size serving for one person. It's also easy to bone at the plate: Just pull back the skin from the top fillet (and munch the bacon wrapping, if you like) and gently lift the meat from the rib bones with your fork, then pull up on the backbone and emptied ribs to remove the rest of the bones from the bottom fillet. Trout is best cooked simply—as here, with mild couscous and zucchini—so the other ingredients don't overwhelm it. If you have extra couscous, just pile it on the platter with the fish.

- 1 tablespoon olive oil, plus more for the baking pan
- 1 shallot, diced
- 1 small zucchini, diced
- ½ cup (85 g) raw whole wheat couscous
- Salt and freshly ground black pepper
- 2 tablespoons chopped fresh basil, plus whole sprigs for garnish
- 4 small whole cleaned rainbow trout (about 2 pounds / 910 g total)
- 6 thin slices bacon, halved horizontally
- 4 thin slices lemon, halved, plus lemon wedges for serving

Preheat the oven to 425°F (220°C). Lightly oil a large broiler-proof baking pan or dish. Put a kettle of water on to boil.

In a heavy 2-quart (2-L) saucepan, heat the oil over medium-high heat. Add the shallot and zucchini and cook, stirring occasionally, until the zucchini is just tender and beginning to brown, about 10 minutes. Stir in the couscous, ¼ teaspoon salt, and ⅛ teaspoon pepper. Add ¾ cup (180 ml) boiling water, stir well, then cover the pan and remove from the heat; let stand until the water is absorbed and the couscous is tender, 10 to 15 minutes. Fluff with a rubber spatula and fold in the chopped basil. Taste and season with more salt and pepper if necessary.

Rinse the fish and pat dry with a paper towel. Season lightly inside and out with salt and pepper. Arrange 3 half-pieces of bacon on a cutting board with the long edges slightly overlapping. Set a fish down on top of them, perpendicular to the slices. Using a spoon or your hand, stuff some of the couscous mixture inside the cavity, along with 2 lemon-slice halves. Wrap the bacon around the fish, pressing on the overlapping ends so they stick together, then put the stuffed and wrapped fish in the baking sheet. Repeat with the remaining fish. Roast until the fish flakes easily when prodded with a small sharp knife, about 15 minutes. To crisp the bacon on top a bit, run the pan under the broiler for a minute. Do not overcook. Use a spatula to transfer the fish to a large platter and serve with basil sprigs and lemon wedges.

TURKEY AND BEEF KIBBEH

Serves 8

This is a simplified version of the traditional Lebanese kibbeh, which are usually made in one of two ways: Bulgur and raw beef are stuffed with a mixture of cooked beef and seasonings, formed into mini-football shapes, and deep fried; or half of the bulgur and raw meat mixture is spread in a baking dish, topped with the cooked meat mixture, and then another layer of bulgur mixture. Here, instead of layering the mixtures I just mix it all together to make a sort of large flat meat loaf—it has all the familiar sweet-spiced kibbeh flavor, but is much easier to pull off. You can also simply form the mixture into patties and pan-fry them instead of baking them—this will give you a crisper crust, but it requires a bit more active time in front of the stove. These are intensely flavorful, best served with a simple green salad and a fluffy warmed pita.

- ¼ cup (½ stick / 55 g) unsalted butter, melted
- 1 onion, diced
- 2 cloves garlic, minced
- 1 teaspoon ground cinnamon
- 1 teaspoon ground allspice
- ½ teaspoon ground cumin
- ¼ teaspoon ground cayenne
- ¾ teaspoon salt
- 3½ cups (665 g) cooked fine- or medium-grind bulgur (page 36), cooled
- 1 pound (455 g) ground chuck
- 1 pound (455 g) ground turkey
- ½ cup (40 g) chopped fresh cilantro
- 2 tablespoons pine nuts (optional)

If making the kibbeh as a baked loaf rather than as patties, preheat the oven to 350°F (175°C) and brush a 9-by-13-inch (23-by-33-cm) baking dish with some of the butter.

In a medium sauté pan, heat 1 tablespoon of the butter over medium-high heat and add the onion. Cook, stirring frequently, for 3 minutes, then add the garlic and cook until the onion is softened and translucent, about 2 minutes. Transfer the onion mixture to a large bowl and spread out to cool to room temperature.

In a small bowl, combine the cinnamon, allspice, cumin, cayenne, and salt.

To the onion mixture, add the bulgur, ground chuck, turkey, cilantro, and spice mixture. Mix with your hands (dampened in cold water) until thoroughly combined.

If making a loaf, scrape the mixture into the prepared baking dish and spread it out evenly. Using a dough scraper (a bench knife) or a metal spatula, cut into 16 rectangles, cutting all the way through. Score an X in each rectangle, pressing the dough scraper only partway down into the meat mixture. Push a pine nut, if using, into the center of each rectangle. Drizzle with the remaining butter. Bake until well browned and cooked through, the internal temperature of the meat is 160°F (70°C), and the rectangles are separate enough to wiggle when you shake the pan gently, 45 minutes to 1 hour. Using a spatula, transfer the rectangles to a platter and serve hot or warm.

If pan-frying the kibbeh, stir the pine nuts, if using, into the meat mixture and shape into 16 (3-inch / 7.5-cm) patties. In a large sauté pan, heat some of the remaining butter over medium heat. Working in batches, add the patties and fry for about 5 minutes on each side, until well browned and cooked through, wiping out the pan and adding more butter as necessary between batches.

BULGUR AND RED BEAN STEW
WITH SMOKED PAPRIKA

Serves 4 | vegetarian

As a lover of meat-based chili of all sorts, I hesitate to call this a chili. It's brighter tasting and perhaps more summery than a dark, long-simmered chili, but otherwise similar to traditional ones, especially when all the fun toppings are piled on.

- 8 ounces (225 g) dried red kidney beans, rinsed and picked over
- 1 tablespoon olive or vegetable oil
- 1 onion, diced
- 1 clove garlic, minced
- 1½ teaspoons ground cumin
- 1 teaspoon dried oregano
- Ground cayenne, to taste (½ to 1 teaspoon)
- ¼ teaspoon freshly ground black pepper
- 1 (14-ounce / 400-g) can whole tomatoes with their juice, pureed
- 1 teaspoon smoked paprika
- Salt
- ½ cup (70 g) raw medium- or coarse-grind bulgur
- Shredded extra-sharp cheddar cheese; sour cream, crème fraîche, or plain yogurt; chopped fresh cilantro; lime wedges; and thinly sliced hot green chiles, to taste

Put the beans in a large heavy saucepan with enough water to cover by 2 inches (5 cm). Bring to a boil, boil for 2 minutes, then remove from the heat, cover, and let soak for 1 hour. Drain in a colander.

In the now-empty saucepan, heat the oil over medium-high heat. Add the onion and garlic and cook, stirring occasionally, until the onion is translucent, about 5 minutes. Add the cumin, oregano, cayenne, and black pepper and stir for 1 minute. Add the beans and enough water to just cover them (about 5 cups / 1.2 L). Bring to a boil, then lower the heat and simmer until tender, uncovered, adding water as necessary to keep the beans covered, 50 to 60 minutes.

Add the tomatoes, smoked paprika, and ¾ teaspoon salt and simmer for 5 minutes. Add the bulgur and simmer until tender, about 10 minutes. Taste and add more salt if necessary. Serve topped with cheese, sour cream, cilantro, lime wedges, and chiles.

BULGUR AND BLACK BEAN BURGERS
WITH CILANTRO MAYONNAISE AND CARROT SLAW
Serves 6 | vegetarian

You can use just about any cooked grain here. Barley adds a whole lot of texture and chewiness to the burgers, while bulgur or quinoa or millet will make a finer-grained patty. Also feel free to substitute any variety of beans, from kidney beans to white beans to chickpeas.

The slaw, mayonnaise, and bread crumb–coated patties can be made up to one day in advance and kept in the refrigerator; put the patties on a waxed paper–lined plate and cover with plastic.

FOR THE SLAW
- ¼ cup (60 ml) cider vinegar
- 1 teaspoon salt
- ½ teaspoon ground cumin
- Pinch of ground cayenne
- 1 teaspoon prepared mustard
- 2 tablespoons olive or vegetable oil
- ½ small head cabbage
- 1 carrot
- 1 teaspoon cumin seeds, toasted

FOR THE MAYONNAISE
- ⅓ cup (80 ml) mayonnaise
- ¼ cup (20 g) chopped fresh cilantro
- Finely grated zest of 1 lime
- Freshly ground black pepper to taste

FOR THE BURGERS
- 1½ cups (255 g) cooked black beans (page 65), or 1 (13-ounce / 370-g) can, drained
- ½ large carrot, grated
- ¼ cup (20 g) chopped fresh cilantro
- Juice of ½ lime
- 4 tablespoons (60 ml) olive or vegetable oil
- 1 teaspoon salt
- ½ teaspoon ground cumin
- ¼ teaspoon ground cayenne
- ½ teaspoon smoked paprika
- 1½ cups (285 g) cooked fine- or medium-grind bulgur (page 36), cooled
- ⅔ cup (70 g) fresh whole wheat bread crumbs
- 6 whole wheat buns, toasted

MAKE THE SLAW
In a large bowl, whisk together the vinegar, salt, ground cumin, cayenne, and mustard. Gradually whisk in the oil to emulsify. Core and very thinly slice the cabbage into shreds; add it to the dressing. Peel the carrot and use the vegetable peeler to shave off long slices. Stack the slices, cut them in half crosswise, then very thinly slice them lengthwise into shreds; add to the cabbage mixture, along with the cumin seeds, and toss well. Keep, covered, in the refrigerator until needed.

MAKE THE MAYONNAISE
In a small bowl, whisk all the ingredients together, cover, and keep in the refrigerator until needed.

MAKE THE BURGERS
In a small food processor, combine the beans, carrot, cilantro, lime juice, 2 tablespoons of the oil, the salt, cumin, cayenne, and smoked paprika and puree until smooth. Add half of the bulgur and process until combined, then transfer the mixture to a large bowl and stir in the remaining bulgur. Shape into 6 patties a little less than ½ inch (12 mm) thick. Spread the bread crumbs on a plate and coat both sides of each patty with crumbs.

In a large sauté pan, heat the remaining 2 tablespoons of oil over medium-high heat. Add the patties and cook until well browned and heated through, about 1½ minutes on each side. Remove to the bottom halves of the buns, spread with the mayonnaise, and cover with slaw and the bun tops. Serve.

OPEN-FACED HUMMUS AND BULGUR SANDWICH
WITH LEMON VINAIGRETTE, SPROUTS, AND TOMATO

Serves 4 | vegan

I thought a bulgur sandwich sounded a bit strange—wheat on bread?—when I read an erroneous tweet about one served at a trendy little sandwich shop in a trendy neighborhood in Brooklyn (turns out they actually use trendy quinoa, not bulgur), but then I thought of pitas filled with tabbouleh, and started reading about other Middle Eastern sandwich-like foods that feature bulgur and decided it was worth a try. Yep. Spread good sturdy bread with a very creamy hummus, dress the bulgur with a very lemony vinaigrette, and use the very best, juiciest tomato you can find, and this could be your new favorite sandwich.

FOR THE HUMMUS

- 1 (15-ounce / 430-g) can chickpeas, drained and rinsed
- Juice of 1½ lemons
- ¾ teaspoon salt
- 1 small clove garlic, chopped
- ¼ cup (60 ml) oil, preferably 3 tablespoons vegetable oil and 1 tablespoon olive oil
- Pinch of hot paprika or ground cumin (optional)

FOR THE VINAIGRETTE

- Juice of ½ lemon
- ¼ cup (60 ml) rice vinegar or white wine vinegar
- ½ teaspoon agave nectar (optional)
- ½ teaspoon salt
- ¼ teaspoon freshly ground black pepper
- 2 tablespoons olive oil

TO SERVE

- 1 cup (190 g) cooked fine- or medium-grind bulgur (page 36), cooled
- 4 large slices crusty bread or bottom halves of crusty rolls
- 2 cups (70 g) alfalfa or broccoli sprouts
- 1 large, very ripe tomato, sliced

MAKE THE HUMMUS

Put all the ingredients in a blender or food processor and puree the living daylights out of it, adding 1 tablespoon water if necessary and scraping down the sides once or twice. Transfer to an airtight container and keep in the refrigerator until needed or up to 1 week.

MAKE THE VINAIGRETTE

In a medium bowl, whisk together the lemon juice, vinegar, agave nectar if using, salt, and pepper. Gradually whisk in the oil until combined. (This is a very tart vinaigrette and won't really emulsify.)

ASSEMBLE AND SERVE THE SANDWICH

Put the bulgur in a small bowl and drizzle in about half of the vinaigrette, tossing to combine; set aside.

Toast the bread on one side under the broiler (or on a cooling rack set over a stovetop burner), then brush the other side with a little of the vinaigrette and toast it. Set the bread on serving plates, vinaigrette side up. Spread generously with hummus (you may not use it all), then divide the bulgur and sprouts among the sandwiches. Drizzle with some of the remaining vinaigrette, top with the tomato slices, drizzle again (you may have some vinaigrette left over), and serve.

CRACKED WHEAT IN SPICED TOMATO SAUCE WITH EGGPLANT AND ZUCCHINI
Serves 4 | vegan

Cracked wheat tinted red with paprika, simmered with a bit of tomato, and studded with pieces of tender braised eggplant and zucchini is one of those hearty one-pan dishes that is so simple it almost shouldn't be as good as it is.

- **3 tablespoons olive oil**
- **½ medium eggplant, diced**
- **1 small red onion, diced**
- **1 clove garlic, minced**
- **½ medium zucchini, diced**
- **½ teaspoon ground cumin**
- **½ teaspoon ground cinnamon**
- **½ teaspoon hot paprika**
- **¼ teaspoon ground coriander**
- **¼ teaspoon ground cardamom**
- **Salt**
- **1 cup (180 g) pureed tomatoes (canned crushed tomatoes is fine)**
- **1 cup (160 g) raw cracked wheat**
- **1 (15-ounce / 430-g) can chickpeas, drained and rinsed (optional)**
- **Juice of ½ lemon**
- **4 sprigs fresh basil**

In a large, deep sauté pan, heat 2 tablespoons of the oil over medium-high heat. Add the eggplant and cook, stirring frequently, until browned and just tender, about 5 minutes. Add the onion, garlic, and zucchini and sauté until the onion is translucent and beginning to brown, about 5 minutes. Add the spices and 1 teaspoon salt and stir for 30 seconds. Stir in the tomatoes, 2 cups (480 ml) water, the cracked wheat, and chickpeas, if using. Bring to a boil, then lower the heat, cover, and simmer, stirring occasionally, until the cracked wheat is tender and most of the liquid has been absorbed, 15 to 20 minutes; add more water if the mixture becomes too dry or starts to stick to the pan. Stir in the lemon juice, taste, and add more salt if necessary. Top with the basil and serve hot.

KAMUT, FETA, AND GRILLED GRAPE SALAD WITH FLANK STEAK
Serves 4

Golden Kamut is marinated in a lemony, garlicky dressing with chunks of feta and crisp spinach and topped with slices of tender grilled flank steak and salty-sweet grilled grapes for a substantial dinner salad that's perfect for company.

- **2 large cloves garlic**
- **Juice of 2 lemons**
- **1 teaspoon salt, or more to taste**
- **1 teaspoon ground cumin**
- **1/2 teaspoon freshly ground black pepper**
- **1/4 teaspoon ground cayenne**
- **1/3 cup (80 ml) olive oil**
- **1 large bunch (435 g) seedless grapes on the stem**
- **1 (1 1/2-pound / 680-g) flank steak**
- **2 cups (340 g) cooked Kamut berries (page 36)**
- **1 shallot, thinly sliced**
- **4 ounces (115 g) feta cheese, cut into 1/2-inch (12-mm) cubes**
- **1/2 cup (40 g) chopped fresh parsley**
- **8 ounces (225 g) baby spinach**

Finely grate the garlic into a large bowl. Add the lemon juice, salt, cumin, black pepper, and cayenne and whisk to dissolve the salt. Gradually whisk in the oil. Dip the grapes into the marinade and set aside in a separate bowl.

Put the steak in a nonreactive baking dish and pour about half of the marinade over it; turn the steak to coat it, then set aside to marinate in the refrigerator for 1 to 2 hours.

Meanwhile, add the Kamut, shallot, and cheese to the bowl with the remaining marinade and toss to combine. Set aside in the refrigerator for up to 2 hours, then add the parsley and spinach and toss to coat. Taste and season with salt if necessary. Set aside at room temperature.

Preheat a charcoal grill to medium-high.

Remove the steak from the marinade with tongs (discard any remaining marinade) and grill until marked on both sides and medium-rare, about 5 minutes per side. Remove to a carving board, cover loosely with aluminum foil, and let rest for 5 minutes.

While the steak is resting, put the grapes on the grill and cook, turning frequently, until charred but not too soft, about 3 minutes.

Pile the salad onto serving plates. Slice the steak across the grain (perpendicular to the lines running the length of the steak) into 1/4-inch-thick (6-mm-thick) slices. Arrange the steak and grilled grapes over the salads. Serve.

VARIATION

★ To make this vegetarian: Omit the steak (obviously), but don't adjust the amount of marinade/dressing. Add 3 cups (540 g) cooked and drained red kidney beans to the salad with the Kamut.

WHOLE WHEAT PASTA
WITH ROASTED RED PEPPER AND GARLIC SAUCE AND PINE NUTS
Serves 3 to 4 | vegetarian

Go ahead and make all of the roasted red pepper and garlic sauce—it's very much like a breadless romesco—and save the rest in the freezer (where it'll keep for several weeks) or refrigerator (where it'll keep for several days). Warm it up, toss it with cooked farro or another hearty grain, add a squeeze of lemon and salt and cracked black pepper to taste, along with some torn fresh basil leaves, and dollop with thick yogurt for a simple dinner.

FOR THE SAUCE (MAKES ABOUT 3 CUPS / 720 ML)
- **4 large red bell peppers**
- **2 whole heads garlic**
- **6 tablespoons (85 ml) olive oil**
- **Salt and freshly ground black pepper**
- **1 cup (135 g) pine nuts or chopped blanched almonds, toasted**
- **1 tablespoon sherry vinegar**

FOR THE PASTA
- **Salt**
- **1 pound (455 g) dried whole wheat penne rigate or other short pasta**
- **1/4 cup (60 ml) heavy cream**
- **Freshly ground black pepper**
- **Handful of fresh basil sprigs, torn**
- **3 tablespoons pine nuts, toasted**

MAKE THE SAUCE
Preheat the oven to 375°F (190°C).

Line a baking sheet or dish with aluminum foil. Put the peppers on the foil and put them in the oven. Cut the heads of garlic horizontally in half and put them together on a piece of foil. Drizzle 2 tablespoons of the oil onto the split garlic and sprinkle with salt and black pepper; gather the foil into a package and squeeze to seal. Put on the baking sheet next to the peppers. Roast the garlic until the cloves are very soft and beginning to caramelize, about 40 minutes; roast the peppers, turning occasionally so the skins blister evenly, until they're collapsed and soft, about 1 hour.

Let the garlic cool, then squeeze the cloves from the skins into a blender. Let the peppers cool, then rub off the skins, cut the peppers in half, and pull out the seeds and stems; put the pepper flesh in the blender with the garlic. Add the remaining 4 tablespoons (55 ml) oil, the pine nuts, vinegar, 1 teaspoon of salt, and 2 tablespoons of water, and puree until smooth. Transfer half of it to a sealable container and reserve for another use; it will keep in the refrigerator for up to 1 week or in the freezer for several weeks.

MAKE THE PASTA
Bring a large pot of salted water to a boil. Add the pasta and stir gently. Bring to a boil and boil until just al dente, about 10 minutes. Drain in a colander.

Pour the sauce into the pasta pot and heat over medium heat until hot, then add the cream, salt and pepper to taste, the pasta, and basil. Toss to combine. Sprinkle with the pine nuts and serve.

HOMEMADE SPELT PASTA

Makes enough for 2 or 3 hearty servings | vegetarian

I confess I don't make fresh pasta all that often, but every time I do I'm reminded how easy it is. When you have a hankering for fresh noodles, you might consider trying this all-spelt version; spelt contains less gluten than wheat and is tolerated by many people who are sensitive to gluten. That said, you can replace the spelt flour here with whole wheat flour, white whole wheat flour, or a combination.

- **2 cups (225 g) whole spelt flour, plus more for kneading**
- **¼ teaspoon salt**
- **2 large eggs**
- **1 teaspoon olive oil**

TO COOK AND SERVE:
- **Salt**
- **1 tablespoon olive oil**
- **Sauce of your choice (see page 171 for ideas)**

In a large bowl (or in the bowl of a stand mixer fitted with the dough hook), combine the flour and salt. Add the eggs, oil, and up to 3 tablespoons water to make a firm dough. Turn out onto a lightly floured counter and knead for 5 minutes, or until smooth (or continue to mix with the dough hook). Cover with a clean cloth or a piece of plastic wrap and let rest for 15 minutes.

Divide the dough into 4 pieces and pass each through a pasta machine to the second- or third-thinnest setting, or roll it out with a rolling pin as thin as you can, flouring the sheet of dough well. Sprinkle with more flour and fold once, then use a pizza wheel or sharp chef's knife to cut into ¼- or ⅛-inch-wide (6- or 3-mm-wide) fettucine-type noodles, gently separating them and piling them loosely on a piece of floured waxed paper. (The dough is too delicate to fold more than once, or to hang to dry.) Let air-dry for about 30 minutes before cooking.

TO COOK AND SERVE
Bring a large pot of salted water to a boil. Add the pasta and stir gently. Bring to a boil and boil for 2 minutes. Drain and toss with the oil, then with sauce.

SAUCE IDEAS FOR HOMEMADE SPELT PASTA OR WHOLE WHEAT DRIED PASTA
Makes enough sauce for 1 pound (455 g) pasta

Whole grain pasta, whether purchased or homemade, is best with hearty, deeply flavorful sauces rather than delicate cream or light wine sauces that can be overwhelmed by the nutty flavor of the noodles themselves. Tomato- or red pepper–based sauces work well, as do simple nut or pestolike treatments. And if you really want to highlight a particular pasta, prepare it as simply as possible: Heat plenty of good olive oil in a heavy sauté pan, add garlic, cracked black pepper, and salt; toss with cooked and drained pasta and a little of its cooking water; and serve showered with freshly grated Parmesan.

EGGPLANT, BASIL, RICOTTA, AND TOMATO
Dice 1/2 eggplant (with or without peel) and lightly salt it; let drain in a colander; rinse and drain well. Heat 2 tablespoons olive oil in a deep sauté pan over medium heat and add the eggplant. Cook, turning frequently with a metal spatula, until nicely browned and tender, 12 to 15 minutes (lower the heat if the eggplant browns too quickly). Mince 2 cloves garlic and add them; cook for 3 minutes. Add 1 (14-ounce / 400-g) can diced tomatoes with their juices (or about 2 cups / 360 g chopped fresh tomatoes), 2 torn-up sprigs fresh basil, and salt and freshly ground black pepper to taste. Cook, stirring frequently, until boiling and heated through, about 2 minutes. Add about 6 tablespoon-size dollops of ricotta and the cooked and drained pasta and toss gently to heat through. Serve with an extra grind of pepper.

TOASTED WALNUT AND PARSLEY SAUCE
In a large heavy sauté pan, toast 1 cup (120 g) walnuts over medium-high heat until fragrant and just colored. Let cool, then pulse in a mini food processor until coarsely ground. Add 1 chopped clove garlic, 1/4 cup (60 ml) olive oil, 1/4 cup (60 ml) heavy cream, 1/2 cup (40 g) chopped fresh parsley, and salt and freshly ground black pepper to taste and pulse until fairly smooth. Transfer to a large bowl and add the cooked and drained pasta, along with a little of the hot pasta cooking water, and toss to coat. Serve with Parmesan shaved over the top.

PATRICIA WELLS'S MEAT AND CELERY SAUCE
Finely dice 3 large ribs celery and 1 small onion. Put in a large sauté pan with 1 tablespoon olive oil, the finely chopped leaves of 1 bunch celery, 1/3 cup (30 g) finely chopped flat-leaf parsley, and 1 bay leaf. Sauté over medium-high heat until the vegetables are just starting to soften, 4 to 5 minutes, then scoot everything to the edges of the pan and add about 1 pound (455 g) lean ground beef to the center. Cook until no longer pink, season with salt and pepper, and stir in 1 (28-ounce / 800 g) can of crushed tomatoes. Cover and simmer over low heat for about 15 minutes. Put the cooked and drained pasta in a large bowl and toss with a couple big spoonfuls of the sauce (you may not need it all; it keeps in the refrigerator and reheats well for days).

FARRO WITH ROAST CHICKEN, BROCCOLI RABE, AND CRISP FRIED LEMON

Serves 4

I could happily eat bitter, tender, garlicky braised broccoli rabe every day of my life, especially if every once in a while it were in a dish like this, with pan-crisped lemon roast chicken and creamy farro and garnished with crisp lightly fried slices of whole lemon. Most of the elements of the dish can be prepared well in advance: The chicken can be roasted, the broccoli rabe blanched, and the farro cooked a couple days ahead of time and kept in the refrigerator, so all you have to do at the last minute is fry the lemons and assemble everything in the same sauté pan.

FOR THE CHICKEN

- 1 (3 1/2-pound / 1.6 -kg) whole chicken
- 1 teaspoon salt
- 1/2 teaspoon freshly ground black pepper
- 1 teaspoon dried thyme
- 1 lemon, thinly sliced

FOR THE BROCCOLI RABE, FRIED LEMON, AND FARRO

- 1 bunch broccoli rabe (1 pound / 455 g), rinsed
- Salt and freshly ground black pepper
- 1/2 cup (60 g) white whole wheat or all-purpose flour
- Pinch of dried thyme
- 1 lemon, sliced into paper-thin rounds
- 1/2 cup (120 ml) olive oil
- 4 cloves garlic, peeled but left whole
- Generous pinch of red pepper flakes
- 2 1/2 cups (420 g) cooked farro (page 36)
- 1 cup (240 ml) chicken stock or water

MAKE THE CHICKEN

Preheat the oven to 450°F (230°C). Arrange the lemon slices in a 9-by-13-inch (23-by-33-cm) baking dish or pan.

Spatchcock the chicken (see Note, page 124), and open it flat like a book. Season on both sides with the salt, pepper, and thyme. Put the chicken in the baking dish over the lemon slices, skin side up. Roast until the internal temperature of a

thigh is 160°F (70°C), the juices run clear, and a drumstick can be easily moved around in its socket, 45 minutes to 1 hour. Let cool to room temperature.

Pull the meat from the bones in bite-size pieces, discarding the skin (keeping the crispest bits for extra flavor, if desired) and large pieces of fat. Set aside.

MAKE THE BROCCOLI RABE, FRIED LEMON, AND FARRO

Trim about 1 inch (2.5 cm) from the bottoms of the broccoli rabe stems and cut crosswise into 2-inch (5-cm) lengths, keeping the florets intact if possible. Bring a large pot of salted water to a boil. Add the broccoli rabe and push it down to submerge it in the water. Cook for 2 minutes, then drain in a colander and transfer to a large bowl of ice water to cool. Drain again and set aside.

Put the flour on a plate and season it with salt, pepper, and the thyme. Dredge the lemon slices in the flour mixture on both sides, pressing gently so that the flour adheres to the lemon. In a large sauté pan, heat all but 1 tablespoon of the oil over medium-high heat until it shimmers but is not smoking. Working in batches, add the lemon slices and fry, turning, until dark brown and crisp, 1 to 2 minutes total; remove to paper towels to drain.

Discard the oil in the pan and wipe out the pan. Put the reserved tablespoon of oil and the garlic in the pan and cook over medium heat until the garlic is soft and well browned, about 8 minutes. Add the chicken and cook, turning with a spatula, until lightly browned and heated through, about 4 minutes. Season with salt and black pepper, add the red pepper flakes, broccoli rabe, farro, and stock, and cook, turning frequently, until the broccoli rabe is tender and everything is heated through and most of the stock has been absorbed, about 4 minutes. Taste and season with more salt and pepper if necessary and serve topped with the fried lemon.

ASPARAGUS AND KABOCHA SQUASH FARROTTO WITH LEMON AND BASIL

Serves 6 | vegan

Farro cooked like risotto makes a lovely, slightly creamy dish, and you don't need to add any cream, butter, or cheese. Leave the peel on the kabocha squash—it may not seem like it, but it gets tender as it cooks. If you don't have kabocha, you can use peeled butternut or acorn squash.

- 1 tablespoon olive oil
- ½ sweet onion, thinly sliced
- 1 clove garlic, minced
- ½ small kabocha squash (about 12 ounces / 340 g), seeds scraped out, peeled if desired, and cut into ¾-inch (2-cm) pieces (see Note, page 176)
- 1¼ cups (45 g) raw farro
- ½ cup (120 ml) white wine
- 3 cups (720 ml) vegetable stock (see below)
- 1 bunch asparagus (about 1 pound / 455 g), tough ends snapped off, cut into 1-inch (2.5-cm) pieces
- Coarsely grated zest and juice of 1 lemon
- Salt and freshly ground black pepper
- 1 large sprig fresh basil, torn (about 6 leaves)

In a large, deep sauté pan, heat the oil over medium-high heat. Add the onion and cook, stirring frequently, until softened and nicely browned, about 10 minutes. Add the garlic, squash, and farro and cook, stirring, for 2 minutes. Stir in the wine and cook for 1 minute, then add just enough of the stock to almost cover the squash and farro (about 2 cups / 480 ml). Bring to a boil, then lower the heat, cover, and simmer, stirring occasionally, until the squash is very soft and the farro is tender, 15 to 20 minutes.

Stir in the remaining stock, the asparagus, and lemon zest and juice. Bring to a simmer and cook just until the asparagus is tender, about 5 minutes, stirring frequently and smashing a few of the squash pieces against the side of the pan to thicken the liquid and make it creamy. Season with salt and pepper to taste and fold in the basil. If the farrotto is too soupy, increase the heat to high and boil until some of the liquid is evaporated. Serve hot.

QUICK STOCKS

When I had a chest freezer (during a brief period of country living), I was all about making big batches of chicken or roasted-vegetable or duck-carcass stock to save for later. Now, in a small kitchen with a single small freezer, I simply cannot allot that much space to stock, even boiled-down concentrated stock. I need that spot for ice cream, and the flank steaks. I'm not entirely willing to give up the stock ideal, though, so when I need stock, I make a quick one, and if it isn't extremely flavorful by the time I'm ready to use it I'll stir in a tiny bit of good-quality stock base and not worry too much about whether it's truly homemade or not.

To make a quick vegetable stock, put a saucepan of water on to boil, adding a few peppercorns, a bay leaf, and whatever vegetables or trimmings you happen to have—a bendy carrot that's been in the crisper drawer a few weeks too long, the ends of the onions or shallots you just cut off, a bunch of parsley stems, leftover fennel stalks, the heel of a bunch of celery; a chicken stock, add a chicken back from the bag in the freezer door; or, if you're making a seafood dish, some shrimp shells or fish trimmings. Simmer it as you cut up vegetables or do other prep for the meal.

THYME FARROTTO
WITH ROASTED RADISHES AND RADISH GREENS

Serves 2 or 3 | vegetarian

I never thought to roast a radish until I saw the gorgeous ones in Rozanne Gold's absolutely dripping-with-genius *Radically Simple*, and I'll never look at those little red root vegetables and their holey green tops the same again. This dish, where the sharp but slightly sweet roasted radishes and crisped leaves are paired with a luxuriously creamy, thyme-infused farrotto, prompted the following reaction from my five-year-old daughter: "Radishes are the best, aren't they?"

- **6 large radishes with plentiful green tops**
- **2 tablespoons olive oil**
- **Salt and freshly ground black pepper**
- **½ onion, thinly sliced**
- **1 clove garlic, minced**
- **1 cup (180 g) raw farro**
- **2½ to 3 cups (600 to 720 ml) vegetable stock**
- **1 teaspoon fresh thyme leaves**
- **1 tablespoon unsalted butter**
- **1 tablespoon crème fraîche, plus more for serving (see page 74)**

Preheat the oven to 400°F (205°C).

Rinse the radishes and their tops and pat them dry. Cut each one in half lengthwise, leaving the tops attached (or cut off and reserve the tops). Spread the roots and tops on one or two baking sheets, drizzle with 1 tablespoon of the oil, sprinkle with salt and pepper, and rub with your fingers to coat everything well. Roast until the roots are tender and the tops are crisp in spots, about 30 minutes. Set aside.

In a large deep sauté pan, heat the remaining 1 tablespoon of oil over medium-high heat. Add the onion and a pinch of salt and cook, stirring frequently, until nicely browned, about 8 minutes, then add the garlic and cook for 2 minutes. Add the farro and stir to coat it with the oil, then stir in about 2 cups of the stock and the thyme. Bring to a boil, then lower the heat and simmer, stirring frequently and adding ½ to 1 cup (120 to 240 ml) more stock, until the farro is tender, 15 to 20 minutes. Stir in the butter and crème fraîche and simmer for 5 minutes. Taste and season with salt and pepper as needed. Spoon into serving dishes and top each serving with a small dollop of crème fraîche and the radish roots and tops. Serve.

WILD RICE SOUP
WITH KABOCHA SQUASH, KALE, AND COCONUT MILK

Serves 4 to 6 | vegan, gluten free

This elegant and beautiful one-pot soup, loaded with tender, frilly kale that conceals its riches of deep-black wild rice at the bottom of the bowl, is so exceedingly simple to make that, if you're like me and tend to make dinner parties more complicated than they need to be, you might hesitate to serve it to guests. But that's exactly why you should.

- 1 tablespoon vegetable oil
- 2 shallots, thinly sliced
- 1 teaspoon ground cumin
- 1 teaspoon ground coriander
- 6 cups (1.4 L) vegetable stock or water
- 1 hot green chile, halved and seeded
- 2 coin-size slices fresh ginger
- 1 (1-inch-wide / 2.5-cm-wide) strip of lime zest; or 1 kaffir lime leaf, torn in a few places but left whole
- 1 cup (180 g) raw wild rice
- ½ small kabocha squash (about 1 pound / 455 g; see below)
- 1 bunch kale
- 1 (13-ounce / 390-ml) can coconut milk
- 2 teaspoons agave nectar
- Juice of 1 lime
- Tamari to taste

In a large heavy saucepan or Dutch oven, heat the oil over medium-high heat. Add the shallots and cook, stirring frequently, until nicely browned, about 5 minutes. Add the cumin and coriander and stir for 15 seconds. Add the stock, chile, ginger, lime zest, and rice. Cover, bring to a boil, then lower the heat and simmer until the rice is almost tender, about 50 minutes.

Meanwhile, scrape the seeds and stringy parts out of the squash (no need to peel) and cut it into 1-inch (2.5-cm) chunks. Wash the kale well and pull the tough inner rib out of each leaf. Roughly chop the kale.

Fish the chile, ginger, and lime zest out of the soup and discard. Stir the coconut milk, agave nectar, lime juice, tamari, and squash into the soup, then increase the heat to medium, bring to a simmer, and cook, covered, until the squash is almost tender, about 8 minutes. Pile the kale on top of the soup, cover, and cook until it is wilted and tender, about 5 minutes, then gently fold it into the soup. Serve hot.

THE OTHER HALF

There are a couple recipes in this book that call for just half a kabocha squash—they're big darn squashes! Wrapped with plastic or sealed up in a freezer bag, the leftover half will keep for quite a while in the crisper drawer of the refrigerator. Here's what to do with it when you're ready to experience this squash as it was truly meant to be enjoyed: Cut into wedges about ¾ inch (2 cm) thick at the widest spot and spread on a baking sheet. Drizzle with olive oil and season generously with salt and pepper. Roast at 350°F (175°C) for about 30 minutes, turning the slices over about halfway through, until nicely browned. (See photo on page 203.)

WILD RICE–STUFFED CORNISH HENS
WITH TARRAGON CRÈME FRAÎCHE

Serves 4 | gluten free

There are few food combinations better than tarragon and crème fraîche, in my opinion, and here they're combined in a classic quick roasting-pan sauce and poured over succulent single-serving hens stuffed with nutty wild rice and dried fruit. It's a fancy but unfussy dish that needs only a plainly dressed green salad and a loaf of bread to complete the meal. You might serve this at a winter dinner party, or for a small family Thanksgiving supper. The rice stuffing, too, is great on its own, and could be doubled and served as a side dish with an unstuffed roast turkey.

- **1 tablespoon unsalted butter**
- **1/2 onion, diced**
- **1 rib celery, diced**
- **1 1/2 teaspoons salt**
- **1/2 teaspoon freshly ground black pepper**
- **1/2 cup (90 g) raw wild rice**
- **1/2 cup (95 g) raw long-grain brown rice**
- **1/4 cup (25 g) dried sour cherries or cranberries**
- **Coarsely grated zest of 1/2 orange**
- **4 small Cornish hens, rinsed and patted dry**
- **1 tablespoon olive oil**
- **1/2 cup (120 ml) white wine**
- **1/3 cup (80 ml) crème fraîche (see page 74)**
- **3 tablespoons chopped fresh tarragon**

In a heavy 2-quart (2-L) saucepan, melt the butter over medium-high heat. Add the onion, celery, 1/2 teaspoon of the salt, and 1/4 teaspoon of the pepper. Cook, stirring occasionally, until the onion is translucent, about 5 minutes. Add the wild rice and 1 1/4 cups (300 ml) water. Bring to a boil, then lower the heat, cover, and simmer for 20 minutes. Add the brown rice, cover, and continue to cook until both rices are just tender and most of the liquid is absorbed, 30 to 40 minutes. Gently fold in the cherries and orange zest, then let cool to lukewarm.

Preheat the oven to 400°F (205°C).

Loosely stuff the hens with the rice mixture, then rub the outside with the oil and season with the remaining 1 teaspoon salt and 1/4 teaspoon pepper. Put in a large flameproof baking pan. (If you like, tie the ends of the drumsticks of each hen together to help it holds its shape.) Roast until the skin is crisp and the temperature of the stuffing registers 165°F (74°C) on an instant-read thermometer, about 1 hour.

Using tongs, carefully remove the hens to a platter and set aside to rest for 10 minutes. Meanwhile, pour off any excess fat from the baking pan and set the pan over medium heat. When the drippings begin to sizzle, add the wine and stir to scrape up any browned bits. When most of the wine has evaporated, stir in the crème fraîche and tarragon and cook to heat the sauce through. Pour the sauce over the hens and serve.

VARIATION

★ To make this with chicken breasts instead of Cornish hens: Buy 4 large (1-pound / 455-g) bone-in chicken breasts with skin. Using a sharp chef's knife, remove the meat of each breast half from the bones in one piece (save the bones for stock). Arrange three pieces of kitchen string on a cutting board and set a breast skin side down on top of and perpendicular to the strings. Holding the knife almost parallel to the surface of the board, slice into the thickest part of the meat and unfold it so it opens like a book, flattening the meat to an even thickness with your palm. Pile some of the rice mixture over the meat, then lift the long edges of the breast over the filling and tie the roll closed with the string. Rub with oil, season with salt and pepper, and roast at 425°F (220°C) for 25 to 30 minutes.

BROTHY CHICKEN AND WILD RICE SOUP
Serves 4 | gluten free

This is such a far cry from the usual chicken and wild rice soup that it doesn't even belong in the same category as that gloopy, cream- or roux-thickened culinary train wreck. The light, Mexican-style broth here is, I think, a much more appropriate medium for good (that is, expensive, special) wild rice: It really lets the flavor of the rice shine.

FOR THE CHICKEN AND BROTH

- **About 2¼ pounds (1 kg) chicken pieces, such as 2 large leg quarters**
- **1 carrot, roughly chopped**
- **1 rib celery, roughly chopped, plus a handful of celery leaves**
- **1 bunch fresh parsley stems**
- **¼ onion, peeled**
- **½ teaspoon whole black peppercorns**

FOR THE SOUP

- **1 tablespoon olive oil**
- **¾ large onion, diced**
- **Salt**
- **1 carrot, diced**
- **½ cup (90 g) raw wild rice**
- **½ cup (95 g) raw long-grain brown rice**
- **1 large tomato, peeled and diced**
- **Juice of 1 lime**
- **Freshly ground black pepper**
- **1 hot green chile, thinly sliced into rounds**

MAKE THE CHICKEN AND BROTH

In a large heavy saucepan or Dutch oven, put the chicken pieces, carrot, celery, parsley stems, onion, peppercorns and enough water to cover the chicken and vegetables generously (about 12 cups / 2.9 L). Bring to a boil, then lower the heat and simmer until the chicken is cooked through and the broth is flavorful, about 45 minutes. Using tongs, remove the chicken to a large bowl. Pour the broth through a fine-mesh sieve into another large bowl or pot; discard the solids. Let cool completely, then skim off the clear fat from the broth. When the chicken is cool enough to handle, pull the meat off in bite-size pieces, discarding the bones, skin, and any excess fat. (You'll have about 2 cups / 300 g meat and 10 cups / 2.4 L broth.)

MAKE THE SOUP

Rinse out the large saucepan and put it over medium-high heat. Add the oil, onion, and a pinch of salt and cook, stirring frequently, until the onion is translucent, about 5 minutes. Add the carrot, 10 cups (2.4 L) broth, and wild rice, bring to a boil, then lower the heat and simmer, covered, for 20 minutes. Add the brown rice and ½ teaspoon salt and continue to simmer, covered, until both rices are tender, about 30 minutes. Add the chicken, tomato, lime juice, and pepper to taste and cook to heat through. Taste and season with more salt if needed. Serve with the chile for scattering over the top.

INJERA (ETHIOPIAN BREAD) WITH STEWED LENTILS AND BRAISED COLLARD GREENS

Makes about 20 small (8-inch / 20-cm) injera; serves 4 to 6 | vegetarian, gluten free

Spongy, pleasantly sour injera is easier to make at home than you might expect. I take the regular-yeast shortcut and let the batter sit at room temperature for a couple days to sour, but you could certainly adapt the recipe if you have a good sourdough starter in your fridge. There are two kinds of whole teff flour that I've found to be readily available: ivory teff and darker, almost cocoa-colored flour labeled simply "teff flour." Both work fine.

The only difficult part of making injera is finding the right pan on which to cook it. Find a good nonstick pan with a lid—the batter is cooked both from the bottom and from the steam it creates. After many attempts with my older nonstick sauté pan (which I keep primarily for the occasional scrambled eggs) and my well-seasoned cast iron griddles and skillets, I finally decided that a new nonstick surface was in order—hey, at this point in the history of cookware, and given that almost all commercial and restaurant injera is made on nonstick mitads rather than the troublesome old-world clay griddles over toxically smoky wood fires, I think we can consider nonstick "traditional." My setup is a relatively cheap but large, flat nonstick griddle with a dome-shaped glass lid from another pan that I position over the injera (and directly on the griddle surface) after I pour in the batter.

FOR THE INJERA

- **3 cups (360 g) whole teff flour**
- **Scant 1 tablespoon instant yeast**

FOR THE COLLARD GREENS

- **1½ pounds (680 g) collard greens**
- **1 tablespoon Niter Qibe (spiced butter, page 66), clarified butter, or vegetable oil**
- **½ onion, diced**
- **Salt**
- **1 clove garlic, minced**
- **1 inch (2.5 cm) fresh ginger, peeled and minced**
- **1 teaspoon nigella seeds (also called kalonji; optional)**

FOR THE LENTILS

- **1 tablespoon Niter Qibe (spiced butter, page 66), clarified butter, or vegetable oil**
- **½ onion, diced**
- **Salt**
- **1 clove garlic, minced**
- **Freshly ground black pepper**
- **2 teaspoons berbere (see Note), or more to taste**
- **1 cup (180 g) split red lentils (masoor dal) or brown lentils**
- **½ cup (90 g) diced peeled tomatoes and their juice (canned is fine)**
- **1 tablespoon tomato paste**

MAKE THE INJERA

In a large bowl, whisk together the flour, yeast, and 4 cups (480 ml) cool water until very smooth. The batter will be very thin. Cover with plastic wrap and set aside to ferment at room temperature for 1½ to 2 days. It will bubble like crazy. If the surface is still covered with foamy bubbles after 1 day, stir it down and re-cover; a dark liquid will collect at the surface. When the batter smells as sour as you'd like it (I prefer the shorter time, which makes it plenty sour), gently pour off the dark liquid, leaving the thick, grayish brown batter in the bowl.

In a small heavy saucepan, bring 1 cup (240 ml) water to a boil. Stir in ½ cup (120 ml) of the batter; it will thicken almost immediately. Lower the heat and whisk until it's as smooth as you can get it, cooking for about 2 minutes—some small lumps are fine. Remove from the heat and let cool to lukewarm, then stir the cooked mixture back into the uncooked batter. Cover the bowl again and set aside until the bubbles return, about 1 hour. It's time to make the injera!

Heat a large, shallow nonstick sauté pan or griddle over medium-high heat until a drop of water dripped onto the surface dances around. Lower the heat to medium and ladle in about ½ cup (120 ml) of the batter, tilting the pan to make a thin pancake. Cover with a lid and cook for about 2½ minutes, until the top looks dry with a few shiny specks and the edges separate from the pan and start to curl up. (Try not

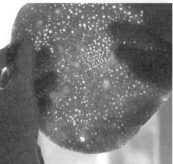

to let condensation from the lid drip onto the injera as you lift it.) Use a spatula to remove the injera to a parchment-lined platter, let cool for a minute, then roll it up if you'd like. Repeat with the remaining batter. If making the injera in advance, let cool, then cover the plate with plastic wrap and keep at room temperature for up to 2 hours.

MAKE THE COLLARD GREENS

Trim the collards and cut out the stems that are thicker than a pencil. Cut the thick stems into 1-inch (2.5-cm) lengths and set them aside separately. Cut the leaves into roughly 2-inch (5-cm) squares.

In a large heavy saucepan or Dutch oven, heat the spiced butter over medium-high heat. Add the onion, collard stems, and a pinch of salt and cook, stirring occasionally, until the onion is translucent, about 5 minutes. Add the garlic, ginger, and nigella, if using, and cook for 1 minute. Add 1½ cups (360 ml) water, pile in the collard leaves, and sprinkle with ½ teaspoon salt. Cover and cook, stirring occasionally and adding more water if it becomes dry, until the collards are very tender, about 1 hour.

MAKE THE LENTILS

In a large heavy saucepan or Dutch oven, heat the spiced butter. Add the onion and a pinch of salt and cook, stirring

occasionally, until the onion is translucent, about 5 minutes. Add the garlic, ½ teaspoon salt, ¼ teaspoon pepper, and the berbere and stir for 1 minute. Add the lentils, tomatoes, tomato paste, and 3 cups (720 ml) water. Bring to a boil, then lower the heat and simmer, stirring occasionally, until the lentils are broken down and the stew is very thick, about 30 minutes. Taste and season with more salt, pepper, or berbere if necessary.

Serve the collards and lentils with the injera.

NOTE: To make a berbere spice mixture: In a small sauté pan over medium-high heat, toast about 12 dried red chiles (small hot ones, such as arbol or cayenne) until lightly browned, about 1 minute. Remove to a bowl to cool. Toast, all together, for about 30 seconds, 1 teaspoon each cumin seeds, coriander seeds, fenugreek seeds, allspice berries, and whole black peppercorns. Add them to the chiles and let cool. Grind in a spice mill until fine, then use your fingers or a fork to stir in 1 teaspoon ground ginger, ½ teaspoon freshly grated nutmeg, and as much hot paprika or ground cayenne as you like to make it as spicy as you can stand (I do about 2 teaspoons paprika for a milder blend).

5

Side Dishes

I've been told that when some people think of "whole grains," they envision a desperately forlorn-looking mound of brown rice or millet, food they're expected to choke down because it's "good for you," cheap, filling, and environmentally sound, but what they'd rather do is compost it (also environmentally sound). I gather that's how whole grains were served in these poor souls' childhood homes, unadorned but for the pile of oversteamed broccoli on top—there's always oversteamed broccoli in these tales of woe. But with just a little imagination, and the occasional dip of the toe into a food culture other than our own, whole grains can be cooked up into side dishes that not only smartly complement the rest of the meal but also compete with it. As with the salads in the earlier chapter, it would take very little effort to turn these into main courses or one-dish meals. Most are so interesting and brightly flavorful in themselves that brilliant meals can be made by quickly cooking up something very simple to go with them—for example, the spicy tomato-stewed millet on page 189 needs nothing more than a nice piece of fish pan-seared in olive oil, seasoned with nothing more than salt and pepper and a squeeze of lemon, or a thick lentil dal, a spoonful of yogurt, and some chunks of cucumber.

AMARANTH "POLENTA"

Serves 2 to 3 | vegetarian, gluten free

Tiny amaranth grains cook up to a porridgelike consistency very similar to that of soft polenta, and while the flavor is altogether different from cornmeal polenta, the amaranth variety can be served in much the same way. Its fresh, almost vegetable flavor makes it well worth trying as an alternative, in addition to being significantly more nutritious than cornmeal. My suggestions for more polenta variations, at right, can be applied to this recipe as well.

- 1 cup (200 g) raw amaranth
- ¼ cup (25 g) freshly grated Parmesan cheese
- 1 tablespoon unsalted butter
- Salt and freshly ground black pepper

In a heavy 2-quart (2-L) saucepan over medium-high heat, toast the amaranth, stirring frequently, until a shade darker and just beginning to crackle. Stir in 3 cups (720 ml) water and bring to a boil, stirring, then lower the heat and simmer briskly, stirring occasionally, until the grains are tender and translucent and the mixture is thick, about 20 minutes. (The mixture won't start to thicken until the last few minutes.) Remove from the heat and stir in the cheese, butter, and salt and pepper to taste. Serve hot.

CLASSIC SOFT POLENTA

Serves 2 or 3 | vegetarian, gluten free

Perfect polenta needs plenty of salt—use just a little at first, then taste again after you stir in the cheese and add more toward the end of cooking.

- 4 cups (960 ml) vegetable stock or water, or more as needed
- Salt and freshly ground black pepper
- 1 cup (160 g) raw coarse- or medium-grind cornmeal, polenta, or corn grits
- 1 tablespoon unsalted butter
- ¼ cup (25 g) freshly grated Parmesan cheese

In a heavy 2-quart (2-L) saucepan, combine the stock, ½ teaspoon salt, and ¼ teaspoon pepper. Bring to a boil, then gradually whisk in the cornmeal. Lower the heat and simmer (it should plop and bubble just once every few seconds), whisking frequently and stirring with a heatproof spatula to prevent it from sticking to the pan, until the cornmeal is thick but still pourable and the individual granules are tender, about 35 minutes for coarse-grind or 15 minutes for medium-grind cornmeal; add ½ cup (120 ml) stock or water if the mixture becomes thick before the granules are tender. Stir in the butter and cheese, then taste and season with more salt and pepper if necessary. Serve hot. (See page 23 for reheating tips.)

VARIATIONS

★ For mascarpone-mushroom polenta: Use the butter to sauté 8 ounces (225 g) sliced mushrooms in a large heavy sauté pan until deeply browned, seasoning with salt, pepper, and fresh thyme leaves. Fold ⅓ cup (80 ml) mascarpone cheese into the polenta before serving and top with the mushrooms. (Try with lemon-roasted chicken, page 172.)

★ For a Mexican-style dish: Toward the end of cooking, stir a seeded, minced large jalapeño and poblano and ¼ teaspoon ground cumin into the polenta and cook until they're just tender. Omit the Parmesan. Sprinkle with crumbled cotija (a firm Mexican cheese) or feta cheese and plenty of chopped fresh cilantro.

BUTTERMILK GRITS WITH PIMIENTO CHEESE
Serves 4 | vegetarian, gluten free

If you're at all surpised by how many kinds of dairy are crammed into this one little side dish, you probably haven't eaten grits in a down-home restaurant in Georgia, where I swear they must fold *whipped cream* into them. Trust me, it's all worth it. I like the fresh tang of buttermilk, which balances the richness in a surprising way, but you could also just use more milk (no need to add it separately) or half-and-half. For lovely cheese grits, omit the pimiento cheese and stir a small handful of just-shredded cheese into the hot grits; sharp white cheddar is good, as is something with a little more kick like a soft-ish asiago.

- **2 cups (480 ml) milk**
- **3/4 teaspoon salt, or more to taste**
- **1 cup (160 g) raw white corn grits or hominy grits**
- **1 cup (240 ml) buttermilk**
- **1/2 tablespoon unsalted butter**
- **1/2 cup (120 g) Pimiento Cheese (page 253)**
- **1/2 teaspoon cracked black peppercorns**

In a heavy 2-quart (2-L) saucepan, bring the milk and salt to a boil. Gradually whisk in the grits, then lower the heat to medium and simmer, whisking frequently, until the mixture begins to thicken, about 1 minute. Add the buttermilk and cook over the lowest heat until the corn grains are tender and mostly translucent and the grits are thick but still pourable, 6 to 8 minutes, or longer depending on the type of grits. Stir in the butter until melted, then let stand off the heat for 5 minutes to thicken further. Season with more salt if necessary. Spoon onto plates or into small bowls and top each serving with 2 tablespoons pimiento cheese and sprinkle with cracked pepper. Serve.

CREAMY, LEMONY HOMINY AND SPINACH

Serves 2 or 3 | vegetarian, gluten free

Like creamed spinach, this is an indulgence, to be sure. But it has a lot more going for it than the old-school classic: A sharp hit of lemon zest and juice brightens the not-too-thick cream sauce, and of course the tender bits of hominy hiding throughout give it a subtle Latin feel. Go all out and serve a steak with it, and hunks of good crusty bread.

- **1 pound (455 g) fresh spinach**
- **1 tablespoon unsalted butter**
- **1 large shallot, minced**
- **Salt**
- **1/2 cup (120 ml) white wine**
- **1 cup (240 ml) heavy cream**
- **Coarsely grated zest of 1/2 lemon**
- **1/4 teaspoon freshly grated nutmeg**
- **1 tablespoon freshly squeezed lemon juice**
- **1 1/2 cups (360 g) cooked hominy (page 23) or 1 (14-ounce / 400-g) can, drained and rinsed**
- **Freshly ground black pepper**

Bring a pot of water to a boil and add the spinach. Cook until wilted and tender, about 3 minutes, then drain well in a fine-mesh sieve, pressing out as much water as possible. Chop the spinach and set aside.

In a small saucepan, heat the butter over medium-high heat. Add the shallot and a pinch of salt and cook, stirring occasionally, until just starting to brown, about 5 minutes. Add the wine and cook until reduced by about half, then add the cream, lemon zest, and nutmeg. Simmer over medium heat until reduced and thickened, about 6 minutes, then whisk in the lemon juice. Fold in the spinach and hominy and cook until just heated through. Season to taste with salt and pepper to taste and serve hot.

OLD-FASHIONED CORNBREAD STUFFING

Serves 4 to 6 | vegetarian

When I was growing up, my mom and dad probably put venison or squirrel or the like on the Thanksgiving table as often as turkey, and my brother and I never missed the bird. But I'll never forget the year my dad decided to make some sort of weird sausage and mushroom stuffing instead of my mom's traditional one. Unforgivable. This cornbread stuffing, while not technically my mom's (hers is based on a mixture of rye, whole wheat, and white French breads), is as simple in spirit and surely would've been welcome on our family table. I suppose I should mention that I would not use this as an actual stuffing, and not just for the usual Alton "Stuffing Is Evil" Brown reasons of poultry-cooking safety. What flavor would be gained from being cooked inside a turkey (for example) is far outweighed by the loss of the crisp, crunchy browning the cornbread achieves when cooked separately. I call it stuffing because I just can't wrap my head around the word *dressing*.

- **5 tablespoons (70 g) unsalted butter, plus more for the baking dish**
- **5 cups (475 g) diced stale cornbread (or 1 recipe of the version on page 243 would work)**
- **2 large ribs celery, diced, plus ¼ cup (15 g) chopped celery leaves**
- **1 onion, diced**
- **¾ teaspoon freshly ground black pepper**
- **½ teaspoon salt**
- **1½ teaspoons minced fresh sage or 1 teaspoon crumbled dried sage**
- **About ½ cup (120 ml) vegetable stock**

Preheat the oven to 400°F (205°C). Butter a 9-by-13-inch (23-by-33-cm) baking dish or pan.

Put the cornbread in a large bowl. In a medium heavy saucepan, melt 4 tablespoons (55 g) of the butter over medium-high heat. Add the celery, onion, pepper, and salt and cook, stirring frequently, until just starting to become tender, about 3 minutes. Scrape into the bowl with the cornbread and add the sage. Toss to combine, then drizzle in the stock, adding just enough to moisten the cornbread evenly. Transfer to the prepared baking dish and dot with the remaining 1 tablespoon of butter. Bake until heated through and crusty on top, 25 to 30 minutes. Serve.

SPICY STEWED MILLET WITH TOMATO, CUMIN, AND MUSTARD SEEDS

Serves 4 | vegan, gluten free

Sautéing the millet and mustard and cumin seeds together before adding the tomatoes and water deepens the flavors of this efficient little stew. My friend and fellow recipe tester Sarah Scheffel says that she likes to add some cooked chickpeas to make a more substantial main course, and I think that's a fine idea, whether you're vegan or not. For vegetarians or omnivores, a generous spoonful of plain yogurt or raita would be good alongside this as well.

- 1 tablespoon olive or vegetable oil
- 1 onion, thinly sliced
- Salt
- 1 teaspoon yellow mustard seeds
- 1 teaspoon cumin seeds
- 1 cup (200 g) raw millet
- 1 (14.5-ounce / 415-g) can whole tomatoes, with their juice
- 2 hot green chiles, split lengthwise but kept whole
- Pinch of hot red pepper flakes
- Juice of 1/2 lemon
- 1/4 cup (20 g) chopped fresh cilantro (optional)

In a heavy medium sauté pan, heat the oil over medium-high heat. Add the onion and a pinch of salt and cook, stirring frequently, until soft and nicely browned, about 10 minutes. Add the mustard seeds, cumin, and millet and cook, stirring, until fragrant and the millet begins to crackle, about 2 minutes. Break up the tomatoes with your hands (or use kitchen shears to cut them up in the can) and add them, along with their juice and 3/4 cup (180 ml) water, to the pan. Add 1/2 teaspoon salt, the chiles, and red pepper flakes and stir well. Bring to a boil, then lower the heat, cover, and simmer until the millet is tender and most of the liquid has been absorbed, about 25 minutes. If the liquid is mostly absorbed but the millet isn't quite tender, drizzle in a few more tablespoons of water and cook for a few more minutes. Taste and add more salt if necessary. Sprinkle with the lemon juice and cilantro, if using, and serve hot, offering the chiles to whoever likes it hottest.

ROASTED CAULIFLOWER AND GARLIC MASHED MILLET

Serves 4 to 6 | vegan, gluten free

My dad had some choice words to say about how this pale mash looked in a photograph I sent to him and my mom, but don't let appearance discourage you—mashed potatoes, for which this millet and cauliflower dish is a delicious and more healthful substitute, aren't particularly attractive either. I roast the olive oil–slicked almonds alongside the garlic and cauliflower—another way to fairly effortlessly add roasty flavor to a simple side dish.

- 1 medium head cauliflower
- 6 cloves garlic
- 8 whole almonds
- 2 tablespoons olive oil, plus more for serving
- Salt and freshly ground black pepper
- 2 cups (350 g) cooked millet (page 24)
- About 1 1/4 cups (300 ml) almond milk (page 71)

Preheat the oven to 400°F (205°C).

Trim the cauliflower and break it into large florets. Put the cauliflower, garlic, and almonds in a 9-by-13-inch (23-by-33-cm) baking dish, drizzle with the oil, and sprinkle with salt and pepper to taste. Toss to coat with the oil. Roast until the cauliflower is very tender and golden brown, 40 to 50 minutes, removing the almonds when they're browned (after about 40 minutes). Coarsely chop the almonds and set aside.

Working in batches if necessary, transfer the cauliflower and garlic to a food processor and add the millet and 1 cup of the almond milk. Puree until fairly smooth, adding more almond milk if needed; the mash will have the consistency of chunky mashed potatoes. Taste and season generously with more salt and pepper. Transfer to a heavy medium saucepan and heat over low heat, stirring frequently, until hot (or reheat in a microwave oven). Transfer to a serving dish, sprinkle with the almonds, drizzle with a little oil, and serve.

THYME-SCENTED MILLET WITH PEPPERS

Serves 4 | vegan, gluten free

This is a quick, simple, unassuming side dish with just a bit of kick from the cracked pepper and richness from the oil. Use a good fruity olive oil here, and it will be appreciated.

- **3 tablespoons olive oil, or more if needed**
- **1 small red bell pepper, diced**
- **1 small yellow or orange bell pepper, diced**
- **1/2 teaspoon salt, or more to taste**
- **1/2 teaspoon cracked black pepper**
- **4 cups (700 g) cooked millet (page 24)**
- **2 teaspoons fresh thyme leaves**

In a large sauté pan, heat the oil over medium heat. Add the bell peppers and cook, stirring frequently, until just tender, about 5 minutes. Add the salt, black pepper, millet, and thyme and turn with a metal spatula to thoroughly combine. Cook until the millet is heated through, about 3 minutes. Taste and season with more salt if necessary, and drizzle with a little more oil if the millet appears dry. Serve hot.

VARIATIONS

★ Hold back on the salt; before serving, top with 1 teaspoon gomashio (page 248) coarsely crushed in a mortar.

★ If keeping the dish vegan or vegetarian isn't an issue, make a more substantial main course (serving perhaps two or three for lunch) by adding a couple handfuls of shredded cooked chicken with the bell peppers and dotting the finished dish with a bit of soft cheese.

MILLET WITH SPINACH, CARAMELIZED ONION, AND RAISINS

Serves 4 | vegan, gluten free

A dish with such a paltry and pedestrian list of ingredients truly should not be allowed to taste as good as this does. The only trick is to not rush the browning and softening of the onion—let it go slowly, and it'll become silky and deeply sweet.

- **1 tablespoon olive oil**
- **1/2 onion, thinly sliced**
- **Salt**
- **3 cloves garlic, chopped**
- **1 cup (200 g) raw millet**
- **1/3 cup (55 g) raisins**
- **Freshly ground black pepper**
- **3 cups (90 g) baby spinach or roughly chopped mature spinach**

In a heavy 3-quart (2.8-L) saucepan, heat the oil over medium-high heat. Add the onion and a pinch of salt and cook, stirring occasionally, until very well browned and soft, at least 10 minutes; lower the heat to medium if it begins to brown too quickly. Add the garlic when the onion is just about done.

Add the millet and stir until crackling and fragrant, about 4 minutes. Add 2 cups (480 ml) water, the raisins, a couple large pinches of salt, and several grinds of pepper. Cover and bring to a boil, then lower the heat and simmer until the millet is tender and most of the water has been absorbed, about 20 minutes.

Fold in the spinach, cover, and cook until the spinach is wilted and heated through, about 2 minutes; season with salt if necessary. Fluff and serve.

TURNIP AND GREENS GRATIN
WITH CRUNCHY MILLET CRUST

Serves 6 | vegetarian, gluten free

When I started asking around for whole grain recipe ideas, both my mom and my aunt sent me a recipe for something they called "millet topping for vegetables." It must be a common way to use millet, but I'd never had anything like it. Here I layer my beloved turnips and their greens with nutty Gruyère and thyme-infused cream, then top the whole thing with a layer of toasty millet enriched with olive oil and cheese, which bakes into a hearty crust.

- 1 tablespoon olive oil, plus more for the baking dish
- 2 cups (480 ml) heavy cream
- 1 clove garlic, smashed but left whole
- 1 sprig fresh thyme
- Pinch of freshly grated nutmeg
- Salt and freshly ground black pepper
- 1 pound (455 g) turnip greens, washed well, large stems removed, roughly chopped
- 1 onion, diced
- 1 cup (200 g) raw millet
- 8 ounces (225 g) Gruyère cheese, shredded
- 2 pounds (910 g) turnips, peeled and sliced ⅛ inch (3 mm) thick
- 1 teaspoon Gomashio (page 248) or sesame seeds (optional)

Preheat the oven to 325°F (165°C). Oil a 9-by-13-inch (23-by-33-cm) baking dish.

In a small heavy saucepan, combine the cream, garlic, thyme, nutmeg, and a pinch each of salt and pepper. Bring to a boil, then remove from the heat, cover, and set aside to steep.

Bring a large pot of water to a boil, add the greens, and blanch for 2 minutes. Drain and transfer to a bowl of cold water to cool. Drain and squeeze dry. Set aside.

In a 3-quart (2.8-L) saucepan, heat the oil over medium heat, add the onion and a pinch of salt, and cook, stirring frequently, until the onion is just beginning to brown, about 5 minutes. Add the millet and cook, stirring, until fragrant, about 5 minutes. Add 2¼ cups (540 ml) water and ¼ teaspoon salt, cover, bring to a boil, then lower the heat and simmer until the water is mostly absorbed and the millet is tender, about 20 minutes. Remove from the heat and let stand for 5 minutes, then gently fold in half of the cheese. Set aside.

Arrange one-third of the turnip slices in a single layer in the baking dish and sprinkle generously with salt and pepper. Top with half of the greens, then half of the remaining cheese. Add another layer of turnips, salt and pepper, greens, and cheese. Top with another layer of turnips and season with salt and pepper. Pour the warm cream evenly over the top, discarding the garlic and thyme. Using a spatula, spread the millet mixture over the top of the casserole, pressing down gently so it sticks together to form a crust. Sprinkle with the gomashio, if using. Bake until the topping is nicely browned, a knife inserted in the center meets no resistance from the turnips, and the cream is bubbling furiously, about 1 hour and 15 minutes. Let stand for 15 minutes, then serve.

VARIATIONS

★ Use thawed and squeezed frozen spinach instead of the turnip greens.

★ Instead of the greens, sauté 1 pound sliced mushrooms in 1 tablespoon olive oil until they release their liquid and are nicely browned and layer them with the turnips.

★ Use half turnips and half russet potatoes.

SAVORY QUINOA CUSTARD

Serves 6 | vegetarian, gluten free

This recipe was graciously given to me by Charles Ramsey, the chef de cuisine at Athens's Five & Ten restaurant, where I was served this custard with a crisp-skinned roasted chicken breast, braised kale, and a lemony salad of shaved celery with pecans. As befits its classy-restaurant origins, this is a simple, highly enriched custard—you want butter, cream, egg yolks, cheese? You've got it. Of course, it would be perfectly acceptable to use whole eggs instead of just the yolks, or use half-and-half instead of cream, and lubricate the cups with a light spray of olive oil instead of soft butter.

- **Softened butter for the cups**
- **12 large egg yolks, or 6 large whole eggs**
- **3 tablespoons heavy cream**
- **3 tablespoons freshly grated Parmesan cheese**
- **1 tablespoon chopped fresh parsley or thyme, or a combination**
- **1 teaspoon salt**
- **3 cups (550 g) cooked quinoa (page 27), cooled**

Preheat the oven to 400°F (205°C). Generously butter six 6- to 8-ounce (180- to 240-ml) custard cups or ramekins. Put a kettle of water on to boil.

In a large bowl, whisk together the egg yolks, cream, cheese, parsley, and salt. Gently fold in the quinoa. Divide the mixture among the prepared custard cups and set them in a baking pan. Pour boiling water in the baking pan to come halfway up the sides of the cups and transfer the pan to the oven. Bake for 18 to 20 minutes, until just set. Remove the cups from the water (use a canning jar lifter if you have one) and let cool for a few minutes or up to 30 minutes. Either serve straight from the cups, or carefully turn each custard out onto a serving plate (loosen the edges with a knife).

SPICED BROWN BASMATI RICE

Serves 4 | vegan, gluten free

This is a dish I used to make a lot for myself when I lived alone and could get away with eating nothing but rice for supper. It's an interesting accompaniment to a simple lentil dal, or gingery curried chickpeas with a few ripe tomatoes grated in. If remaining vegan isn't a concern, try using ghee in place of the oil, and be sure to include a spoonful of plain yogurt on your plate.

- **1 cup (195 g) raw brown basmati rice**
- **1 tablespoon olive or vegetable oil**
- **1 teaspoon cumin seeds**
- **4 whole cloves**
- **½ teaspoon green cardamom pods, lightly crushed**
- **Pinch of ground cinnamon**
- **½ teaspoon salt**

Rinse the rice in at least three changes of water, until the water is clear; drain well and put in a bowl with 1½ cups (360 ml) water. Let soak for 30 minutes.

In a heavy 2-quart (2-L) saucepan, heat the oil over medium-high heat and add the cumin, cloves, cardamom, and cinnamon. Cook, stirring, for 1 minute. Add the rice and its soaking water and the salt and bring to a boil over high heat. Stir once, then cover and lower the heat to very low; cook until all the water is absorbed and the rice is tender, without stirring, 20 to 25 minutes. Remove from the heat and let rest, covered, for 5 minutes. Fluff gently with a heatproof spatula and serve.

TURNIP RICE
Serves 4 | vegan, gluten free

Turnip rice. Sounds *lovely*, doesn't it? But oh, my goodness, it is! Little nuggets of pleasantly bitter turnips are blanched and briefly sautéed together with pureed turnip greens (absolutely loaded with calcium), a touch of tingly ginger, and classic curry spices, then fluffy basmati rice is folded in to make a substantial side dish. If you're not a turnip lover—yet—feel free to substitute the greens with other, milder cruciferous braising greens like collards or kale, and pair them with cauliflower or sweet potatoes instead of the turnips if you like. For further simplicity, you can thaw a block of frozen chopped spinach and skip the blanching and pureeing altogether.

- 2 medium turnips, peeled and diced (about 2 cups / 260 g)
- 1 large carrot, peeled and diced (optional)
- 5 packed cups chopped turnip greens (about 8 ounces / 225 g)
- 1 hot green chile, seeded and chopped (optional)
- 1 tablespoon olive oil
- ½ onion, diced
- Salt
- 1 teaspoon minced fresh ginger
- 1 teaspoon ground coriander
- ½ teaspoon ground cumin
- ¼ teaspoon turmeric
- 3 cups (585 g) cooked brown basmati rice (pages 29–30)

Fill a large bowl with ice water. Bring a large pot of water to a boil and add the turnips and carrot, if using; return to a boil and cook until just barely tender, about 4 minutes. Using a slotted spoon, transfer the vegetables to the ice water to cool. Add the turnip greens to the boiling water, shoving them down into the water as they wilt. Cook until the stems are tender, about 8 minutes, then pour into a sieve and rinse under cold running water to cool. Put the greens in a mini food processor with the chile, if using, and a splash of water (up to about ¼ cup / 60 ml) and puree until smooth. Set the blanched vegetables and turnip-greens puree aside.

In a large deep sauté pan, heat the oil over medium-high heat. Add the onion and a pinch of salt and cook, stirring frequently, until translucent, about 5 minutes. Add the ginger, coriander, cumin, turmeric, and 1 teaspoon salt and stir for 30 seconds. Add the blanched turnips and carrot and stir to coat them with the onion-spice mixture. Add the turnip-greens puree and stir until evenly incorporated. Cover and cook, stirring occasionally, until the turnips and carrot are tender, about 5 minutes, uncovering the pan at the end to let excess moisture evaporate. Gently fold in the rice and cook to just heat through, about 2 minutes. Serve.

VARIATIONS

★ To make this a vegan main dish: Add 1 drained and rinsed (14-ounce / 400-g) can chickpeas (about 1½ cups) to the sauté pan with the blanched turnips and carrots.

★ To make this a vegetarian main dish: Add the chickpeas, as above, and either serve with a generous mound of plain yogurt alongside or stir a generous dollop of plain yogurt into the mixture just before adding the rice.

FRESH CRANBERRY RICE
Serves 4 | vegetarian, gluten free

I saw a recipe in an old rice cookbook years ago that used fresh cranberries in what was described as a "Swedish" rice dish, though since then, I have not been able to find reference to any traditional Swedish preparation of rice involving fresh cranberries. Perhaps it's Swedish in the same way that I always thought of challah as "Swiss bread" (thanks to my mom and a long-ago-clipped Pillsbury ad with a recipe for "Golden Braid of Berne"). This deep-pink, tart-sweet rice, with a hint of fresh dill, would be excellent with simply smoked or roasted fish and a slice of dense whole rye pumpernickel—or, if the occasion is particularly festive, a torn-off piece of buttery challah!

If cranberries are out of season, look for frozen ones, which work just as well here as fresh: Just give them a quick rinse in a colander.

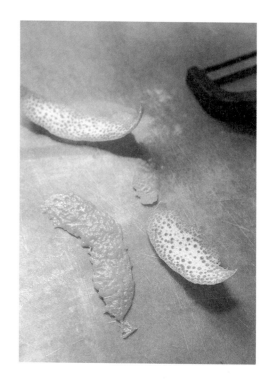

- **8 ounces (225 g) fresh cranberries**
- **3 tablespoons freshly squeezed orange juice**
- **1 teaspoon coarsely grated orange zest, plus thin strips for garnish**
- **2 tablespoons honey**
- **2 tablespoons sugar, or more to taste**
- **Salt and freshly ground black pepper**
- **3 cups (585 g) cooked long-grain brown rice (pages 29–30)**
- **1 teaspoon chopped fresh dill**

In a heavy 3-quart (2.8-L) saucepan, combine the cranberries, orange juice and grated zest, honey, sugar, and a pinch each of salt and pepper. Cook over medium heat, stirring frequently, until all the cranberries have burst and the liquid is somewhat thickened, 5 to 7 minutes. Taste and season with more sugar if necessary; it should be tart but sweet enough to be, you know, edible. Gently stir in the rice and dill and cook to heat through. Serve hot, sprinkled with strips of orange zest.

(VERY) DIRTY RICE
Serves 6 | *gluten free*

At a wacky potluck in a doublewide dance hall somewhere in Cajun country one evening years ago, I had my first lesson in dirty rice from an older couple. In their sixties, they partied (not to mention danced) better than I did in my twenties—and were kind enough not only to serve me some rice but to tell me how to make it myself when I got back to New York and started missing it. They told me to first make a roux, a step I no longer take since the absurdity of using *flour* in a *rice* dish dawned on me. Here's a very slightly lighter version, and see the variation for one that's even more so.

Dirty rice, in addition to being delicious and easy to make, is a friendly entrée into the nose-to-tail lifestyle. In fact, if you have a chicken back or neck in the freezer, go ahead and toss it into the pot with the gizzards and discard it with the bay leaf—the bones will give the broth body and more flavor.

- **1 pound (455 g) chicken gizzards and hearts, plus a few livers**
- **1 bay leaf**
- **Freshly ground black pepper**
- **1 teaspoon plus 1 tablespoon vegetable oil**
- **1 onion, diced**
- **2 ribs celery, diced**
- **1 teaspoon salt**
- **1/2 to 1 teaspoon ground cayenne, or more to taste**
- **1 1/2 cups (285 g) raw long-grain brown rice, rinsed at least three times**
- **4 scallions, thinly sliced**
- **Vinegary cayenne hot sauce, such as Crystal or Tabasco**

Put the gizzards, bay leaf, and a few grinds of black pepper in a medium saucepan, cover with cold water (at least 3 cups), and bring to a boil. Lower the heat and simmer for 30 minutes. Using tongs, remove the gizzards to a cutting board (discard the bay leaf) and set aside. Pour the broth through a fine-mesh sieve into a large glass measuring cup and set aside.

In a small sauté pan, heat the 1 teaspoon oil over medium-high heat. Add the chicken livers and hearts and cook, turning occasionally, for 5 minutes. Remove to the cutting board with the gizzards and let cool for a few minutes.

In a large, deep sauté pan or Dutch oven, heat the remaining tablespoon of oil over medium-high heat and add the onion. Cook, stirring occasionally, until translucent and beginning to brown, about 8 minutes.

Meanwhile, chop the gizzards, livers, and hearts until the largest pieces are about the size of a piece of the celery (and the hearts especially are no longer recognizable as such). Add them to the pan with the onion and cook until no pink remains and the onion is nicely browned and sticking to the bottom of the pan. Stir in the celery, salt, 1/2 teaspoon black pepper, the cayenne, and rice. Add 2 1/2 cups (600 ml) of the strained broth and stir to scrape up the browned bits. Cover the pan and bring to a boil, then lower the heat and simmer until the rice is tender and the liquid is absorbed, 45 to 50 minutes. If the rice is tender but the mixture is still soupy, uncover and increase the heat to high until the excess liquid is evaporated. Fold in the scallions and cook until heated through and wilted, about 3 minutes. Serve with hot sauce at the table.

VARIATION

★ For a quicker, much lighter dish using ground pork (or turkey) and cooked brown rice, omit the gizzards and hearts and livers and skip the broth making. Simply sauté the onion and celery together until lightly browned, about 8 minutes, then add 1 pound (455 g) ground pork or turkey and cook until the excess liquid in the pan is evaporated and the pork is lightly browned and no longer pink, about 5 minutes. Stir in the salt, cayenne, and black pepper to taste, then gently fold in the scallions and about 4 cups (780 g) cooked and cooled brown rice. Cook, turning frequently, until heated through. Serve with hot sauce.

SESAME AND CASHEW BROWN BASMATI RICE
Serves 3 or 4 | vegan, gluten free

This simple and surprisingly filling rice, with fragrant fresh curry leaves, toasty sesame seeds, and crunchy roasted cashews, is a simplified and lightened version of a classic Indian sesame rice featured in Neelam Batra's delightfully hefty *1,000 Indian Recipes*. If you can't find curry leaves, which are available at any Indian grocery store and many Asian ones (and which will keep for weeks in a sealed bag in the crisper drawer), just leave them out—the dish is worth making even without them.

- **1 cup (190 g) raw brown basmati rice**
- **Salt**
- **3 tablespoons sesame seeds**
- **1/2 teaspoon crushed red chile**
- **1 tablespoon olive or vegetable oil**
- **1/2 cup (65 g) coarsely chopped roasted unsalted cashews**
- **16 fresh curry leaves**
- **3 scallions, thinly sliced**

Rinse the rice in at least three changes of water, until the water is clear; drain well and put in a heavy 2-quart (2-L) saucepan with 1 1/2 cups (360 ml) water. Let soak for 30 minutes. Add 1/2 teaspoon salt and bring to a boil over high heat. Stir once, then cover and lower the heat to very low and cook until all the water is absorbed and the rice is tender, without stirring, 20 to 25 minutes. Remove from the heat and let rest, covered, for 5 minutes.

Heat a large deep sauté pan over medium-high heat. Add the sesame seeds and cook, stirring, until brown and fragrant, about 2 minutes. Scrape into a bowl. Add the crushed red chile to the hot pan and stir, off the heat, until darkened a shade, about 15 seconds. Scrape into the bowl with the sesame seeds and set aside.

Wipe out the pan, return it to medium-high heat, and add the oil. Add the cashews and curry leaves and cook, stirring, until the cashews are golden brown, about 1 1/2 minutes. Add the scallions and stir for 15 seconds. Add the rice and the sesame-chile mixture and gently fold with a heatproof spatula to combine and heat through. Season with more salt, if necessary, and serve hot.

RYE BERRIES WITH BRAISED RED CABBAGE, APPLES, AND DRIED CURRANTS

Serves 6 | vegetarian

To me, the flavor of rye berries cannot be separated from that of caraway. Without the slightly sweet caraway, rye berries seem—perhaps unfairly—to lack an essential part of their very character. Here they're both added to tender braised red cabbage and apple, and spiked with a little crushed red pepper, a splash of cider vinegar, and a handful of tangy dried currants. It makes a substantial Thanksgiving-type side dish that would also be especially nice under a thick-cut pan-roasted pork chop or alongside a good beer-simmered sausage.

- 1 tablespoon olive oil
- 1 tablespoon unsalted butter
- 1 onion, thinly sliced
- Salt
- 1 large apple, preferably Golden Delicious, quartered, cored, and cut crosswise into $1/4$-inch (6-mm) slices
- 1 tablespoon brown sugar
- 1 teaspoon caraway seeds, lightly crushed
- Pinch of crushed red pepper
- $1/2$ small head red cabbage, cored and cut crosswise into $1/4$-inch (6-mm) slices
- $1/2$ cup (120 ml) vegetable stock or water
- $1/4$ cup (60 ml) cider vinegar
- $2^1/2$ cups (440 g) cooked rye berries (page 31)
- $1/4$ cup (25 g) dried currants

In a large deep sauté pan or Dutch oven, heat the oil and butter over medium-high heat. Add the onion and a pinch of salt and cook, stirring frequently, until just starting to become tender, about 4 minutes. Add the apple and cook, stirring occasionally, until the apple and onion are lightly browned, about 8 minutes. Sprinkle in the brown sugar, caraway seeds, and crushed red pepper and stir for 1 minute. Add the cabbage and cook until just starting to wilt, about 2 minutes, then add the stock, vinegar, rye berries, currants, and $1^1/2$ teaspoons salt. Cover and cook until the cabbage is tender and most of the liquid is absorbed, about 15 minutes. Serve.

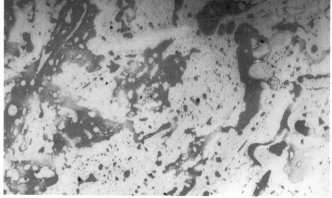

CREAMY SORGHUM
AND CABBAGE SLAW

Serves 8 | vegetarian, gluten free

Serve this classic slaw (well, classic except for the *sorghum*) with a pile of pulled-pork barbecue, or chicken pieces grilled Cornell style (marinated in vinegar, vegetable oil, herbs, whisked egg, and lot of salt), perhaps with a tall square of cornbread.

- **1 cup (240 ml) plain yogurt**
- **½ cup (120 ml) buttermilk**
- **Juice of 1 lime**
- **¾ teaspoon salt, or more if needed**
- **½ teaspoon freshly ground black pepper, or more if needed**
- **1 clove garlic**
- **4 scallions**
- **1 small (1½-pound / 680-g) green cabbage**
- **3 cups (480 g) cooked sorghum (page 32), chilled**

In a large bowl, whisk together the yogurt, buttermilk, lime juice, salt, and pepper. Using a fine grater, grate in the garlic; whisk to combine.

Thinly slice the scallions and add them to the bowl. Quarter and core the cabbage, then finely chop it (cut into ½-inch / 12-mm wedges, then thinly slice across several wedges at a time) and add it to the bowl. Add the sorghum and fold it into the dressing and vegetables. Taste and season with more salt and pepper if necessary. Serve, or set aside to chill in the refrigerator for up to 4 hours before serving.

CHARD-FLECKED COUSCOUS
WITH LEMON ZEST AND PINE NUTS

Serves 4 | vegan

Red-stemmed chard will tint this couscous a pretty, faint pink, but you can use white or yellow chard, spinach, or kale instead; if using kale, remove the tough stems and increase the sautéing time a bit to be sure it's tender before adding the water and couscous.

- **1 tablespoon olive oil**
- **½ bunch red chard, washed well, stems trimmed and thinly sliced, leaves chopped**
- **1 teaspoon salt**
- **¼ teaspoon freshly ground black pepper**
- **1 cup (170 g) raw whole wheat couscous**
- **½ teaspoon grated lemon zest**
- **3 tablespoons pine nuts**

In a heavy 2-quart (2-L) saucepan, heat the oil over high heat. When it shimmers, add the chard, salt, and pepper and cook, stirring frequently, until wilted, about 3 minutes. Add 1½ cups (360 ml) water and bring to a boil. Stir in the couscous and lemon zest, cover, and remove from the heat; let stand until all the water is absorbed and the couscous is tender, 10 to 15 minutes.

Meanwhile, in a small heavy sauté pan over medium-high heat, toast the pine nuts until lightly browned and fragrant, about 3 minutes. Fluff the couscous and fold in the pine nuts; serve hot.

CURRIED CRACKED WHEAT
AND GREEN LENTILS WITH YOGURT

Serves 2 to 4 | vegetarian

This hearty Indian-spiced dish would be great as part of a meal of several different dishes, such as tomato-stewed okra, plain basmati rice or warm flatbread, a spoonful of spicy pickle from the cupboard, and a simple cooling salad of thinly sliced cucumbers, fresh mint, lime juice, and salt.

- ¼ cup (60 ml) plain yogurt, plus more for serving
- 1 tablespoon olive oil
- ½ onion, diced
- ½ teaspoon cumin seeds
- ½ teaspoon yellow or brown mustard seeds
- ½ teaspoon turmeric
- ¼ teaspoon ground cayenne
- 1 teaspoon grated fresh ginger
- 1 clove garlic, grated
- ½ cup (95 g) green lentils, rinsed
- ½ cup (80 g) raw cracked wheat
- 1 teaspoon salt, or more to taste

Whisk the yogurt into 1½ cups (360 ml) water and set aside.

In a large sauté pan, heat the oil over medium-high heat. Add the onion and cook, stirring frequently, until soft and nicely browned, about 8 minutes. Add the cumin and mustard seeds, turmeric, cayenne, ginger, and garlic and cook, stirring, for 30 seconds. Add the yogurt-water, lentils, and cracked wheat. Bring to a boil, then cover, lower the heat, and simmer until the lentils and wheat are tender, about 30 minutes, adding the salt and ¾ cup (180 ml) more water about halfway through the cooking time and stirring occasionally. Serve with generous dollops of yogurt on the side.

VARIATION

★ For a more substantial dish or main course: Add 2 or 3 handfuls of random vegetables (such as chopped green beans, diced carrots, and sweet corn kernels) to the pan when the lentils and wheat are almost tender, cover, and continue to cook until the vegetables are tender, 5 to 10 minutes.

THAI HERB COUSCOUS
WITH BROWNED BUTTER AND SHALLOTS

Serves 3 or 4 | vegetarian

Here, the herby couscous is served with some ginger-garlic sautéed bok choy and roasted kabocha squash (page 176), but it would also be delicious with a nice piece of pan-seared fish and a salad of greens with pureed ginger-and-carrot dressing. Or make a quick-cooked ratatouille of sorts: Sauté a big pile of yellow squash and zucchini with garlic, grate in a couple of fresh tomatoes, tear in a few Thai basil leaves, and add some drained canned white beans to heat through.

- **2 tablespoons unsalted butter**
- **2 large shallots, very thinly sliced**
- **Salt**
- **1 cup (170 g) raw whole wheat couscous**
- **2 kaffir lime leaves, center rib removed, minced**
- **1/4 cup (20 g) chopped fresh cilantro**
- **1/4 cup (20 g) chopped fresh mint**
- **1/4 cup (20 g) chopped fresh Thai or regular basil**

Put a kettle of water on to boil.

In a heavy 2-quart (2-L) saucepan, melt the butter over medium-high heat. Add the shallots and a pinch of salt and cook, stirring frequently, until the shallots are very well browned and crisp. Using a slotted spoon, remove the shallots to a paper towel and set aside. Return the pan to medium heat and continue to cook the butter until deep golden bits appear. Stir in the couscous, kaffir lime leaves, 3/4 teaspoon salt, and 1 1/2 cups (360 ml) boiling water, cover the pan, and remove from the heat. Let stand until the water is absorbed and the couscous is tender, 10 to 15 minutes, then fluff with a rubber spatula and fold in the cilantro, mint, and basil. Transfer to a serving bowl, top with the shallots, and serve.

FARRO WITH BACON,
SHAVED BRUSSELS SPROUTS, AND ROASTED CHESTNUTS
Serves 4 to 6

I could imagine this dish on a traditional Thanksgiving table as a stand-in for bread-based stuffing: It's festive, with bits of bacon and freshly roasted chestnuts throughout the slightly crisped-up Brussels sprouts and tender farro. As soon as you see small local chestnuts in your market, snatch some up and roast them—the small American chestnuts are easier to peel and have a more vibrant flavor and color than the Asian ones. Put the whole peeled nuts in a freezer bag, suck out the air, seal, and freeze for up to 2 months. You can also, of course, use jarred or bagged roasted and peeled chestnuts.

- **4 ounces (115 g) bacon, diced**
- **½ onion, diced**
- **1 pound (455 g) Brussels sprouts, rinsed, trimmed, and very thinly sliced**
- **1 pound (455 g) small fresh chestnuts, roasted (see Note) and coarsely chopped**
- **2½ cups (420 g) cooked farro (page 36)**
- **2 tablespoons sherry vinegar, or to taste**
- **Salt and freshly ground black pepper**
- **Pinch of freshly grated nutmeg, or to taste**

In a large deep sauté pan, cook the bacon over medium heat until the fat is rendered and the bacon is crisp, about 8 minutes. Using a slotted spoon, remove the bacon to a paper towel to drain. Set aside.

Return the sauté pan with the bacon drippings to medium-high heat. Add the onion and cook, stirring frequently, until the onion is nicely browned, about 8 minutes. Add the Brussels sprouts and chestnuts and cook, stirring frequently, until the greens are wilted and beginning to brown, about 5 minutes. Fold in the farro and vinegar and cook to heat through. Season with salt, pepper, and nutmeg to taste, and add more vinegar if necessary. Serve hot.

NOTE: To roast chestnuts, set each chestnut on a cutting board flat side down and using a sharp knife (serrated works best) cut an X in the shell on the curved side. Arrange them X side up in a roasting pan and roast in a 400°F (205°C) oven for 20 to 25 minutes, until the X opens up and reveals the nut inside. Working quickly, while the chestnuts are still hot (hold them with a towel, if necessary, to protect your hands), peel the shell and inner brown papery skin off with your fingers.

FARRO WITH BUTTER-BRAISED CELERY AND TARRAGON
Serves 4 | vegetarian

Mild farro with braised celery and tarragon, enriched with good butter and plenty of black pepper, makes a creamy, unctuous, rich, comforting, unchallenging side dish—often just what a family needs on a cool fall evening.

- **3 tablespoons unsalted butter**
- **1/2 small onion, diced**
- **6 ribs celery, cut on the bias into 1/2-inch (12-mm) pieces, plus leaves from 1 bunch celery**
- **3/4 teaspoon salt, or more to taste**
- **1/2 teaspoon freshly ground black pepper**
- **2 1/2 cups (420 g) cooked farro (page 36)**
- **2 tablespoons chopped fresh tarragon**
- **Juice of 1/2 small lemon**

In a heavy 3-quart (2.8-L) saucepan over medium heat, melt the butter. Add the onion and cook, stirring frequently, until translucent, about 5 minutes. Add the celery (reserve the leaves) and cook, stirring occasionally, until just tender but still a bit crisp. Stir in the salt, pepper, farro, and 1/2 cup (120 ml) water. Increase the heat to high and bring to a boil. Cook, stirring frequently, until the farro is heated through, the celery is quite tender, and the liquid in the pan is creamy, reduced somewhat, and emulsified, about 8 minutes. Chop the celery leaves and stir them into the pan along with the tarragon and lemon juice. Cook for 2 minutes, then taste and add more salt if necessary. Serve hot.

VARIATIONS

★ This also works well with hulled barley, or a mixture of barley and farro or barley and wheat berries.

★ Use 1 teaspoon chopped fresh thyme instead of the tarragon.

SPELT WITH ESCAROLE AND MILK-POACHED GARLIC

Serves 4 | vegetarian

Escarole is an underused, underappreciated braising green that I believe deserves more attention. Its bitterness and the crunch at the pale green center of each leaf are nicely balanced by the tender, nutty spelt and mild poached garlic. Be sure to wash the escarole well; it's usually grown in sandy soil, and the leaves tend to hold on to grit. Fill a salad spinner bowl or a clean sink with water and swish the separated leaves around in it for a while, then let stand for a few minutes so the sand can settle at the bottom before lifting out the leaves.

- 1 head garlic, cloves separated and peeled
- ³/4 cup (180 ml) milk
- 1 tablespoon olive oil
- 1 small head or ¹/2 large head escarole, torn into pieces and washed well
- Salt and freshly ground black pepper
- 2 cups (390 g) cooked spelt berries (page 36)
- ¹/4 cup (25 g) freshly grated Parmesan cheese

Put the garlic and milk in a small saucepan and bring to a simmer over medium heat. Lower the heat and cook until the garlic is very soft, about 25 minutes. Remove with a slotted spoon and set aside. (Reserve the milk for use in a gratin, or drink it to build up your immune system—or just your character.)

In a large sauté pan, heat the oil over medium heat and add the poached garlic cloves, escarole, and a few pinches of salt and pepper. Cover and let steam for 1 to 2 minutes, then uncover and cook, turning the escarole with a spoon or spatula, until it is wilted and tender and the thick white parts of the leaves are almost translucent, about 3 more minutes. Add the spelt and gently fold it into the escarole and garlic. Cook until heated through and most of the liquid has evaporated, about 5 minutes. Taste and season again, then sprinkle with the cheese and serve.

VARIATION

★ Instead of escarole, use about 12 ounces (340 g) baby bok choy: Trim the stem ends and slice the heads crosswise into ¹/2-inch (12-mm) strips.

6

Sweets, Snacks, and Baked Goods

I love crusty, holey-crumbed white breads and delicate chiffon cakes as much as the next person, but even more I appreciate the deeper, richer flavors and varied textures of baked goods and desserts made with whole grains. Slightly chewy oatmeal cookies. Savory cornmeal muffins with no sweetener other than the natural sugars in blueberries and cornmeal. A creamy, extra-tangy custard pie of Greek yogurt and good eggs with plenty of fresh lime juice in a nutty Graham-style crust. Dark, dark chocolate squares full of crisp popped amaranth and chewy dried cherries. Thin rye crackers when you need something crunchy or to serve as delivery mechanisms for copious amounts of pimiento cheese (or hummus, or shards of a special cheese). Yes, these sweets, snacks, and baked goods are whole grain (one hundred percent), but there will be no doubt as you taste each one that it is a truly special treat. Trust me, you won't miss the refined stuff.

BLUEBERRY CORNMEAL MUFFINS
Makes 12 | vegetarian

In the old days, I'm told, muffins were not sweet. They were whipped up quickly in the early evening, just in time to serve with supper—on the plate next to pot roast, say, rather than for breakfast. Even blueberry muffins would be served with the main meal of the day, and they too would be savory at heart (if a little fruit-sweet and tangy). I think these muffins would be wonderful to serve to a group of friends in a basket on a big pine farm table with a hearty roast with pan gravy for sopping up and a platter of rosemary roasted fall vegetables.

- 6 tablespoons (85 g) unsalted butter, melted, plus more for the pan
- 1½ cups raw fine yellow cornmeal
- 1 cup (140 g) white whole wheat flour
- 4 teaspoons baking powder
- 1 teaspoon salt
- 1 cup fresh or frozen (not thawed) blueberries
- 1½ cups (360 ml) milk
- 1 large egg

Preheat the oven to 425°F (220°C). Generously butter a standard 12-cup muffin pan or spray it with nonstick cooking spray.

Into a large bowl, sift the cornmeal, flour, baking powder, and salt. Spoon 2 tablespoons of the mixture into a small bowl, add the blueberries, and toss to coat. Set aside.

In a glass measuring cup, whisk together the milk, egg, and butter. Pour into the large bowl with the dry ingredients and fold in with a rubber spatula until the dry ingredients are just moistened; do not overmix. Gently fold in the blueberries. Spoon the batter into the prepared muffin cups. Bake until golden brown at the edges, 15 to 20 minutes, rotating the pan halfway through so the muffins bake evenly. Transfer the pan to a wire rack and let cool for 5 minutes, then loosen the edge of each muffin in several places with a thin knife and lever them out with the knife. Let cool completely on the rack.

VARIATION
★ For slightly sweeter, fruitier olive oil muffins, add 3 tablespoons agave nectar or honey to the wet ingredients, and replace the butter with olive oil.

APPLE OAT MUFFINS

Makes 12 | vegetarian

Lightly sweetened and just right for a quick breakfast, these will be more familiar, as muffins, than the more austere ones on page 210. Try using other fruits instead of the apple—a pear or a cup of frozen raspberries or cherries would work well. If you like, stir a handful of toasted walnuts or pecans into the batter, or top each muffin with a pinch of sliced almonds, or a mixture of chopped nuts and coarse sugar before baking.

- ½ cup (120 ml) milk
- ½ cup (120 ml) plain Greek yogurt
- 1 cup (160 g) raw rolled oats
- ⅓ cup (80 ml) olive oil, vegetable oil, melted unsalted butter, or a combination, plus more for the pan
- 1 cup (140 g) white whole wheat flour
- 4 teaspoons baking powder
- Pinch of salt
- 1 teaspoon ground cinnamon
- 1 large egg
- 1 teaspoon pure vanilla extract
- ¼ cup (50 g) sugar
- 1 apple, peeled, cored, and diced

In a large bowl, combine the milk, yogurt, and oats and set aside to soak for 30 minutes to 1 hour.

Preheat the oven to 375°F (190°C). Generously butter a standard 12-cup muffin tin or spray it with nonstick cooking spray.

In a large bowl, whisk together the flour, baking powder, salt, and cinnamon. To the oats mixture, add the egg, vanilla, sugar, and oil and whisk until thoroughly combined. Add to the dry ingredients and stir with a spatula until just combined; do not overmix. Fold in the apple. Spoon into the prepared muffin tin, filling each hole about three-quarters full. Bake until a toothpick inserted in the center comes out clean and the tops are browned, about 25 minutes, rotating the tin halfway through. Loosen the edges of the muffins with a knife and transfer them to a wire rack to cool. The muffins will keep, stored in an airtight container at room temperature, for up to 3 days.

RYE AND PARMESAN SUPPER MUFFINS

Makes 12 | vegetarian

I wonder why you don't see many savory muffins made with rye. Studded with caraway seeds and topped with grated Parmesan for a toasty, crisp cap, these would be excellent alongside a roast, or with a tangy tomato soup for dunking. They're also good gently split in half with a sharp serrated knife, toasted under the broiler, and buttered. But then, what bakery product *wouldn't* be good split, toasted, and buttered?

- 1¼ cups (170 g) white whole wheat flour
- ¾ cup plus 2 tablespoons (85 g) whole rye flour
- 4 teaspoons baking powder
- 1 teaspoon caraway seeds, lightly crushed in a mortar
- ½ teaspoon salt
- 1 cup (240 ml) milk
- 1 large egg
- ½ cup (120 ml) vegetable oil
- ¼ cup (25 g) freshly grated Parmesan cheese

Preheat the oven to 425°F (220°C). Generously butter a standard 12-cup muffin pan or spray it with nonstick cooking spray.

In a large bowl, whisk together the flours, baking powder, caraway, and salt. Set aside.

In a glass measuring cup, whisk together the milk, egg, and oil. Pour into the large bowl with the dry ingredients and fold in with a rubber spatula until the dry ingredients are just moistened; do not overmix. Spoon the batter into the prepared muffin cups and sprinkle the tops with the cheese. Bake until golden brown, 15 to 20 minutes, rotating the pan halfway through so the muffins bake evenly. Transfer the pan to a wire rack and let cool for 5 minutes, then loosen the edge of each muffin in several places with a thin knife and lever it out with the knife. Let cool completely on the rack.

OATY BISCUITS

Makes 8 large or 16 small cookies | vegetarian

This is one of those recipes you may wish to commit to memory, and not just because the quantities are so easy to remember. In the universe of cookies made with whole grains, there may be none better for serving with an impromptu pot of tea with a friend than the very U.K. ones known as oaty biscuits. These cookies somehow straddle the line between substantial and delicate, sweet and savory (try them with a hunk of good cheese). You can have them mixed, in the oven, and the bowl and saucepan cleaned and in the dish drainer in about ten minutes.

They're also easily varied with different flours and grain flakes and judicious quantities of add-ins—see the variations for a couple ideas, but know that as long as the resulting dough can be formed into rough disks, you can add just about anything (as I write, my five-year-old daughter is cutting up a stale marshmallow to stir into her own *very loose* adaptation of oaty biscuit dough; hey, whatever keeps her busy for a few minutes, right?).

- **6 tablespoons (85 g) unsalted butter**
- **1/3 cup (75 g) brown sugar**
- **1 cup (160 g) raw rolled oats**
- **1 cup (140 g) white whole wheat flour**
- **1 teaspoon baking powder**
- **1/4 teaspoon salt**
- **1 large egg, beaten**

Preheat the oven to 350°F (175°C). Line a baking sheet with parchment paper.

In a small heavy saucepan, melt the butter with the brown sugar; let cool for 5 minutes.

In a medium bowl, combine the oats, flour, baking powder, and salt. Stir in the butter mixture, then the egg. Use a 1/4-cup (60-ml) measure to scoop out 3-tablespoon blobs of the dough (for large cookies) or 1 1/2-tablespoon blobs (for small) and drop them onto the prepared baking sheet, patting the dough with your palm to 1/4-inch-thick (6-mm-thick) circles at least 1 1/2 inches (4 cm) apart. Bake in the center of the oven until firm and golden brown at the edges, about 20 minutes. Let cool on the pan for 5 minutes, then transfer to a wire rack to cool completely. The cookies will keep in an airtight container for up to 1 week.

VARIATIONS

★ Add a small handful of diced dried fruit and 1/2 teaspoon ground cinnamon to the dough.

★ Add 2 tablespoons shredded unsweetened coconut and 1/4 cup (30 g) chopped pecans or roasted unsalted cashews to the dough.

★ Use a combination of rolled oats and barley, rye, and wheat flakes.

BROWNED-BUTTER OATMEAL COOKIES

Makes about 14 large cookies | vegetarian, gluten free*

The toasted oats and browned butter give these hearty cookies a deep nutty flavor. For softer cookies, underbake them by a few minutes.

- 4 cups (640 g) raw rolled oats (not quick or instant oats)
- ½ cup (70 g) extra-fine brown rice flour
- 1½ teaspoons baking soda
- ¼ teaspoon salt
- 1 cup (2 sticks / 225 g) unsalted butter
- 1¼ cups (275 g) packed brown sugar
- 1 large egg
- 1 teaspoon pure vanilla extract
- 1 cup (165 g) raisins

Preheat the oven to 375°F (190°C). Line two baking sheets with parchment paper.

In a large sauté pan over medium-high heat, toast the oats, stirring frequently, for 4 to 5 minutes, until fragrant. Let cool completely, then put 2 cups (320 g) of the oats in a food processor and grind as finely as possible (this takes about 1½ minutes in my mini food processor). Add the brown rice flour, baking soda, and salt and process to combine. Set aside.

Wipe out the sauté pan and put the butter in it. Heat over medium-low heat until melted, then continue to cook, stirring occasionally, until the bits of solids at the bottom of the pan start to brown, 5 to 6 minutes; remove from the heat and let cool to lukewarm.

In a large bowl, beat the brown sugar together with the browned butter until well combined; beat in the egg and vanilla. Stir in the ground oat mixture, then the oats and raisins; the dough will be a little crumbly. Shape into slightly flattened 2-inch (5-cm) balls by squeezing the dough between your palms, and place them 1½ inches (4 cm) apart on the prepared baking sheets. Bake until golden brown at the edges but still soft in the centers, 12 to 14 minutes, rotating the pan halfway through so the cookies bake evenly. Let cool on the pans for 5 minutes, then transfer to wire racks to cool.

* See page 25.

MASA ZALETTI
(CORNMEAL COOKIES)

Makes about 28 cookies | vegetarian, gluten free

I'd been making zaletti, the not-too-sweet Italian cornmeal cookies, for years before my mom told me they're even better when made with at least some portion of masa harina, and she's right: The tortilla-like flavor of the masa brings them back to the New World and renders the cookies a bit more savory than when made with the slightly sweeter cornmeal.

- ⅓ cup (35 g) dried currants
- 1½ cups (190 g) masa harina (preferably "for tortillas")
- 1 cup (140 g) raw fine yellow cornmeal
- Pinch of salt
- 10 tablespoons (140 g) unsalted butter, melted
- 3 large egg yolks, beaten
- ⅓ cup (65 g) sugar
- ½ teaspoon baking soda
- Grated zest of 1 large lemon

Preheat the oven to 375°F (190°C). Line two baking sheets with parchment paper.

Put the currants in a bowl and cover with hot water; let soak until soft.

Meanwhile, in a large bowl, whisk together the masa harina, yellow cornmeal, and salt. Using a rubber spatula, stir in the butter.

In a medium bowl, whisk together the egg yolks, sugar, baking soda, and lemon zest. Pour the mixture into the masa harina mixture and stir to combine. Drain the currants, reserving the soaking water; add the currants to the dough and knead gently in the bowl with your hands until the dough is thoroughly combined, sprinkling in up to 4 tablespoons (60 ml) of the currant soaking water a little at a time to make a dough that holds together when you squeeze it. Scoop up a rounded-tablespoon-size chunk of dough and squeeze it into a ball; flatten it between your palms to make a ¼-inch-thick (6-mm-thick) round and place it on the prepared baking sheet. Repeat with the remaining dough, and arrange the rounds 1 inch (2.5 cm) apart. Bake until golden brown at the edges and firm in the centers, about 12 minutes, rotating the pans halfway through so they brown evenly. Let cool on the pans for 5 minutes, then transfer to wire racks to cool.

SALTED RYE COOKIES

Makes about 48 cookies | vegetarian

This fairly straightforward and versatile dough can be made as drop cookies instead of icebox-style sliced logs: Chill the dough, then scoop it into rounded-tablespoon-size balls, roll in the salt-sugar mixture, arrange at least 1½ inches (4 cm) apart on the baking sheet, and flatten slightly. In addition, you can substitute just about any kind of flour for the rye.

- 1 cup (2 sticks / 225 g) unsalted butter, at room temperature
- ¾ cup (150 g) granulated sugar
- 1 large egg
- Kosher salt
- ½ teaspoon finely grated orange zest
- 2½ cups (230 g) whole (dark) rye flour
- 3 tablespoons coarse sparkling sugar or turbinado sugar

In a large bowl, using an electric mixer, cream the butter and granulated sugar together until light and fluffy. Beat in the egg, a pinch of salt, and the orange zest. Gradually mix in the flour. Divide the dough into two portions and place each on a sheet of plastic wrap. Shape into logs about 2 inches (5 cm) in diameter and wrap tightly. To shape the soft dough log into a more perfect cylinder, use a paper-towel tube: Cut the tube open vertically along one side and nest the wrapped log inside, then tape or rubber-band the tube closed. Chill in the refrigerator until firm, about 1 hour.

Preheat the oven to 350°F (175°C). Line two baking sheets with parchment paper.

On a sheet of waxed paper, combine 1½ teaspoons salt and the sparkling sugar. Unwrap the dough logs and roll them in the mixture to coat well. Place each log on a cutting board and cut into ⅛-inch-thick (3-mm-thick) rounds, arranging the rounds 1 inch (2.5 cm) apart on the prepared baking sheets. Bake until lightly browned at the edges, about 16 minutes, rotating the pans halfway through so the cookies bake evenly. Remove to wire racks to cool completely. The cookies can be stored at room temperature in an airtight container for up to 1 week.

VARIATION

★ For black walnut teff cookies: Instead of the rye flour, use 1⅔ cups (225 g) teff flour and 1 cup (115 g) whole spelt flour. Omit the orange zest and add ½ cup (60 g) chopped black walnuts to the dough. Roll the dough logs in maple sugar, if you like.

CORNMEAL OLIVE OIL CAKE WITH BASIL GLAZE

Serves 8 to 12 | vegetarian

This cake is a real treat: sweet and light-textured, with a simple basil-scented glaze that drips attractively down the side of the cake before it firms up into a crusty icing. If your olive oil is an especially fruity extra-virgin one you might want to cut it with a little neutral vegetable oil to mellow the flavor a bit. You can use medium- or coarse-grind cornmeal if that's all you have; just sift out the larger pieces of corn before measuring so the cake isn't gritty. The vegan variation that follows is not at all similar in consistency or appearance, but is equally delicious.

FOR THE CAKE

- 1$\frac{1}{2}$ cups (170 g) whole spelt flour or white whole wheat flour
- $\frac{1}{2}$ cup (70 g) raw fine yellow cornmeal
- $\frac{3}{4}$ cup (150 g) sugar
- 4 teaspoons baking powder
- $\frac{1}{2}$ teaspoon salt
- 2 large eggs
- 1 cup (240 ml) plain yogurt (nonfat is fine)
- Finely grated zest of 1 large lemon
- 1 teaspoon pure vanilla extract
- $\frac{1}{2}$ cup (120 ml) olive oil

FOR THE GLAZE

- $\frac{1}{4}$ cup (60 ml) half-and-half or heavy cream
- 1 sprig fresh basil, torn up, plus 6 additional whole sprigs for garnish
- 1 cup (100 g) confectioners' sugar
- 2 tablespoons freshly squeezed lemon juice

MAKE THE CAKE

Preheat the oven to 350°F (175°C). Lightly oil a 9-inch (23-cm) springform pan or spray it with nonstick cooking spray. (Alternatively, use a deep 9-inch / 23-cm round regular pan.)

In a large bowl, whisk together the flour, cornmeal, sugar, baking powder, and salt.

In a separate medium bowl, whisk together the eggs, yogurt, lemon zest, and vanilla, then whisk in the oil. Pour the mixture into the dry ingredients and fold with a rubber spatula until just combined; do not overmix. Scrape the batter into the prepared pan and smooth the top. Bake on the center rack of the oven until a toothpick inserted in the center comes out clean and the cake has pulled away from the side of the pan, 35 to 40 minutes. Set the pan on a wire rack to cool slightly.

MAKE THE GLAZE

While the cake is baking, combine the half-and-half and torn basil in a small heavy saucepan, and bring to a boil. Remove from the heat, cover, and let steep for 20 minutes. Sift the confectioners' sugar into a small bowl and pour the cream through a fine-mesh sieve into the bowl. Whisk until smooth, then whisk in the lemon juice.

Remove the outer ring of the cake pan. (If you used a regular pan, run a knife around the edge to loosen it, then invert onto a second rack, carefully remove the pan, then reinvert so the cake is right side up.) Slide a piece of waxed paper under the rack to catch drips of glaze. While the cake is still warm, spoon about half of the glaze over the top and let it drip prettily down the sides. When the glaze is set, after about 15 minutes, spoon on some more of the glaze (you may not use all of it). Let the cake cool completely, then transfer to a cake plate (with or without the pan bottom), and garnish with the basil sprigs.

VARIATION

★ To make a vegan cornmeal cake, increase the flour to 1$\frac{3}{4}$ cups (200 g). Omit the eggs. Instead of the yogurt, use 1$\frac{1}{4}$ cups (300 ml) plain nut, soy, or rice milk plus 2 tablespoons freshly squeezed lemon juice. In the glaze, use nut, soy, or rice milk instead of half-and-half. The cake will be moister and denser than the nonvegan version, sort of like a brownie, with an addictively chewy, caramel-flavored edge, and the glaze will be more of a syrup that soaks into the cake than an icing that sits atop it.

CARDAMOM APPLE CRISP
Serves 4 to 6 | vegetarian

Fruit crisps are usually afterthoughts in my family, desserts Mom throws together with some nut-butter-oat topping from the freezer and sticks in the oven just before supper's ready. But this one, with cardamom, is just special enough to plan to make and serve for guests. If you have cast-iron mini cocotte dishes or single-serving-size ovenproof cups, you can divide the fruit and topping among them and arrange them on a sheet pan to bake.

- **6 tablespoons (85 g) unsalted butter, softened, plus more for the pan**
- **2¹/₂ pounds (1.2 kg) apples (about 6), preferably a mix of sweet and tart**
- **¹/₂ cup (60 g) whole wheat or white whole wheat flour**
- **¹/₂ cup (55 g) raw rolled oats**
- **¹/₂ cup (110 g) brown sugar**
- **1¹/₄ teaspoons ground cardamom**
- **¹/₂ teaspoon freshly grated nutmeg**
- **Milk for serving (optional)**

Preheat the oven to 375°F (190°C). Lightly butter a 9-inch (23-cm) square baking pan.

Peel (if you like), core, and slice the apples ¹/₄ inch (6 mm) thick and put them in the prepared baking pan.

In a medium bowl, combine the remaining ingredients, working the butter into the dry ingredients with your fingertips. Scatter the mixture over the apples, pinching some of it into clumps. Bake until the topping is nicely browned and the apples are tender, about 30 minutes. Serve warm in bowls, with a splash of milk, if using.

VARIATIONS

★ To make gluten-free crisp topping, use brown rice flour, quinoa flour, buckwheat flour, or almond meal instead of wheat flour, and be sure to use gluten-free oats.

★ Try pears, peaches, nectarines, or plums instead of or in addition to the apples.

★ Use ground cinnamon instead of cardamom and add ¹/₂ teaspoon ground cloves to the topping.

★ Add a handful of chopped walnuts or pecans to the topping, and stir some raisins (plumped in rum or brandy, perhaps) into the apples.

★ Sprinkle the fruit with a little rosewater or grate in some orange zest and add a handful of chopped pistachios to the topping.

LIME CUSTARD PIE WITH ALMOND AND "GRAHAM-FLOUR" CRUST

Serves 8 | vegetarian

The standard four-ingredient Key lime pie (graham-cracker crust from the store, bottled Key lime juice, sweetened condensed milk, egg yolks—period) is hard to beat, I'll admit that right away. But this pie does it. By a wide margin. Let's start with the crust, which combines whole wheat pastry flour (made from soft white wheat) and coarser wheat bran and/or germ to approximate hard-to-find true Graham flour. The ground almonds contribute to the crumbly, crunchy texture and enrich the crust with a little more fat. The filling is simplicity itself: a quick whisk of whole eggs, Greek yogurt, lime juice, and a touch of sugar to balance the double hit of tanginess that bakes into a delicate, light, trembling custard. I tend to serve the pie just straight up, but a drift of whipped cream would be splendid too.

FOR THE CRUST

- **1 cup (110 g) whole almonds**
- **1/3 cup (65 g) sugar**
- **1 cup (130 g) whole wheat pastry flour**
- **1/4 cup (20 g) wheat bran or toasted wheat germ, or a combination**
- **1/2 teaspoon salt**
- **1/2 cup (1 stick / 110 g) unsalted butter, melted**

FOR THE FILLING AND TO SERVE

- **3 large eggs**
- **1 1/2 cups (360 ml) plain Greek yogurt**
- **2/3 cup (130 g) sugar**
- **2/3 cup (160 ml) freshly squeezed lime juice**
- **Lightly sweetened whipped cream (optional)**
- **Very thinly sliced lime (optional)**

MAKE THE CRUST

In a food processor or blender, process the almonds and sugar until finely ground. Transfer to a medium bowl and add the flour, wheat bran and/or germ, and salt and whisk to combine. Drizzle in the butter and use a rubber spatula to stir with a quick cutting motion until the dry ingredients are evenly moistened. Pat the mixture firmly into a 9- or 9 1/2-inch (23- or 24-cm) glass pie dish, making sure the crust is even and that it extends all the way up the sides. Set aside in the refrigerator to chill for 30 minutes.

Preheat the oven to 400°F (205°C).

MAKE THE FILLING

In a large bowl, whisk the eggs, yogurt, and sugar together until smooth, then whisk in the lime juice until smooth and the sugar is dissolved. Set aside.

Bake the empty crust in the center of the oven for 10 minutes. Pour in the filling and carefully return the pie dish to the oven. Immediately lower the oven temperature to 325°F (165°C) and bake until the filling is just set in the center (it'll still be jiggly) and the crust is nicely browned, 55 to 60 minutes. Let cool on a wire rack for 2 hours, then refrigerate until very cold, at least 2 hours.

Slice and serve with whipped cream and lime, if you'd like. The pie will keep, covered in plastic wrap in the refrigerator, for up to 1 day.

SWEET LEMON QUINOA CUSTARDS WITH PAPAYA SYRUP

Serves 6 | vegan, gluten free

This elegant, clean-tasting dessert couldn't be simpler. In fact, the only challenge might be finding enough sort-of-matching custard cups and the agar powder or flakes (check the baking aisle or bulk-spice sections of the health food store, or the specialty or "organic" area of a good supermarket). If keeping it vegetarian isn't the goal, you can also make these pseudo-custards with unflavored gelatin: In a small saucepan, stir 1 teaspoon gelatin into ¼ cup (60 ml) water and let soak for 5 minutes, then heat it over very low heat, stirring just until it's dissolved, then continue with the recipe, stirring in the almond milk, sugar, and so on. Also, feel free to use regular whole milk if you like.

FOR THE CUSTARDS

- **2 cups (370 g) cooked quinoa (page 27)**
- **Grated zest of 1 lemon**
- **1 teaspoon agar powder, or 2 tablespoons agar flakes**
- **2 cups (480 ml) almond milk (page 71)**
- **⅔ cup (130 g) sugar**
- **Pinch of salt**

FOR THE PAPAYA SYRUP

- **1 small ripe papaya, peeled, halved, seeded, and chopped**
- **½ cup (100 g) sugar**

MAKE THE CUSTARDS

Set six 6-ounce (180-ml) custard cups or ramekins in a baking pan or on a plate. (If you want to serve them in the cups, you can use pretty mismatched teacups, as they won't need to be heated in this recipe, just chilled.)

Put the quinoa and lemon zest in a large bowl and set aside.

In a small heavy saucepan, bring ¼ cup (60 ml) water to a boil. Add the agar and stir well. Remove from the heat and let soak for 5 minutes. Stir in the almond milk, sugar, and salt and bring to a simmer over medium heat, stirring constantly. Simmer for 1 minute (the mixture will start to thicken), then pour over the quinoa mixture. Stir well, then divide the "custard" among the custard cups. Put in the refrigerator until set and chilled, about 2 hours (it will set in less than half that time, but it should be served completely cold). If not serving right away, cover with plastic wrap.

MAKE THE PAPAYA SYRUP

Put the papaya, sugar, and ½ cup (120 ml) water in a heavy saucepan and bring to a boil. Lower the heat and simmer until the papaya is very tender and the thinner edges start to become translucent, 15 to 25 minutes depending on the ripeness of the fruit. Transfer to a bowl or other container and refrigerate until chilled, about 2 hours.

To serve, loosen the edge of each custard with a knife and turn it out onto a serving plate. Spoon the papaya syrup and slices over the top and serve.

VARIATIONS

★ For a vanilla custard: Omit the lemon zest and add 1 split and scraped vanilla bean to the custard mixture. (After simmering, rinse, pat dry, and reserve the vanilla bean pod for another use.)

★ For a coconut custard: Replace 1 cup (240 ml) of the almond milk with coconut milk and add 1 tablespoon unsweetened shredded coconut to the custard mixture.

★ Use 2 mangoes instead of a papaya.

QUINOA AND CHICKPEA-FLOUR SWEETS WITH CARDAMOM

Makes 24; serves 6 | vegan, gluten free

These pan-fried sweets are a sweet, quinoa-enhanced take on French panisse, or chickpea-flour fries. I've always loved panisse in theory, as a low-glycemic substitute for fried potatoes, more than in practice: The soft, custardlike interior always seemed just a little off to me, and the chickpea flour (aka besan) a little bland. Quinoa and cardamom to the rescue! Quinoa gives the batter some needed structure and texture, and cardamom sort of clarifies and grounds the flavor of the besan.

- About ¹⁄₂ cup (120 ml) vegetable oil, plus more for the pan
- 1 cup (130 g) chickpea flour (besan), plus more for dredging
- ¹⁄₂ teaspoon ground cardamom
- Pinch of salt
- ¹⁄₄ cup (55 g) brown sugar
- 1¹⁄₂ cups (275 g) cooked quinoa (page 27), cooled
- 2 tablespoons confectioners' sugar

Lightly oil a 9-inch (23-cm) square baking pan.

Sift the 1 cup chickpea flour, the cardamom, and salt into a heavy 2-quart (2-L) saucepan. Whisk in the brown sugar, then whisk in 1 cup (240 ml) water until fairly smooth. Whisk in another 1 cup (240 ml) water. Place the pan over medium-high heat and cook, stirring frequently with a heatproof spatula and scraping the flour paste from the bottom and the corners of the pan, until the mixture is a thick paste, about 8 minutes. Remove from the heat and quickly stir in the quinoa, then spread the mixture out evenly in the prepared pan about ¹⁄₂ inch (12 mm) thick, patting it smooth with your dampened hands as necessary. Transfer the pan to the refrigerator until cooled and firm, about 15 minutes.

Cut the chickpea-flour "cake" into 24 small triangles. Spread some chickpea flour on a plate and dredge the rectangles in the flour to coat both sides, shaking off the excess.

In a large, heavy sauté pan, preferably *not* nonstick, put enough oil to cover the bottom. Heat over medium-high heat. When the oil is shimmering, add some of the chickpea-flour triangles in a single layer, being careful not to crowd the pan. Cook without turning for 3 to 4 minutes, until deep golden brown on the bottom (you'll notice the bottom edges beginning to brown). Using a thin metal spatula, turn the triangles over and brown the other side. Remove to paper towels to drain. Repeat with the remaining triangles, wiping out the pan and adding more oil as necessary. (The sweets can be made up to 2 hours in advance and warmed and crisped in a clean dry sauté pan just before serving.)

Put the confectioners' sugar in a sieve and sift it over the sweets. Serve warm.

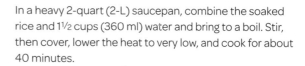

BLACK RICE PUDDING
WITH COCONUT MILK AND CANDIED SWEET POTATO
Serves 6 | vegan, gluten free

A couple years ago, my friend Regan Huff brought over an old yogurt tub of black rice pudding she'd made, and we ate it. Out of her colorful woven-plastic-tape market bag that I've come to consider infused with some kind of culinary magic, she also pulled a second yogurt tub. This one, labeled BLACK RICE PUDDING FOR LATER, contained raw black rice, one of those awesome mini cans of Thai coconut milk, and a handwritten recipe.

- 1 cup (190 g) raw black rice, soaked overnight and drained
- ⅔ cup (150 g) brown sugar or turbinado sugar
- 1 small sweet potato, peeled and diced
- ½ (13.5-ounce / 400-ml) can coconut milk (about ¾ cup / 80 ml), plus more for serving
- ¼ teaspoon salt
- Toasted sesame seeds or chopped roasted peanuts

In a heavy 2-quart (2-L) saucepan, combine the soaked rice and 1½ cups (360 ml) water and bring to a boil. Stir, then cover, lower the heat to very low, and cook for about 40 minutes.

Meanwhile, in a separate small saucepan, combine ⅓ cup (75 g) of the sugar and 1 cup (240 ml) water and add the sweet potato. Bring to a boil, stirring frequently, then lower the heat and simmer briskly until the sweet potato is a bit translucent at the edges and very tender but still holds its shape, 25 to 30 minutes; the syrup will be reduced and the water almost completely evaporated, so watch closely toward the end of the cooking and stir or lower the heat as necessary to prevent sticking. Transfer the sweet potato to a bowl and set aside.

In the same saucepan, combine the coconut milk, salt, and remaining ⅓ cup (75 g) sugar and bring to a boil, stirring to dissolve the sugar and salt.

When the rice is tender and most of the liquid has been absorbed, pour in the coconut milk mixture and stir well. Bring to a boil and cook, stirring frequently, until the mixture is the consistency of thin rice pudding. Spoon small portions into small dessert bowls, top with the sweet potato and sesame seeds, drizzle with more coconut milk, if desired, and serve warm or at room temperature. The pudding and sweet potato can be made up to 1 day in advance and refrigerated. Warm the pudding over very low heat, adding a little water if necessary to loosen it, before serving.

SWEET CRACKED-WHEAT PUDDING WITH CARDAMOM AND CASHEWS

Serves 4 | vegan

Only slightly sweet for an after-supper pudding, but very comforting and homey nonetheless, this fairly classic Indian dessert can withstand all sorts of whims and fancies: Use another grain instead of cracked wheat and adjust the cooking time and water quantity as necessary (millet, quinoa, and short-grain rice would all work well). Use any kind of milk (soy milk, rice milk, or regular cow's milk for a nonvegan version); any sweet-dessert spices and flavorings you find appealing (just a pinch each of ground cloves and cinnamon, some grated orange zest from the freezer door, a used vanilla bean pod); and any nuts that would go well— or even fresh cut-up fruit or berries.

- 1 cup (160 g) raw cracked wheat
- 3 cups (720 ml) almond milk (page 71)
- ¼ cup (55 g) packed brown sugar
- ½ teaspoon ground cardamom
- ¼ cup (35 g) roasted unsalted cashews

In a heavy 2-quart (2-L) saucepan, combine the cracked wheat, milk, brown sugar, and cardamom. Bring to a boil, then lower the heat and simmer until the cracked wheat is tender, about 20 minutes. Serve warm in small bowls, sprinkled with cashews, or put in the refrigerator until very cold; stir well and sprinkle with cashews before serving chilled.

VARIATIONS

★ This is also great with freekeh, or cracked green wheat, instead of the regular cracked wheat.

★ Add a splash of rosewater just before serving.

★ For a thicker pudding, add ¼ cup (40 g) rolled oats along with the cracked wheat. Or if you aren't concerned with keeping it vegan, put 1 large egg yolk in a small bowl and, using a fork, gradually whisk in a spoonful of the hot cracked-wheat mixture; gradually stir the egg-yolk mixture back into the saucepan and cook, stirring frequently, for 5 minutes— do not boil.

DOUBLE-QUINOA VANILLA PUDDING

Serves 4 to 6 | vegetarian, gluten free

You know how you crave vanilla pudding when you're sick, or sad, or just bone tired? Maybe that just runs in my family. Anyway, this is the same sort of dessert. Creamy, a little sweet, and very soothing. The quinoa—both whole and thin rolled flakes sold as a quick-cooking breakfast porridge—boosts the nutritional content, which I think can only make it more comforting. When I'm healthy, I like it with tart fresh fruit or berries and crunchy nuts as counterpoints to the rich, soft pudding— but when I'm not, the plain custard itself is all I want or need.

- 3 cups (720 ml) milk
- ⅓ cup (65 g) sugar
- ½ cup (85 g) raw ivory quinoa, well rinsed
- ½ cup (50 g) quinoa flakes
- 1 large egg yolk
- ½ teaspoon pure vanilla extract
- 2 ripe peaches, nectarines, or plums, pitted and diced
- Toasted sliced almonds, toasted pepitas, toasted sesame seeds, and/or ground cinnamon, to taste (optional)

In a heavy 2-quart (2-L) saucepan, combine the milk, sugar, and whole quinoa. Bring to a boil, watching carefully to make sure it doesn't boil over, then lower the heat and simmer, stirring occasionally, until the quinoa is tender, about 20 minutes. Stir in the quinoa flakes and simmer, stirring occasionally, for 3 minutes. Put the egg yolk in a small bowl and very gradually whisk in about ½ cup (120 ml) of the hot quinoa mixture, then gradually whisk it back into the saucepan; do not let the pudding boil after you've added the egg yolk. Cook over low heat for 2 minutes, whisking frequently. Whisk in the vanilla and remove from the heat. Let stand for 5 minutes to thicken, then spoon into small bowls and top with the peaches. If you like, top with toasted almonds, pepitas, sesame seeds, and/ or cinnamon.

Alternatively, after adding the vanilla, transfer to a bowl, put a piece of plastic wrap directly on the surface, and refrigerate until very cold, about 2 hours; serve chilled with the peaches and add the other toppings as desired.

WHOLE WHEAT COCONUT AND PISTACHIO LADOO
(INDIAN SWEETS)
Makes about 14 sweets | vegetarian

Ladoo are Indian sweetmeats made by melting ghee and stirring in flour and flavorings, cooking until thick and toasty, then either forming the resulting dough into little walnut-size spheres while it's still hot or pressing it into a pan and cutting into squares when it's firm and cool. The little treats are most often made with chickpea flour (besan), but they're just as melt-in-your-mouth—and even more flavorful, I was happy to discover—when made with whole wheat flour. This is an excellent time to use a good stone-ground whole wheat flour, whose coarse texture and darker flavor work better here than in many baked goods in which they can become overpowering.

- 1 cup (2 sticks / 225 g) unsalted butter, or ¾ cup (85 g) ghee
- 1¾ cups (200 g) whole wheat flour
- ¼ cup (25 g) unsweetened shredded coconut
- ½ cup (110 g) packed dark brown sugar
- ½ teaspoon pure vanilla extract
- ¼ cup (30 g) shelled pistachios (salted or unsalted), ground or very finely chopped

If using butter, in a heavy 2-quart (2-L) saucepan, melt the butter over medium-high heat. Continue to cook at a brisk simmer until the foam on top dissipates and turns to larger bubbles, about 5 minutes. Carefully pour into a heatproof container and let stand for a few minutes; wipe out the saucepan. Spoon off any white solids from the top of the butter and discard. Slowly pour the clear butter back into the saucepan, leaving the white solids at the bottom in the container; discard the solids. (If using ghee, simply melt it in the saucepan over medium heat.)

Add the flour and coconut and cook over medium heat, stirring constantly with a heatproof spatula, for 5 minutes, or until the flour smells toasty and no longer raw. Add the brown sugar and vanilla and cook, stirring, until the sugar is melted and thoroughly incorporated, about 5 minutes. Scrape the mixture into a baking pan or dish and pack it tightly with the spatula into a layer about ½ inch (12 mm) thick, squaring

off or trimming the edges as evenly as you can. Sprinkle the pistachios over the top and press with the spatula or your palm to make them adhere. Let cool for 5 minutes, then cut into squares and let cool completely on a wire rack. Store in an airtight container in the refrigerator; the sweets will keep for up to 1 week.

* See page 25.

227

CHEWY CHOCOLATE-TAHINI PUFFED-GRAIN SQUARES

Makes 16 | vegetarian

These chewy, dense squares were inspired by a recipe in Terry Walters's brilliant book *Clean Food*. There's very little in here that isn't good for you, and yet my daughter—who is certainly no stranger to real sweets—absolutely loves them. Parents in particular should appreciate the value of a treat-snack you don't really have to think twice about allowing. These keep nicely for up to two weeks in the refrigerator.

If you want to keep it gluten free, use puffed brown rice or millet or a combination of the two. You might also consider substituting sunflower seeds for the almonds (allergenic to many kids) if you plan to pack one of these into a kid's school lunchbox or send them to school as a treat for the class.

- **1 cup (110 g) whole almonds**
- **4 cups (60 g) unsweetened puffed Kamut, brown rice, spelt, or millet, or a combination**
- **2 tablespoons shredded unsweetened coconut (optional)**
- **1 tablespoon flax seeds, coarsely ground**
- **3 tablespoons olive or vegetable oil**
- **½ cup (120 ml) honey or maple syrup**
- **2 ounces (55 g) bittersweet chocolate, chopped**
- **2 tablespoons tahini**
- **Pinch of salt**

In a food processor or blender, pulse the almonds until finely ground. Dump into a large bowl and add the puffed grains, coconut, if using, and flax seeds.

In a small heavy saucepan, combine the oil, honey, chocolate, tahini, and salt. Cook over medium heat just until the chocolate is melted and the mixture is semi-uniform. Pour over the mixture in the bowl and stir with a rubber spatula until well coated. Dump the mixture into a 9-inch (23-cm) square baking pan or dish and press firmly with your palms or the spatula to an even layer. Use a bench knife or metal spatula to cut into 16 squares, then cover and put in the refrigerator until firm, about 15 minutes. Transfer to an airtight container and store in the refrigerator for up to 2 weeks.

VARIATION

★ For vanilla squares (pictured): Add ½ cup (35 g) nonfat dry milk powder to the puffed-grains mixture. Use 3 ounces (85 g) white chocolate instead of the bittersweet. Use 2 tablespoons butter instead of the oil. Add ½ teaspoon pure vanilla extract to the liquid mixture after you remove it from the heat.

AMARANTH AND DRIED CHERRY CHOCOLATES

Makes about 16 chocolates | vegetarian, gluten free

Add value to a block of good chocolate with crisp puffed amaranth and fancy dried cherries—preferably sour cherries, if you can find them—and give these tiny confections as a holiday gift. They'll keep for a good while at room temperature, as the melted chocolate is effectively tempered by seeding, adding unmelted chocolate a little at a time. However, to minimize the risk of melting or getting messy in their wrappers they're best refrigerated.

- 8 ounces (225 g) good-quality dark chocolate, at least 60% cacao solids and preferably around 72%
- Pinch of salt
- 1¼ cups (75 g) popped amaranth (page 20)
- ¼ cup (25 g) chopped dried cherries

Line the bottom of a small tray or baking sheet with parchment paper.

Finely chop the chocolate and put half of it in a heatproof bowl set over a saucepan of simmering water; don't let the water touch the bottom of the bowl. Heat the chocolate, stirring constantly, until most of it is melted. Remove the bowl from the saucepan and dry off the bottom of the bowl to remove any condensation (you don't want any water to get into the chocolate). Stirring constantly with a spatula, add the remaining chocolate a little at a time, stirring until each bit is mostly melted before adding more; it should take at least 5 minutes to add the remaining chocolate. If the chocolate cools to lukewarm before it's all melted, set the bowl back over the hot water (off the heat) and keep stirring. When all the chocolate is melted, add the salt, 1 cup (60 g) of the popped amaranth, and the dried cherries and stir well.

Scrape the mixture into the prepared tray and spread out to about ¼ inch (6 mm) thick. Smooth the top as well as you can. Sprinkle the remaining popped amaranth evenly over the top and press lightly with your palm so it adheres. Transfer to the refrigerator to cool for about 5 minutes, until set but not completely hard. (The chocolate is easier to cut when still just a bit soft.) Lift the chocolate slab out of the tray and onto a cutting board; peel off the paper and cut into pieces. Return to the refrigerator until very firm, at least 30 minutes. Serve. To store the chocolates, wrap each piece in waxed paper and keep in an airtight container in the refrigerator or in a cool spot.

VARIATION

★ Use chopped toasted and skinned hazelnuts or toasted almonds instead of or in addition to the dried cherries. Any other dried fruit would be nice too—especially tiny currants or blueberries.

LEDA'S ALEGRÍAS
(MEXICAN PUFFED AMARANTH SWEETS)

Makes 24 sweets | vegetarian, gluten free

Serve these little squares of sweet, chewy, crisp amaranth and sesame seeds with a bowl of sliced ripe mango sprinkled with fresh lime juice, following a light supper—I'm thinking the chicken and wild rice soup (on page 179), or corn tortillas filled with cumin-spiced braised greens (on page 180) and a spoonful of black beans (on page 65). And because these are, I think, as close as anyone's going to get to healthful Rice Krispy treats, other than the nut-enriched sweets on the opposite page, I wouldn't hesitate to tuck one into a kid's lunchbox.

- ¼ cup (½ stick / 55 g) unsalted butter, plus more for the baking dish
- 2 cups (120 g) popped amaranth (page 20)
- ½ cup (75 g) sesame seeds, toasted
- ¼ cup (60 ml) maple syrup
- 2 tablespoons molasses
- ¼ teaspoon ground cinnamon
- ⅓ cup (45 g) diced dried apricots or dried currants

Butter a 9-by-13-inch (23-by-33-cm) baking dish or pan. Put the amaranth and sesame seeds in a large bowl and set aside.

In a small heavy saucepan, combine the maple syrup, molasses, butter, cinnamon, and apricots. Bring to a boil over medium heat, then lower the heat and cook, stirring constantly with a silicone spatula or wooden spoon, until the mixture thickens to a syrup consistency. Pour over the amaranth mixture and stir to coat evenly. Press the mixture firmly and evenly into the prepared baking dish. Let cool completely, then cut into squares. The sweets will keep, in an airtight container at room temperature, for at least 5 days.

DON'T GET LOVE SICK [SIC]

Among many hikers, backpackers, bikers, and other gluttons for punishment, the phrase "Don't get love sick" is as engrained in the psyche as the orthography of *lovesick* apparently is in my own. The first letters of the mneumonic device stand for: **D**AIRY, **G**RAINS, **L**EGUMES, **S**EEDS.

Meat, eggs, and other animal-derived proteins provide on their own all the essential amino acids our bodies need to ingest in order to survive—they're complete proteins, in other words. But each food in the categories above generally needs to be combined with a food from a category on one or the other side of it in the sequence to make

a complete protein that contains all the amino acids. So dairy and grains (preferably whole grains, of course), grains and legumes (beans, peanuts), and legumes and oily seeds or nuts will together provide a complete protein. Though it isn't necessarily true that the imperfect proteins must be consumed at the same meal, at the same time, to be fully used by the body as a complete protein, countless classic food pairings are the result of that long-held belief: beans and rice, lentils and rice (see page 148 for a stellar example), chickpeas and tahini (in traditional hummus), milk and cereal, peanut butter and bread, cheese and crackers.

TRAIL BARS

Makes 16 bars | vegan, gluten free*

This is a soft, not-too-sweet oat bar that would be perfect for tucking into a lunch box or picnic basket, and an ideal trail snack: Its whole oats, nuts, and seeds make a complete protein, and the dried fruit is filling and energy-dense.

- ⅓ cup (80 ml) vegetable oil, plus more for the pan
- 1 cup (200 g) mixed dried fruit, such as raisins, cranberries, and chopped apricots
- ½ cup (75 g) halved and pitted dates
- 1 cup (90 g) mixed, unsalted nuts, such as walnut or pecan halves, sliced or slivered almonds, and hazelnuts
- 2 tablespoons flax or sesame seeds
- 2 cups (320 g) raw rolled oats
- ½ teaspoon salt
- ½ cup (125 g) unsweetened applesauce

Preheat the oven to 350°F (175°C). Lightly oil a 9-inch (23-cm) square baking pan.

Put the dried fruit and dates in a heatproof bowl and cover with boiling water. Let soften for about 5 minutes, then drain, pressing out excess water. Set aside.

Toast the nuts in a small sauté pan over medium-high heat until fragrant and lightly colored, about 3 minutes. Transfer to a small food processor and pulse 2 or 3 times to coarsely chop. Transfer to a large bowl.

In the food processor (no need to clean it out), grind the flax seeds and 1 cup (160 g) of the oats until very fine (it's okay if most of the flax seeds remain whole). Add to the nuts in the bowl, along with the salt and the remaining 1 cup (160 g) of oats.

Again using the food processor, puree the softened dried fruit. Add the oil and applesauce and pulse to combine. Pour into the oat mixture and stir well with a rubber spatula. Press the mixture firmly and evenly into the prepared pan using the spatula or, better, your palm to pack it down. Using a metal spatula or a bench knife, cut the dough into 16 squares in the pan. Bake in the center of the oven until firm and lightly browned, about 20 minutes. Place the pan on a wire rack and let cool to room temperature, then remove from the pan, wrap each square in waxed paper, and store in an airtight container at room temperature for up to 1 week.

* See page 25.

OLD-FASHIONED POPCORN

Makes about 2 quarts (60 g) | vegan, gluten free

Air popping is fine and all, but who has room for an air popper? My popcorn-obsessed mom and dad, that's who. They have every imaginable item of popcorn paraphernalia, including a Plexiglass-enclosed movie-theater-style popcorn popper with an enormous countertop footprint to which they don't seem to mind devoting kitchen space. But I believe they're outliers. To make popcorn on the stove, the way it was *meant* to be made, you don't need to use nearly as much oil as some folks claim, just a tablespoon for eight cups (60 g) of popped corn, and the improvement in flavor over air popped is worth every drop.

- **1 tablespoon vegetable or olive oil**
- **½ cup (80 g) raw popping corn**
- **Seasonings, as desired**

Have one or two large bowls ready.

In a heavy 4-quart (3.8-L) saucepan or pot with a lid, heat the oil and 1 kernel of the popcorn over high heat with the lid on. When the kernel pops, lift the lid and carefully add the remaining popcorn. Immediately put the lid back on, but leave it slightly ajar. Holding the lid with a pot holder, shake the pan back and forth vigorously over the heat until the popping seems to have slowed, about 2 minutes, then remove it from the heat. Keep shaking until the popping has mostly stopped, then dump the popcorn into one of the large bowls.

If you like (and especially if you're planning to use the popcorn for caramel corn, as on page 234), remove the unpopped kernels: Shake the bowl so the heavy kernels fall to the bottom. Lift the popped corn out of the bowl and transfer it to the second bowl; discard or repop the unpopped kernels. Toss with seasonings, if desired, and serve.

- Fine salt (grind kosher or table salt to a powder in a mortar)

- Nutritional yeast

- Gomashio (page 248), ground to a powder

- Roasted and ground nori seaweed

- Sweet fall spices: 1 tablespoon ground cinnamon, 1 teaspoon ground allspice, 1 teaspoon freshly grated nutmeg, and ½ teaspoon ground cloves

- A teaspoon or two of Chinese five-spice powder

- A teaspoon or two of chaat masala

- A few teaspoons of Cajun spice blend: ¼ cup ground cayenne; 1 tablespoon each paprika, ground coriander, and black pepper; 2 teaspoons ground cloves; 1½ teaspoons garlic powder; 1 teaspoon dried thyme, crumbled; and salt to taste if desired. (The remaining spice blend will keep indefinitely in a lidded jar.)

- My current favorite: Finely grind salt and citric acid together (citric acid is often available in the canning supplies section of grocery stores, or in the bulk spices section of health food stores) and sprinkle on generously. It's like salt-and-vinegar potato chips.

- Mince garlic and sauté until golden in olive oil (and use olive oil for cooking the popcorn). Season with plenty of fine salt and maybe some dried rosemary.

- Combine ground cayenne and a little raw sugar in a mortar and grind together before sprinkling over the popcorn.

- Melted butter, ground cinnamon, and a pinch of sugar and salt.

- Sprinkle with a little soy sauce and wasabi powder.

- Finely grate lemon zest right over the bowl (to catch the flavorful lemon oil that sprays out as you grate), then sprinkle with fine salt and/or sugar.

- Finely grate lime zest into the popcorn, then sprinkle with finely grated Parmesan, ground cayenne, and ground cumin.

- Grate dark chocolate over hot popcorn and season with ground cinnamon, ground cayenne, grated orange zest, perhaps a little sugar, and fine salt.

- Combine unsweetened cocoa powder, confectioners' sugar, and ground cinnamon and sprinkle over (ideally, buttered) popcorn.

- Monica's Indian-spiced popcorn: Before popping the corn, combine ½ teaspoon ground cumin, ½ teaspoon ground cayenne, and ¼ teaspoon turmeric and add the mixture to the hot oil with the popcorn kernels. Season the spiced popcorn with fine salt, then toss with roasted unsalted peanuts, diced red onion, and minced fresh cilantro. Serve with lemons for squeezing over the popcorn at the last minute.

SESAME-COCONUT CARAMEL CORN
WITH AGAVE NECTAR

Makes about 4 quarts (460 g) | vegetarian, gluten free

Here's a basic, nearly foolproof baked caramel corn; a few ideas for variations follow. It is important that you employ a candy thermometer or an instant-read thermometer, as the temperature of the caramel rises quickly, and the hard-ball test is too time-consuming and, in my opinion, just too annoying to be useful. (In case you still want to use that test, drip a drop of the caramel into a cup of cold water. If it forms a hard ball that is just barely squeezable between your thumb and finger, it's ready.)

- **4 quarts (120 g) popped corn (two batches Old-Fashioned Popcorn; page 232), unpopped kernels removed**
- **1/2 cup (75 g) sesame seeds, toasted**
- **1/2 cup (45 g) unsweetened shredded coconut, toasted**
- **1/2 cup (1 stick / 110 g) unsalted butter**
- **1/3 cup (80 ml) agave nectar**
- **1/2 cup (110 g) brown sugar**
- **3/4 teaspoon salt**
- **1/4 teaspoon baking soda**

Preheat the oven to 250°F (120°C). Lightly grease two 9-by-13-inch (23-by-33-cm) baking dishes or pans or three smaller ones.

Put half of the popcorn in each of two large heatproof bowls (or one huge bowl if you have one); pile the sesame seeds and coconut on top and set aside.

In a heavy 2-quart (2-L) saucepan, melt the butter over medium-high heat. Stir in the agave nectar, brown sugar, and salt. Bring to a boil, without stirring after you see the first bubbles. Insert a candy thermometer. Boil until the caramel reaches 265°F (130°C—hard ball stage), about 3 1/2 minutes from the time the bubbles cover the surface (the temperature will rise quickly toward the end, so keep your eye on it). Remove from the heat and immediately stir in the baking soda. The caramel will foam and turn opaque. Carefully pour it over the popcorn and stir with a heatproof spatula or wooden spoon to lightly coat. Turn out into the prepared

baking dishes. Bake for 45 minutes, stirring and rotating the pans every 15 minutes. Let cool in the pans on wire racks, then gently break the popcorn into pieces. Store in an airtight container at room temperature for up to 1 week.

VARIATIONS

★ For Mom's honey-orange caramel corn: Omit the sesame seeds and coconut. Use 1/2 cup (120 ml) honey instead of the agave nectar. Add 1 1/2 teaspoons minced orange zest with the baking soda.

★ For sorghum-chocolate caramel corn: Use 1/2 cup (120 ml) sorghum syrup instead of the agave nectar. Use 1/4 cup (30 g) cacao nibs instead of the sesame seeds and coconut. Add 2 teaspoons vanilla extract with the baking soda (do this carefully, as it will sputter!).

★ For agave-chile caramel corn: Omit the sesame seeds and coconut. Use 3/4 cup (150 g) white granulated sugar instead of the brown sugar. Add 1/2 teaspoon ground cayenne or 1 teaspoon chipotle chile flakes with the baking soda. If you like, add 1 tablespoon tequila to the caramel (do this carefully, as it will sputter!).

★ For maple-bacon caramel corn (not vegetarian): Omit the sesame seeds and coconut. Cook 8 ounces (225 g) bacon until crisp, drain, and crumble it into the popcorn. Use 1/2 cup (120 ml) maple syrup instead of the agave nectar (a caramel made with maple syrup will take longer to come to temperature, about 7 minutes). If you have it, use part or all maple sugar for the brown sugar. If you like, use bacon drippings instead of oil to cook the popcorn.

GRANDMA FREDLEY'S KETTLE CORN
(MINUS THE BACON)

Makes about 2 quarts (100 g) | vegan, gluten free

I've always loved salty, just slightly sweet, crisp county-fair-style kettle corn, even more than its darker, crunchier cousin, buttery caramel corn. It's definitely in the treat category rather than the everyday-snack category of popcorn preparations, but the way I make it, it's fairly light and clean tasting.

I burned many a batch of poorly executed kettle corn before I thought to ask my popcorn-fanatic mother how to make it. Turns out she had a recipe passed down from my grandma that was significantly different from all the others I'd seen: First, she used copious amounts of bacon drippings, which also took care of the salt content (and you're free to do so too, if you wish—use two tablespoons of drippings and omit the additional salt); I replace this with plain old vegetable oil. And second, she added water with the popcorn. Insanity, you say—but it works. The water ensures that the popcorn has time to heat up and pop before the sugar burns, and that the resulting caramel coats the popcorn lightly and evenly.

- **⅓ cup (55 g) raw popping corn**
- **¼ cup (50 g) sugar**
- **2 tablespoons vegetable oil**
- **½ teaspoon salt, ground to a powder in a mortar**

Have two large bowls ready. In a cup, combine the popcorn and ¼ cup (60 ml) water and have it close to the stovetop. Measure the sugar and have it close by as well.

In a heavy 4-quart (3.8-L) saucepan or pot with a lid, heat the oil and 1 kernel of the popcorn over high heat with the lid on. When the kernel pops, lift the lid and sprinkle in the sugar. Carefully add the popcorn and water and immediately put the lid back on, but leave it slightly ajar. Holding the lid with a pot holder, shake the pan back and forth vigorously over the heat. It'll steam and hiss like all heck for about 90 seconds, then when the water has evaporated, the kernels will start to pop. Keep shaking over the heat for about 40 seconds longer, and when the popping seems to have reached its peak—the *second* you hear it start to slow and no later—remove it from the heat. Keep shaking until the popping has mostly stopped, then immediately dump the kettle corn into one of the large bowls. Let cool for a few minutes.

Now you need to remove any unpopped kernels (there shouldn't be too many): Agitate the kettle corn with a spoon, breaking apart the pieces that are stuck together and letting the heavy kernels fall to the bottom of the bowl. Lift the popped corn out of the bowl and transfer it to the second bowl; discard the unpopped kernels. Toss the kettle corn with the salt and serve.

QUICK RYE CRACKERS

Makes 32 crackers | vegan

A few years ago, bread guru Peter Reinhart published a little article on whole wheat crackers in the *L.A. Times* that—not to put too fine a point on it—changed my life. I can make crackers! And do anything I want to them! I've been making these whole rye crackers ever since, and as I was writing this, I went back to my printout of Reinhart's recipes and found that, no surprise, I'd strayed pretty far from his gospel. Oh, well. Just more evidence that unleavened breads like crackers are forgiving and adaptable. Feel free to use other whole-grain flours besides rye (as long as you choose ones that have at least a little gluten so the dough can be rolled out easily—like spelt, wheat, or triticale), and mix up the seasonings at will. And if you want a very thin cracker, more like a whole grain chip, try running the dough through a pasta machine to get it as thin as you'd like, then transfer the sheet to the pans, cut them into pieces, brush, top, and bake—just keep a close eye on them so the thin chips don't burn.

- 2½ cups (230 g) whole (dark) rye flour, plus more for dusting
- 1 teaspoon salt, plus more for sprinkling
- 1 teaspoon caraway seeds, plus more for sprinkling
- 3 tablespoons olive or vegetable oil
- 1 tablespoon agave nectar
- 1 teaspoon cornstarch or agave nectar, mixed with 2 tablespoons hot water
- Poppyseeds and/or sesame seeds, for sprinkling

Preheat the oven to 300°F (150°C). Set racks in the middle and lower thirds of the oven. Line two baking sheets with parchment paper.

In a medium bowl, combine the flour, salt, and caraway seeds. Make a well in the center and pour in ¾ cup (180 ml) water, the oil, and agave nectar. Stir with a rubber spatula to make a soft dough; it will be a little sticky, and you can add a little more flour if you need to. Divide the dough in half and put one-half on a work surface dusted with flour. Using a floured rolling pin, roll a rough rectangle a little less than ⅛ inch (3 mm) thick, frequently lifting the sheet of dough with a bench knife or metal spatula to make sure it isn't sticking. Transfer the sheet of dough to one of the prepared baking sheets (by loosely rolling it up onto and then off of the rolling pin). Repeat with the remaining dough and the remaining baking sheet.

Brush the sheets of dough with the cornstarch mixture. Sprinkle with salt, caraway seeds, and poppyseeds and/or sesame seeds. Gently roll over the seeds to press them into the dough. Use a pizza cutter or knife to cut each sheet of dough into 16 rectangles, then scoot the rectangles apart slightly on the baking sheets.

Bake for 15 minutes, then rotate the baking sheets top to bottom and front to back and bake for another 15 to 20 minutes or until the crackers are several shades darker and no longer limp when you lift one. Transfer to wire racks to cool completely (they'll crisp up a bit as they cool). The crackers can be stored in an airtight container at room temperature for at least 1 week; if they soften, put them on a baking sheet and heat them in a hot oven for a few minutes.

PLAID CRACKERS
Makes 4 large flatbreads | vegan

If you have a little more time, try these yeast-dough flatbreads instead of the quicker crackers. While the quick unleavened ones (see page 237) are crunchier, these are shattery-crisp: You bake them in whole sheets, then break the sheets into irregular shards for serving. An herb and yogurt dip (page 108), hummus (page 165), or a wedge of good cheese are all fine accompaniments, as is a bottle of cold white wine. Feel free to use, say, all whole wheat flour, or whole spelt flour—anything with at least some gluten will work well here.

- 1 teaspoon agave nectar or honey
- 2 teaspoons instant yeast
- ¼ cup (60 ml) olive oil, plus more for the bowl
- 1 teaspoon caraway seeds, plus more for sprinkling
- 2 cups (185 g) whole (dark) rye flour
- 1 cup (115 g) whole wheat flour, or more if needed
- 1 teaspoon salt, plus more for sprinkling
- 1 teaspoon cornstarch or agave nectar, mixed with 2 tablespoons hot water
- Poppyseeds, for sprinkling
- Sesame seeds, for sprinkling

Put 1 cup (240 ml) warm water in a large bowl and stir in the agave nectar, yeast, oil, and the caraway seeds. Stir in the flours (you may need a little more or a little less) and the salt and work the dough into a smooth ball, kneading it a few times on a lightly floured work surface. Clean out and oil the bowl, and return the dough to the bowl, turning it to coat the top with oil. Cover with plastic wrap and let rise in a warm spot for about 1 hour.

Preheat the oven to 400°F (205°C). Set a rack at the lowest level. Line a baking sheet with parchment paper.

Divide the dough into 4 portions. Keeping the others covered, use a rolling pin to roll out one portion as thinly as possible, flouring the work surface and rolling pin lightly as necessary (the oil in the dough makes it fairly easy to work with), into a rough rectangle (misshapen is fine, as are minor tears in the dough—this is rustic baking). Transfer the dough to the prepared baking sheet, brush with the cornstarch mixture, and sprinkle with salt, caraway seeds, poppyseeds, and sesame seeds in a plaid pattern. Gently roll over the salt and seeds to press them into the dough. Slide the parchment paper with the flatbread off the baking sheet onto the bottom rack of the oven. Bake until nicely browned and crisp, 6 to 8 minutes (watch it closely!), then slip the baking sheet under the paper and remove the flatbread and paper to a wire rack to cool. Repeat with the remaining dough portions (you can pull the paper from underneath the first flatbread to reuse it). Break into shards and serve. The shards can be stored in an airtight container at room temperature for at least 1 week.

SUPER-GRAIN BREAD
Makes 1 loaf | vegetarian

It may seem like a lot of steps, but this is a very easy bread for even a busy person to pull off. You could start the whole grain soak and the sponge on a Saturday evening, party all night, then mix everything together in the morning to have bread ready for lunch a few hours later, and for sandwiches throughout the week. If you have to retard the process at any point, stick the covered bowl or bowls in the refrigerator, then pull them out when you're ready to continue. I've done this for several days as schedules change and events conflict, with no appreciable decline in quality. The loaf is heavily seeded, studded with nutritious and textural whole grains, and perfect for hearty sandwiches or as a base for a spread of fresh cheese and jam.

Mixing up the sponge and covering it with the dry ingredients to be stirred in the next morning is a method I first learned from Rose Levy Berenbaum's *The Bread Bible*; despite the multi-step process, you really only have to flour up the kitchen once—brilliant.

FOR THE SOAK
- 1¼ to 1½ cups (200 g) mixed raw whole grains, such as rolled oats or barley, cornmeal, cracked wheat, bulgur, millet, amaranth, or well-rinsed quinoa
- Scant 1 cup boiling water

FOR THE SPONGE
- 1 cup (140 g) whole wheat or whole rye flour
- 1 tablespoon vital wheat gluten (see Note, page 242)
- ¼ teaspoon instant yeast

FOR THE DRY INGREDIENTS
- 1¾ cups (200 g) white whole wheat flour
- 2 tablespoons vital wheat gluten
- 1 teaspoon instant yeast
- 2 tablespoons coarsely ground flax seeds, or whole sesame, poppy, or sunflower seeds, or a mixture
- 1 tablespoon kosher salt

TO FINISH
- Olive or vegetable oil for the bowl

MAKE THE SOAK
In a medium bowl, combine the grains and boiling water. Cover with plastic wrap.

MAKE THE SPONGE
In a large bowl (the bowl of your stand mixer if you have one), whisk together the whole wheat flour, vital wheat gluten, yeast, and 1 cup (240 ml) of warm water.

ADD THE DRY INGREDIENTS
On top of the sponge you just made, spread the white whole wheat flour, vital wheat gluten, yeast, flax seeds, and salt; do not stir the dry ingredients into the sponge yet. Cover the bowl with plastic wrap and set it and the soaking whole grains aside for 6 hours or overnight at room temperature.

MIX THE DOUGH
Uncover the bowls. If using a stand mixer, put the mixer bowl in the mixer and attach the dough hook. (If mixing by hand, fit your hand with a rubber spatula or wooden spoon.) Mix on medium-low speed to stir the dry ingredients into the wet sponge. Dump in the soaked grains (they'll have absorbed all the liquid) and continue to mix until a sticky, stiff, but stretchy dough is formed, 6 to 8 minutes. (If working by hand, mix as well as you can in the bowl, then turn out onto a lightly floured work surface and knead the heck out of it for about 10 minutes. It will be a little sticky, but use only enough flour to make it workable.) Let the dough rest on the counter while you rinse out and lightly oil the bowl. Shape the dough into a tight ball and put it in the bowl; cover with plastic wrap and set aside in a warm spot to rise until almost doubled in volume, about 1½ hours.

SHAPE AND BAKE THE LOAF

Remove from the bowl and gently press into a 9-by-6-inch (23-by-15-cm) rectangle. Roll up into a tight, 9-inch-long (23-cm-long) loaf, pinch the seam to secure the loaf shape, and fit it seam side down into a large loaf pan; cut a lengthwise slash ½ inch (12 mm) deep in the top. (Alternatively, to make a freestanding loaf, fold the two corners on the far side of the rectangle down to meet at the center, then fold the point that results at the top down to the center and roll toward you to shape into a loaf with pointed ends—a torpedo. Place on a baking sheet dusted with flour and cut 3 diagonal slashes in the top.) Cover loosely with plastic wrap and let rise until the top of the loaf is 1 to 2 inches (2.5 to 5 cm) above the lip of the pan (or the freestanding loaf has risen dramatically), about 1 hour.

Meanwhile, preheat the oven to 400°F (205°C). Bake the loaf in the center of the oven for 10 minutes, then lower the oven temperature to 375°F (190°C) and bake for 30 to 35 minutes, until nicely browned. Transfer to a wire rack and let cool completely before slicing. The bread will keep at room temperature, in a plastic bag or wrapped in plastic, for up to 5 days.

HONEY WHOLE WHEAT SANDWICH BREAD

Makes 1 loaf | vegetarian

One bowl, two short rises, and this loaf is ready to bake into a perfectly slice-able sandwich bread.

- **2 tablespoons honey**
- **1 scant tablespoon instant yeast**
- **1 scant cup (220 ml) milk or buttermilk**
- **1 cup (115 g) whole wheat flour**
- **2 ¾ cups (385 g) white whole wheat flour**
- **2 tablespoons vital wheat gluten (see Note)**
- **2 ½ teaspoons salt**
- **Olive or vegetable oil for the bowl**
- **1 teaspoon unsalted butter (optional)**

In a large bowl (the bowl of your stand mixer if you have one), combine 1 scant cup warm water (220 ml) and the honey, then sprinkle the yeast over the top and stir. Add the milk, flours, vital wheat gluten, and salt. If using a stand mixer, put the bowl in the mixer and fit it with the dough hook. (If mixing by hand, fit your hand with a rubber spatula or wooden spoon.) Mix on medium-low speed until a smooth, stretchy dough is formed, 6 to 8 minutes. (If working by hand, mix as well as you can in the bowl, then turn out onto a lightly floured work surface and knead the heck out of it for about 10 minutes. It will be a little sticky, but use only enough flour to make it workable.) Let the dough rest on the counter while you rinse out and lightly oil the bowl. Shape the dough into a tight ball and put it in the bowl; cover with plastic wrap and set aside in a warm spot to rise until doubled in volume, about 1 hour.

Remove from the bowl (dump the dough out so the smooth top is down) and gently press into a 9-by-6-inch (23-by-15-cm) rectangle. Roll up into a tight, 9-inch-long (23-cm-long) loaf, pinch the seam to secure it to the loaf, and fit it seam side down into a large loaf pan; make sure that the top surface is tight and smooth. Cover loosely with plastic wrap and let rise until the top of the loaf is 1 to 2 inches (2.5 to 5 cm) above the lip of the pan, about 1 hour.

Preheat the oven to 400°F (205°C).

Bake the loaf in the center of the oven for 10 minutes, then lower the oven temperature to 375°F (190°C) and bake for 35 to 40 minutes, until deeply browned. Tip the loaf out of the pan and tap the bottom, which should sound hollow. Transfer to a wire rack (if you'd like a softer crust, spread a little butter on top while it's still hot); let cool completely before slicing. The bread will keep at room temperature, in a plastic bag or wrapped in plastic, for up to 4 days.

NOTE: Vital wheat gluten is the high-protein part of the wheat kernel and is available in powdered form in the baking section of most supermarkets and in the bulk bins at many health food stores. I've found it very useful in my experiments with quicker rising 100-percent whole-grain breads, where it contributes to a stronger, stretchier dough that rises better and results in a pleasantly chewy crumb that doesn't crumble and disintegrate when you slice it and use it for sandwiches.

SOUTHERN CORNBREAD
Serves 8 | vegetarian

My husband just came home from getting his hair cut and, as it happens, had to listen to the woman with the trimmers rail about the travesty that one of the local restaurants here in Athens sells as "cornbread": Lord have mercy, it has bits of *corn* in it! Hoo-boy, are people opinionated about cornbread down here. True Southern cornbread must not have any sugar (whoever it was who gave us the witticism "Keep your sugar out of my cornbread and your tea out of my tea" was a keen observer of this region), and the cornmeal must under no circumstances be yellow. Unless, that is, it *should* have some sugar and must *always* be yellow cornmeal. Add a little sugar to this if you'd like, or try the variations—it'll be delicious, even if I wouldn't risk serving it to any born Southerner over the age of sixty-five.

- ¼ cup (½ stick / 55 g) unsalted butter, melted, plus more for the pan
- 1½ cups (160 g) raw fine white or yellow cornmeal
- 1 cup (140 to 170 g) white whole wheat flour, whole spelt flour, or whole wheat pastry flour
- 4 teaspoons baking powder
- 1 teaspoon salt
- 1½ cups (360 ml) milk
- 1 large egg

Preheat the oven to 425°F (220°C). Butter a 9-inch (23-cm) square baking pan.

Into a large bowl, sift the cornmeal, flour, baking powder, and salt. In a separate bowl, whisk together the milk, egg, and butter. Pour the wet ingredients into the dry and stir with a rubber spatula until just combined. Scrape into the prepared pan and smooth the top. Bake in the center of the oven until nicely browned and a toothpick inserted in the center comes out clean, about 20 minutes. Let cool for a few minutes on a wire rack, then cut into squares and serve warm or at room temperature.

VARIATIONS

★ For bacon cornbread (not vegetarian): Cook 4 ounces (115 g) diced bacon until crisp; drain on a paper towel. Use the rendered fat to grease the baking pan, and sprinkle the bacon over the batter right before you put the cornbread in the oven. (Alternatively, cook the bacon in a well-seasoned 10-inch / 25-cm cast-iron skillet; remove the bacon to a paper towel to drain, then pour off all but about 1 tablespoon of the rendered fat. Scrape the cornbread batter directly into the hot skillet, sprinkle with the bacon, and transfer to the oven to bake. Cut into wedges to serve.)

★ For maple-bacon cornbread (not vegetarian): Make bacon cornbread as above, but add 3 tablespoons maple syrup to the wet ingredients.

★ For chile cornbread: Dice 2 large roasted poblano chiles and pat dry with a paper towel. Mince 2 chipotle chiles in adobo and add them, along with the poblanos, to the wet ingredients.

★ For fresh-corn cornbread: Add 1 cup (170 g) fresh (un-cooked is fine) or frozen (thawed) sweet corn kernels to the wet ingredients. And don't tell my husband's barber.

★ For buttermilk or yogurt cornbread: Use 1 cup (240 ml) buttermilk or plain yogurt instead of the milk. Increase the eggs to 2. Reduce the baking powder to 2 teaspoons and add ½ teaspoon baking soda.

HOT COCOA WITH CORNMEAL OR MASA

Serves 3 or 4 | vegan, gluten free

Champurrado, a chocolate drink thickened with cornmeal or masa, has been consumed in Mexico for centuries, and for a time it was thought of as almost a daily necessity. Friar Ilarione da Bergamo, an Italian missionary traveling in Mexico in the 1760s, describes the Mexicans' odd-sounding diet in his fascinating journal. He reports that they would generally drink atole, a thick cornmeal porridge often flavored with chocolate, twice a day, first while still in bed, then again in the late afternoon. Should anyone be forced to "go without chocolate, champurrado, or atole for just one morning," he writes, "he or she would be regarded as a most unfortunate person, wretched, and on the verge of desperation."

I wouldn't go that far (unless it were *coffee* we were discussing), but neither would I wish to go a winter without indulging in a few warm mugs of this puddinglike cocoa.

- ¼ cup (40 g) raw fine cornmeal (yellow, white, or blue) or masa harina
- ¼ cup (20 g) unsweetened cocoa powder
- Pinch of salt
- 2½ cups (600 ml) rice milk, soy milk, or almond milk
- 1 cinnamon stick, plus more for serving
- 3 tablespoons agave nectar or ⅓ cup (65 g) sugar
- ½ teaspoon pure vanilla extract

Into a medium bowl, sift the cornmeal, cocoa powder, and salt. Add ½ cup (120 ml) of the rice milk and whisk until smooth. Set aside.

In a heavy 2-quart (2-L) saucepan, bring the remaining 2 cups (480 ml) rice milk and the cinnamon stick to a simmer, then whisk in the cocoa mixture and agave nectar. Return to a very slow simmer and cook, stirring or whisking frequently, until thickened to the consistency of melted ice cream, about 15 minutes. Stir in the vanilla and remove and discard the cinnamon stick. Pour into a 4-cup (960 ml) glass measuring cup for easier pouring, then divide among mugs and serve with fresh cinnamon sticks for stirring. The cocoa will thicken and take on a light puddinglike quality as it cools in the mugs.

BARLEY TEA

Serves 2 | vegan

I first encountered roasted barley tea when I worked at a publishing company in Manhattan's Koreatown. It's refreshing whether served hot or chilled, and it has a slightly sweet, nutty flavor that makes it ideal for serving with meals or with a little sweet afternoon treat. Roasted unhulled barley for making tea is sold in Asian grocery stores (mugicha in Japanese, boricha in Korean), but you can concoct a fair approximation of it at home by toasting regular hulled or pearl barley and steeping it. If you like, toast a larger batch of barley and keep it in an airtight jar in the cupboard for up to two months.

- ½ cup (100 g) raw hulled barley
- Agave nectar (optional)

In a large heavy sauté pan over medium heat, toast the barley, stirring frequently, until deep brown and fragrant, 6 to 10 minutes. Transfer to a saucepan and add 3 cups (720 ml) water. Bring to a boil, then lower the heat and simmer until the water is about the color of light beer, 15 to 20 minutes. Pour through a sieve into a heatproof tea pot or pitcher, sweeten if you like, and serve hot or chill and serve over ice. Discard the barley itself, or if you are feeling thrifty, return it to the saucepan, add water to cover, cook until tender, drain, and refrigerate for another use

CARAWAY-SAGE SPELT BREADSTICKS

Makes about 64 thin breadsticks | vegan

This super-basic yeasted dough, made primarily with lower-gluten whole spelt flour, is quite versatile: Cut and roll it into ropes for breadsticks, as here, or omit the caraway and sage and divide it into a dozen small sandwich rolls, let rise in a warm spot for a couple hours, then bake. Or you can make it into four balls, let rise, then stretch and roll out thinly to make individual-size pizzas; top with a little sauce and cheese and bake on a preheated pizza stone at 500°F (260°F).

- 1½ cups (360 ml) warm water
- 1 teaspoon agave nectar
- 2 teaspoons instant yeast
- ¼ cup (60 ml) olive oil, plus more for the bowl
- 3¾ cups (430 g) whole spelt flour
- ¾ cup (115 g) whole wheat flour, or more as needed
- 1 scant tablespoon salt
- 2 teaspoons caraway seeds
- 1 teaspoon rubbed dried sage

In a large bowl (the bowl of your stand mixer if you have one), combine the warm water and agave nectar, then sprinkle the yeast over the top and stir. Add the oil, flours, and salt. If using a stand mixer, put the bowl in the mixer and fit it with the dough hook. (If mixing by hand, fit your hand with a rubber spatula or wooden spoon.) Mix on medium-low speed until a smooth, stretchy dough is formed, 6 to 8 minutes. (If working by hand, mix as well as you can in the bowl, then turn out onto a lightly floured work surface and knead the heck out of it for about 10 minutes. It will be a little sticky, but use only enough flour to make it workable.) Let the dough rest on the counter while you rinse out and lightly oil the bowl. Shape the dough into a tight ball and put it in the bowl; cover with plastic wrap and set aside in a cool spot to rise until doubled in volume, about 6 hours.

Turn the dough out onto a floured work surface and divide into 4 portions.

Knead one-quarter of the caraway seeds and sage into each portion of dough. Let rest for 15 minutes. Divide each portion into 16 pieces and roll each into a thin rope 12 to 14 inches (30 to 35 cm) long. Arrange on two baking sheets lined with parchment paper and cover loosely with plastic wrap. Let rise in a warm spot for 30 minutes. Preheat the oven to 400°F (205°C). Bake in the center and lower thirds of the oven until browned and crisp, 18 to 20 minutes, rotating the pans halfway through. Transfer to wire racks to cool.

Homemade Condiments to Have on Hand

Making whole grains a part of your life doesn't have to be difficult. You don't have to reinvent the wheel every time you put a pot of grains on the stove to simmer. Sometimes just plain grains with a simple dressing or topping, a dollop or sprinkle of this or that, is all you need to make a satisfying, enriching side dish (or, if it's one of those days, your whole meal). Following are a few of those embellishments you can make when you feel like being in the kitchen for a bit and keep at the ready in the refrigerator or pantry for days when you don't.

GOMASHIO

Makes ½ cup (70 g) | vegan, gluten free

Gomashio (also spelled *gomasio*) is a classic topping for simple grains dishes, and instantly transforms them from boring hippie food to . . . *delicious* hippie food. And there was a time when the world seemingly wouldn't let you write a vegetarian cookbook that didn't mention the fact that steamed broccoli was more palatable when topped with the salty, toasty stuff. You can buy it premade, but it's so easy to make at home, where you can also adjust the salt and either grind it or leave the seeds whole, that there's really no reason to buy it. Look for reasonably priced sesame seeds in the bulk section of health food stores, or in Asian, Mexican, or Indian grocery stores.

The method below, in which the seeds are lightly toasted and then cooked in saltwater until the moisture evaporates, leaving the seeds coated with salt, comes from Makiko Itoh, the author of *The Just Bento Cookbook* and the Just Bento blog. It allows the seeds to become evenly seasoned without being ground, so the gomashio can be kept longer.

- ½ cup (70 g) white, brown, and/or black sesame seeds
- 1 to 1½ teaspoons salt (use the lesser quantity if adding seaweed)
- 1 teaspoon dulse flakes, toasted, or crushed toasted nori seaweed (optional)

In a small sauté pan over medium heat, toast the sesame seeds, stirring constantly with a heatproof spatula, until fragrant and a shade darker, about 2 minutes. Add ½ cup (120 ml) water and the salt and cook, stirring constantly, until the water is completely evaporated and the seeds are dry, matte rather than shiny, and coated with the salt. Let cool in the pan. If you'd like, put the sesame seeds, in batches, in a mortar or spice grinder with a few pieces of toasted dulse or wakame seaweed and coarsely grind. Transfer the gomashio to an airtight container; stored in a cool, dark cupboard, it will keep for up to 1 month if ground or longer if the seeds are left whole (if you like, you can grind just as much as you need at a time).

SEEDY NUT TOPPING

Makes about ¾ cup (90 g) | vegan, gluten free

I'd sprinkle this mixture of nutrient-rich nuts and seeds on pretty much anything. Not just the obvious choices, like oatmeal or another breakfasty porridge, or a bowl of wheat or rye berries, but also plain or lightly sweetened yogurt, fresh fruit, steamed vegetables like broccoli or cauliflower, bitter greens braised in stock with a little ginger and soy sauce, green beans, snow peas, sweet potatoes . . . or any combination of vegetables and grains. It'll keep for a month or so in the cupboard, so go ahead and double the recipe. And it goes without saying that while this is a combination I find to be especially versatile and useful (and of course tasty), feel free to use whatever nuts and seeds you like.

- ⅓ cup (20 g) pepitas (hulled pumpkin seeds)
- ⅓ cup (35 g) sliced almonds
- 3 tablespoons sesame seeds
- Pinch of salt
- 3 tablespoons flax seeds

In a small heavy sauté pan over medium-high heat, toast the pepitas, tossing and stirring constantly, until they swell and begin to color. Transfer to a bowl. Return the pan to the heat and toast the almonds until fragrant and just beginning to brown, then scrape them into the bowl. In the hot pan, off the heat, toast the sesame seeds until they glisten and turn golden brown; sprinkle with salt and add them to the bowl. In a spice grinder, pulse the flax seeds until most of them are cracked, and add them to the bowl. Let cool, then transfer to a jar with a lid and store in a cool dark spot for up to 1 month.

BASIC VINAIGRETTE FOR GRAINS

Makes 1 scant cup (220 ml) | vegan, gluten free

Vinaigrettes and salad dressings used with grains need to have a bit more acid—vinegar, citrus—than most of those used with greens, or they'll taste bland. Here's a simple one you can make in a large-ish batch and keep in the refrigerator to drizzle over grains and chopped vegetables for quick, substantial salads. Often, when I make a salad I'll make double or triple the amount of vinaigrette—then pour some of it into a jar to save for another use, and toss the greens, grains, and vegetables in the bowl with the remainder.

- 1 clove garlic, lightly crushed but left whole
- ½ cup (120 ml) white- or red-wine vinegar, or Champagne vinegar or sherry vinegar
- 2 tablespoons freshly squeezed lemon juice (optional)
- 1 teaspoon salt
- ½ teaspoon freshly ground black pepper
- 2 teaspoons grainy mustard
- ⅓ cup (80 ml) olive oil

Rub the inside bottom of a medium bowl with the garlic and drop it in, then whisk together the vinegar, lemon juice, if using, salt, pepper, and mustard until the salt is dissolved. Gradually add the oil, whisking to emulsify. Remove the garlic (save it for another use, if you'd like), then pour into a clean jar (a half-pint / 240 ml glass canning jar works well), cover, and refrigerate for up to 3 weeks. Put the jar in a saucepan of hot water for a few minutes to warm and liquefy the oil, then shake well before using the vinaigrette.

BUTTERMILK-YOGURT DRESSING
WITH CHIVES

Makes 1½ cups (360 ml) | vegetarian, gluten free

This is a creamy but super-healthful dressing, excellent folded into cold grains for a quick salad, or as a thin sandwich spread in place of mayonnaise. Try it drizzled into a whole wheat pita stuffed with chilled bulgur, sliced tomatoes and cucumbers, cooked chickpeas, grated carrot, sprouts, and toasted pepitas.

- **1 cup (240 ml) buttermilk**
- **½ cup (120 ml) plain yogurt**
- **¼ cup minced fresh chives**
- **1 tablespoon grated onion**
- **½ teaspoon salt**
- **¼ teaspoon freshly ground black pepper**

In a large bowl, whisk all the ingredients together until smooth. Transfer to an airtight container and store in the refrigerator for up to 1 week.

VARIATIONS

★ To make a large batch (3 cups / 720 ml) of a thicker dip for raw vegetables or breadsticks (on page 242), or a spread for sandwiches: Omit the buttermilk and plain yogurt and use ¾ cup (180 ml) plain Greek yogurt pureed in a mini food processor with 1¾ cups (1 pound / 455 g) cottage cheese. Increase the salt to ¾ teaspoon and the pepper to ½ teaspoon or to taste. Increase the onion to 2 tablespoons and squeeze out excess liquid before adding it.

★ For a very herby dressing, instead of the chives use about 2 tablespoons minced fresh basil, 2 tablespoons minced fresh parsley, and 1 teaspoon minced fresh marjoram or oregano.

CARAMELIZED ONIONS
WITH THYME AND BALSAMIC VINEGAR

Makes about 3 cups (720 ml) | vegan, gluten free

Spoon these soft, sweet onions onto cooked whole wheat couscous, quinoa, or millet, or fold them into brown rice or farro.

- **5 pounds (2.3 kg) sweet onions, sliced**
- **2 tablespoons olive oil**
- **1 teaspoon salt**
- **4 sprigs fresh thyme, stemmed**
- **1 tablespoon balsamic vinegar**

Put the onions, oil, salt, thyme, and vinegar in a large heavy pot or Dutch oven and cook over medium-low heat, stirring occasionally, until golden and very soft, about 1½ hours—don't let them brown too quickly; if they start to brown before they soften into a velvety mass, add a splash of water and cover the pot for a few minutes. Let cool, then put in freezer bags and freeze for up to several months, or keep in the refrigerator for up to 1 week.

PIMIENTO CHEESE

Makes about 4 cups (800 g) | vegetarian, gluten free*

Last year during college football (known outside the South as "fall" or "autumn"), I was seized by a desire to make pimiento cheese for the first time. It was the beginning of what promises to be a long and beautiful relationship with the old-school, newly hip bright orange spread. The version below, my latest but probably not my last, is heavy on the roasted peppers (I like either homemade oven-roasted or jarred "fire-roasted" red peppers, which have a bit of smoky char to them, rather than the bland preminced pimientos), and not so heavy on the mayo (I use cream cheese or even softer Neufchâtel to fill out the spread). This is excellent on rye crackers (page 237) and of course it could be dolloped liberally on grits, polenta, or even steel-cut oatmeal. (It's also wonderful in an omelet or with raw vegetables.)

Don't use preshredded cheese, which, besides being coated in additives you don't need, won't get mushy enough to melt with the other ingredients.

- **1 pound (455 g) good-quality extra-sharp cheddar cheese, shredded**
- **8 ounces (225 g) cream cheese, at room temperature**
- **¼ cup (60 ml) good-quality mayonnaise**
- **1 tablespoon freshly squeezed lime juice**
- **½ to 1 teaspoon hot paprika, to taste**
- **1 cup (135 g) roasted and peeled red bell peppers (about 2 large), or jarred roasted red peppers in brine, very well drained**

In a medium bowl, with a rubber spatula, beat together the cheeses, mayonnaise, lime juice, and paprika until thoroughly combined. Mince the roasted peppers and stir them into the cheese. Cover and refrigerate for at least 1 hour or up to 1 week.

---

* If gluten is an issue, definitely don't use preshredded cheese, whose additives may not be gluten free.

SUN-DRIED TOMATO MUHAMMARA

Makes about 2½ cups (600 ml) | vegan

In this dip (or spread or condiment), based on the Syrian and Lebanese muhammara, softened sun-dried tomatoes take the place of hot or sweet dried chiles, lending it a tangy rather than spicy edge. Serve a few spoonfuls with any whole grain, perhaps thinned with a little water or broth, or spread on grilled or broiled whole grain bread and drizzle with a little olive oil as a between-meal snack or appetizer.

- **1 whole head garlic**
- **4 tablespoons (60 ml) olive oil**
- **Salt and freshly ground black pepper**
- **1 packed cup (110 g) sun-dried tomatoes (drained if packed in oil)**
- **1 (½-inch-thick / 12-mm-thick) slice of country bread**
- **½ teaspoon ground cayenne**
- **½ cup (60 g) chopped walnuts, toasted**
- **3 tablespoons pomegranate molasses (see Note)**

Preheat the oven to 375°F (190°C). Cut the head of garlic horizontally in half and put it on a piece of aluminum foil. Drizzle 1 tablespoon of the oil into the slit garlic and sprinkle with salt and black pepper; gather the foil into a package and squeeze to seal. Put it on the rack in the oven and roast until the cloves are very soft and beginning to caramelize, about 40 minutes.

Meanwhile, put the sun-dried tomatoes and bread in a blender and pour boiling water over them to just cover. Let soak until the tomatoes are very soft, about 30 minutes. Squeeze the garlic cloves from the skins into the blender and add the remaining 3 tablespoons of oil, ¾ teaspoon of salt, the cayenne, walnuts, and pomegranate molasses. Blend until very smooth, adding up to ⅓ cup (80 ml) water if necessary to make a puree the consistency of thick hummus. Transfer to a sealable container; the sauce will keep in the refrigerator for up to 1 week.

NOTE: Tart, dark-red pomegranate molasses is a key ingredient in muhammara; it can be found in Middle Eastern grocery stores (the Lebanese brands are the best in my experience—but make sure you can see that the pomegranate molasses is pourable and not dried out and thick), in most Indian grocery stores, and in the international foods aisle of some good supermarkets. If you can't find it, you can add balsamic vinegar to taste, or, better, balsamic vinegar that has been boiled until reduced to a syrup with a little agave nectar (see page 89).

NICOLE'S SPICY RED-TOMATO CHUTNEY

Makes about 2 pints (960 ml) | vegan, gluten free

The recipe for this very British chutney was given to me by my friend Nicole Mitchell and is adapted from one by the grand dame of English cookery, Delia Smith. When she gave me a jar last year, I came to rely on it almost daily. A little spoonful of it is all you need to make a quickly steamed bowl of whole wheat couscous, bulgur, or cracked wheat something special, and it's also welcome anywhere there's cheese—I love it on a rough hunk of bread with a thick shard of good cheddar or a crumbling slab of Stilton or something similar. Try it in buckwheat crêpes (page 59) too.

- 1 pound (455 g) ripe tomatoes, coarsely chopped
- 1 large Granny Smith apple, cored and coarsely chopped
- 1 medium onion , coarsely chopped
- 1 cup (170 g) golden raisins
- 2 cloves garlic, minced
- 1 teaspoon salt
- ½ teaspoon ground cayenne
- ½ teaspoon ground ginger
- 1 cup (220 g) packed brown sugar
- 1¼ cups (300 ml) malt vinegar or cider vinegar
- Cheesecloth or muslin bag of pickling spices: ½ teaspoon mustard seeds, ½ teaspoon allspice berries, ½ teaspoon whole black peppercorns, 2 whole cloves, ½ cinnamon stick (optional)

In a food processor, in batches if necessary, process the tomatoes until pureed, and then the apple, onion, and raisins until finely minced; put them all in a heavy 4-quart (3.8-L) nonreactive (stainless-steel or enameled) saucepan. Add the garlic, salt, cayenne, ginger, brown sugar, and vinegar. If you're using the spice bag, attach it with a binder clip to the side of the pan so that the spices are submerged. Bring to a boil, then lower the heat and simmer, stirring occasionally, until the chutney is thick, jammy, and deep brown in color, about 2½ hours—stir more frequently toward the end to keep it from sticking. Discard the spice bag. Ladle into 2 clean, hot pint-size glass jars, let cool to room temperature, then cover and refrigerate. The chutney will keep for at least 1 month in the refrigerator.

Appendix

MEASURING FLOUR

The most accurate way to measure flour for baked goods is to use a scale: You just put the bowl on the scale, zero it out, and add flour until you have the right amount—no measuring cups needed.

If you don't have a kitchen scale, use the spoon-and-level method for measuring the flour volume quantities in the baking recipes: Stir the flour a bit in the bag or other container to loosen and aerate it and break up any lumps. Set your dry measuring cup on a piece of waxed paper and spoon in the flour until it overflows. Use a knife or the straight side of a spoon handle to sweep the top level with the rim of the cup. Dump the excess from the waxed paper back into the flour bag or container.

Note, too, that you may need to use more flour (or dampen your dough-kneading hands to add more moisture) depending on the humidity in your kitchen from day to day. This is especially true for bread recipes. I've found that flour weights and measures can vary quite a bit depending on the weather, and as accurate and consistent as I've tried to be here I'm sure you'll find you need to add a little more or a little less. Luckily we're not attempting any fancy sponge cakes— all the baking in this book is . . . well, let's call it rustic.

GRAIN COOKING CHEAT SHEET

Salt is optional and a matter of taste; as a general rule, add it toward the end of cooking. For more details about basic grain-cooking techniques, please see the individual grain descriptions on pages 18 to 39. Grains marked with * can be cooked in larger quantities by scaling up the proportions with no loss of quality; † indicates that the grains are good to freeze.

GRAIN	QUANTITY	WATER	SIMMER	YIELD
Amaranth*	1 cup (200 g)	3 cups (720 ml)	20 min.	2 cups (330 g)
Barley: hulled or hull-less*†	1 cup (200 g)	3 cups (720 ml)	40 min.	2½ to 3 cups (400 to 480 g)
Buckwheat: groats or roasted (kasha)*† *Toast in pan with egg or fat.*	1 cup (165 g)	1½ cups (360 ml)	10 min.	3½ cups (600 g)
Corn: whole hominy*†	1 cup (160 g)	3 cups (720 ml)	40 min.	2½ cups (600 g)
Cornmeal: medium- or coarse-grind (grits or polenta)* *Whisk into boiling water. Stir while simmering.*	1 cup (160 g)	4 cups (960 ml)	15–35 min.	4 cups (960 g)
Cornmeal: fine-grind* *Whisk into boiling water. Stir while simmering.*	1 cup (160 g)	4 cups (960 ml)	5–10 min.	4 cups (960 g)
Millet† *Toast in dry pan or oil.*	1 cup (200 g)	2 cups (480 ml)	20–25 min.	4 cups (700 g)
Oats: oat groats*†	1 cup (180 g)	3 cups (720 ml)	20 min.	2½ cups (560 g)
Oats: steel-cut oats* *Stir while simmering.*	½ cup (90 g) 1 cup (180 g)	2 cups (480 ml) 4 cups (960 ml)	25–30 min. 25–30 min.	1½ to 1¾ cups (370 to 430 g) 3 to 3 ½ cups (740 to 860 g)
Oats: Scottish or pinhead oats* *Stir while simmering.*	½ cup (90 g) 1 cup (180 g)	2 cups (480 ml) 4 cups (960 ml)	10 min. 10 min.	1¾ cups (430 g) 3½ cups (860 g)

GRAIN	QUANTITY	WATER	SIMMER	YIELD
Oats: extra-thick rolled oats* *Stir while simmering.*	½ cup (80 g) 1 cup (160 g)	1¼ cups (300 ml) 2½ cups (600 ml)	10–15 min. 10–15 min.	1 cup (240 g) 2 cups (480 g)
Oats: rolled oats* *Stir while simmering.*	½ cup (80 g) 1 cup (160 g)	1 cup (240 ml) 2 cups (480 ml)	6–8 min. 6–8 min.	1 cup (240 g) 2 cups (480 g)
Quinoa*† *Rinse well.*	1 cup (170 g)	1½ cups (360 ml)	15–20 min.	3 cups (560 g)
Rice: basmati or long- or short-grain brown rice*† *Rinse well.*	1 cup (190 g)	2 cups (480 ml)	30 min.	3 to 4 cups (600 to 800 g)
Rice: Chinese black rice*† *Rinse, soak 4–8 hours, drain before cooking.*	1 cup (190 g)	2 cups (480 ml)	40 min.	2½ cups (500 g)
Rice: Wehani or other red rice*†	1 cup (190 g)	2 cups (480 ml)	30 min.	2½ cups (500 g)
Rye berries*†	1 cup (180 g)	3 cups (720 ml)	50 min.	2½ cups (440 g)
Sorghum*†	1 cup (190 g)	2 cups (480 ml)	45–50 min.	3 cups (480 g)
Teff* *Toast in dry pan. Stir while simmering.*	½ cup (100 g)	1½ cups (360 ml)	20 min.	1 cup (250 g)
Triticale berries*†	1 cup (180 g)	3 cups (720 ml)	40 min.	2 cups (320 g)
Wheat: wheat berries, hard red or white*†	1 cup (175 g)	3 cups (720 ml)	50 min.	2½ cups (475 g)

GRAIN	QUANTITY	WATER	SIMMER	YIELD
Wheat: wheat berries, soft white*†	1 cup (175 g)	3 cups (720 ml)	30 min.	2½ cups (475 g)
Wheat: spelt berries*†	1 cup (175 g)	3 cups (720 ml)	35 min.	2½ cups (475 g)
Wheat: Kamut*†	1 cup (175 g)	3 cups (720 ml)	40 min.	2½ cups (475 g)
Wheat: farro*†	1 cup (180 g)	1½ cups (360 ml)	15–20 min.	2½ cups (420 g)
Wheat: bulgur, fine- or medium-grind (no. 1 or 2)*† *Add to boiling water, cover, remove from heat, let stand.*	1 cup (140 g)	1¼ cups (300 ml)	10–15 min. (off heat)	3 cups (540 g)
Wheat: bulgur, coarse-grind (no. 3)*† *Add to boiling water, cover, simmer.*	1 cup (140 g)	2 cups (480 ml)	15 min.	3 cups (540 g)
Wheat: cracked wheat or freekeh*† *Toast in dry pan or oil. Stir while simmering.*	1 cup (160 g)	1½ cups (360 ml)	10–12 min.	2 cups (360 g)
Wheat: whole wheat couscous* *Add to boiling water, cover, remove from heat, let stand.*	1 cup (170 g)	1½ cups (360 ml)	5 min. (off heat)	3 cups (480 g)
Wild rice: brown or black wild rice*†	½ cup (80 g)	1½ cups (360 ml)	35–50 min.	1½ cups (240 g)

Grains marked with * can be cooked in larger quantities by scaling up the proportions with no loss of quality; † indicates that the grains are good to freeze.

SOURCES

Anson Mills

ansonmills.com
phone: 803-467-4122
1922-C Gervais Street
Columbia, SC 29201

These people at this South Carolina organic grower and milling company know their grits, especially, but also their rice and whole grain flours (and—shh!—artisan-quality white flours, too: I covet the ni-hachi sobakoh and the farina di pizzaiolo). Truly, they have some of the most interesting cornmeal and hominy products available anywhere: pencil cobb grits (read about 'em on the website), blue and white and yellow corn grits in various grinds, even yellow whole hominy corn and culinary lime for making your own hominy. Rare graham flour, farro piccolo, roasted farro (or spelt), stone-cut oats, buckwheat flours. You could spend all day reading the artful descriptions of these special products, which are available to order in small or very large quantities.

Arrowhead Mills

arrowheadmills.elsstore.com
phone: 800-434-4246
The Hain Celestial Group, Inc.
4600 Sleepytime Drive
Boulder, CO 80301

Arrowhead Mills stocks organic whole grains (buckwheat groats, millet, amaranth, oat groats, long-grain brown rice, brown basmati rice, quinoa), organic whole-grain flours, and gluten-free buckwheat flour and yellow cornmeal. Many are available in grocery stores, and they can be ordered in sensible quantities online.

Bob's Red Mill

bobsredmill.com
phone: 800-349-2173
5000 SE International Way
Milwaukie, Oregon 97222

Miller of conventional, organic, and certified gluten-free grains and flours, Bob's Red Mill also packages nuts, seeds, beans, baking mixes, and so on. Many of these products are available in grocery stores, but there's a much wider selection online and, presumably, in the brick-and-mortar store in Oregon. I'm fairly certain that every grain product used in this book is available from Bob's Red Mill by mail or Internet order.

Haldeman Mills

haldemanmills.com
phone: 717-665-2339
1720 Locust Grove Road
Manheim, PA 17545

Brinser's Best and Stauffer's Home roasted cornmeal (made by Haldeman Mills) is not available online, but you can find a store that sells it with a bulk-store-finder tool.

Kalustyan's

kalustyans.com
phone: 800-352-3451
123 Lexington Avenue
New York, NY 10016

Kalustyan's is a real-world and online seller of specialty rices and other grains, spices, nuts, flours, extracts, dried fruits, lentils, dried beans, and condiments. If you're ever in Manhattan, stop by the store and stock up.

King Arthur Flour

kingarthurflour.com
phone: 800-827-6836
135 U.S. Route 5 South
Norwich, VT 05055

King Arthur Flour's catalog and online ordering system offer not just the whole wheat and white whole wheat flours commonly available in grocery stores across the country, but also sparkling white sugar, vital wheat gluten, whole cornmeal, steel-cut and rolled oats, oat flour, whole spelt flour, high-fiber barley flour, brown rice flour, and sorghum flour.

Nuts Online

nutsonline.com
phone: 800-558-6887
125 Moen Street
Cranford, NJ 07016

This is an online retailer of nuts and nut flours, whole grains, flours, dried fruits, and gluten-free products. One advantage of ordering grains from these folks is that they're available in smaller quantities; it's easier to try out unusual grains when you don't have to commit to them by the case.

Red Mule Grits

Tim and Alice Mills
redmulegrits.us
Mills Farm
150 Harve Mathis Road
Athens, GA 30601

Red Mule Grits is a local-to-me microproducer of excellent organic corn grits, cornmeal, Polenta de Georgia (coarse-grind cornmeal), and English porridge (a mixture of different grains). Their mill is mule powered.

INDIAN GROCERY STORE LOCATORS

There are a couple of currently working Indian grocery store locators online. The URLs have a certain fly-by-night quality about them, but I wanted you to at least know that there is such a thing as an Indian grocery store locator and that theoretically you can use one to find purveyors of inexpensive spices, fresh curry leaves, lentils, and rices local to you.

thokalath.com/grocery/
diggsamachar.com/grocery/grocery.htm

FURTHER READING

Whole Grains Council
wholegrainscouncil.org
A respected resource for all information whole grain. Up-to-date nutrition information, whole grains in the news, and links to health and nutrition studies.

USDA National Nutrient Database for Standard Reference
ndb.nal.usda.gov
Find detailed nutrition information for a wide range of foods, from plain foods like "rice, brown, medium-grain, cooked" to ready-to-eat brand-name cereals.

Gramene: A Resource for Comparative Grass Genomics
gramene.org
For those three or four of you who are interested in more cereal grain taxonomy, this is a useful database.

INDEX

ACKNOWLEDGMENTS

Thanks first must go to my editor at Stewart, Tabori and Chang, Natalie Kaire, who first approached me about writing this book and who was a constant source of enthusiastic encouragement throughout the process. Elinor Hutton deserves a special thank you for her thoughtful edits and suggestions, all of which improved the book immeasurably; I'm lucky to have had her as a developmental editor. Ellie also shepherded the book through the final stages of photography and design with grace and impeccable taste. I'd also like to thank my friend Marisa Bulzone for her invaluable advice and support.

Special thanks go to my good friend and frequent collaborator Leda Scheintaub, a cookbook author and editor, who read recipes as I was working on them, offering ideas and advice and support, and then also copyedited the completed manuscript with her legendary eagle eye and recipe smarts. Thanks, too, to my friend Sarah Scheffel, recipe tester and editor, for her work on many of the vegan and vegetarian dishes. I'd also like to thank, as usual, my good friend Regan Huff, one of the best cooks I've ever known, who loaded me up with inspiring ideas right from the beginning and then was kind enough to take container after container of food—some of it tasty, some just edible—off my hands and out of my crazy crowded refrigerator so I could keep cooking more food week after week, month after month. She also, thoughtfully as always, made sure I often had occasion to enjoy entirely grain-free meals with her as I was working on this book.

Once again a cookbook is far better for having in large part been made in Athens, Georgia, a small town with perhaps an unlikely concentration of people who enjoy and produce excellent food—and photographs of food. Rinne Allen is truly the best photographer I could have hoped to have shot the pictures for this book. She and the talented and creative prop and food stylist Lucy Allen Gillis are directly responsible for how delicious and beautiful all the whole grains in these pages look. Thank you, Rinne and Lucy, for making it all incomparably gorgeous—and fun. And thank you to Chrissy Reed, for making the shoot much, much easier than it could have been. The Four Coursemen also deserve my sincerest gratitude for allowing us to use their space—and really use it hard—for several weeks. I'd like to thank Charles Ramsay and Mimi Maumus at the Five & Ten restaurant as well: Charles for his amazing quinoa custard recipe and Mimi for some last-minute true frisée.

As always, thank you to my parents, Dave and Diana Fredley, for ideas, old and new recipes, spurtles, and every other kind of support you can imagine them providing from thousands of miles away. Finally, thank you to my patient and supportive husband and daughter, Derek and Thalia, my best friends, my loves, for everything.